PUBLIC RELATIONS, SOCIETY AND THE GENERATIVE POWER OF HISTORY

Public Relations, Society and the Generative Power of History examines how histories are used to explore how the past is constructed from the present, how the present is always historical, and how both past and present can power imagined futures.

Divided into three distinct parts, the book uses historical inquiry as a springboard for engaging with interdisciplinary, critical and complex issues in the past and present. Part I examines the history of corporate PR, the centrality of the corporation in PR scholarship and the possibility of resisting corporate hegemony through PR efforts. The theme of Part II is 'Historicising gender, ethnicity and diversity in PR work,' focusing on how gendered and racialised identities have been constructed and resisted both within the profession and through the result of its work. Part III engages with 'Histories of public relations in the political sphere,' bringing together work on the different ways in which public relations has evolved in changing political contexts, both formally as a function within political institutions and in the context of contributions to broader narratives of nationalism and identity.

Featuring contributions from leading academics, this book challenges traditional PR historiography and contests the 'lessons' derived from existing literature to address the implications of key areas of critically engaged PR theory. This volume is a valuable teaching resource for upper-level undergraduates and postgraduates studying public relations, strategic communications, political communication and organisational communication.

Ian Somerville is Head of the School of Media, Communication and Sociology at the University of Leicester. His research has been published in international communication, PR, politics and sociology journals and in various edited collections. His most recent book is *International Public Relations: Perspectives from Deeply Divided Societies* (Routledge, 2017).

Lee Edwards is Associate Professor at the London School of Economics and Political Science. She teaches and researches strategic communication from a critical perspective. She is the author of books, book chapters and empirical studies in the leading journals in the field of communication scholarship.

Øyvind Ihlen is Professor in the Department of Media and Communication at the University of Oslo and co-director of POLKOM – Centre for the Study of Political Communication. He has over 120 publications where he applies theories of rhetoric and sociology to the study of public relations.

PUBLIC RELATIONS, SOCIETY AND THE GENERATIVE POWER OF HISTORY

Edited by Ian Somerville, Lee Edwards and Øyvind Ihlen

Routledge
Taylor & Francis Group

LONDON AND NEW YORK

First published 2020
by Routledge
2 Park Square, Milton Park, Abingdon, Oxon OX14 4RN

and by Routledge
52 Vanderbilt Avenue, New York, NY 10017

Routledge is an imprint of the Taylor & Francis Group, an informa business

© 2020 selection and editorial matter, Ian Somerville, Lee Edwards and Øyvind Ihlen; individual chapters, the contributors

The right of Ian Somerville, Lee Edwards and Øyvind Ihlen to be identified as the authors of the editorial material, and of the authors for their individual chapters, has been asserted in accordance with sections 77 and 78 of the Copyright, Designs and Patents Act 1988.

All rights reserved. No part of this book may be reprinted or reproduced or utilised in any form or by any electronic, mechanical, or other means, now known or hereafter invented, including photocopying and recording, or in any information storage or retrieval system, without permission in writing from the publishers.

Trademark notice: Product or corporate names may be trademarks or registered trademarks, and are used only for identification and explanation without intent to infringe.

British Library Cataloguing-in-Publication Data
A catalogue record for this book is available from the British Library

Library of Congress Cataloging-in-Publication Data
A catalog record has been requested for this book

ISBN: 978-1-138-31710-9 (hbk)
ISBN: 978-1-138-31711-6 (pbk)
ISBN: 978-0-429-45128-7 (ebk)

Typeset in Bembo
by Newgen Publishing UK

Printed and bound by CPI Group (UK) Ltd, Croydon, CR0 4YY

CONTENTS

CONTRIBUTORS

Patricia A. Curtin is professor and associate dean for undergraduate affairs at the University of Oregon, Eugene. Her 13 years of professional communication experience encompass public relations work for start-ups and agencies, specialising in employee relations. She received her M.A. and Ph.D. from the University of Georgia and taught for ten years at the University of North Carolina-Chapel Hill, where she directed graduate programs within the School of Journalism and Mass Communication. She joined the University of Oregon faculty in 2006 as the endowed chair in public relations. Her research encompasses agenda building, international public relations, public relations history and development of critical/postmodern approaches to public relations theory, particularly the cultural-economic model. She is the author of approximately 75 refereed research studies and two books and has won research awards from the Association for Education in Journalism and Mass Communication, the International Communication Association and the International Public Relations Conference.

Lee Edwards is Associate Professor at the London School of Economics and Political Science. She teaches and researches strategic communication from a critical perspective, with a focus on how power circulates in and through strategic communications work. She is the author of numerous articles, books and book chapters, publishing theoretical interventions and empirical studies in many of the leading journals in the field of communication scholarship.

Johanna Fawkes is Visiting Professor, University of Navarra and Visiting Research Fellow at the University of Huddersfield. As Principal Research Fellow at Huddersfield University (2016–2018) she managed the international research project to construct a Global Capability Framework (GCF) for public relations and communication management. Before joining Huddersfield she was Senior Lecturer in Public Relations at Charles Sturt University (2011–2016) where she was Course Director for the Doctor of Communications. Jo is an academic with over 15 years' teaching experience in UK universities (following 15 years as a PR practitioner in the public sector). After leading the Leeds Met B.A. PR until 2004, she was an independent scholar and research consultant to a range of clients. She completed her Ph.D. looking at professional ethics from a Jungian perspective in 2011. Her book, *Public Relations Ethics and Professionalism: the Shadow of Excellence*, was published by Routledge in 2015.

Kate Fitch is Senior Lecturer in the School of Media, Film and Journalism at Monash University in Melbourne, Australia, where she coordinates the public relations specialisation. Dr Fitch previously worked at Murdoch University, where she founded the public relations major and chaired the program for ten years. Her current research investigates sociocultural perspectives on public relations, focusing on gender and history. Her book, *Professionalizing Public Relations: History, Gender and Education*, published by Palgrave in 2016, offered a sociological history of Australian public relations in the twentieth century drawing on archival and interview research. Recent publications focus on women in public relations, history and historiography and celebrity public relations. She is currently working on a co-authored book on popular culture and social change. Dr Fitch is on the editorial board of *Public Relations Inquiry* (2015–ongoing) and previously served on the editorial board of *Public Relations Review* (2010–2018).

Ruth Garland spent 28 years in public sector strategic communications before starting her Ph.D. in Media and Communications at the London School of Economics in 2012. She was awarded her doctorate in February 2017 for her thesis 'Between Media and Politics: Can Government Press Officers Hold the Line in the "Age of Political Spin"?' She has taught at the LSE and Brunel University, and since 2017 has been a Lecturer in Media Cultures at the University of Hertfordshire. Her research focus is on public communication and the relationship between media and politics, taking an interdisciplinary approach that encompasses media sociology, political communication and public relations. She worked as a publicist at the BBC for 19 years and has an enduring interest in British television. Her current research interests include the recent history of UK government communication, and a thematic content analysis of the ITV daily live programme *Loose Women*.

Owen Hargie is Emeritus Professor in the School of Communication at the University of Ulster. He is a Chartered Member, Registered Practitioner and Associate Fellow of the British Psychological Society. He is an elected member of the prestigious Royal Norwegian Society of Sciences and Letters, and a Fellow of the UK Academy of Social Sciences. He has published 70 book chapters, 126 articles in refereed journals, 11 major research reports, and 22 books, including *Key Issues in Organizational Communication* (2004), *Communication Skills for Effective Management* (2017), *Skilled Interpersonal Communication: Research, Theory and Practice*

(2010) and *Auditing Organizational Communication: A Handbook of Research, Theory and Practice* (2009). He acts as consultant on communication for numerous public and private sector organisations. In 2007 he was awarded a Senior Distinguished Research Fellowship by the University of Ulster in recognition of his research contributions over three decades.

Jochen Hoffmann is Associate Professor of Organizational and Public Communication at Aalborg University, Denmark. He is mainly doing research on the intersections of organisational communication, public relations and political communication. Current projects focus on public relations education, corporate political advocacy and public affairs.

Kevin Hora is Programme Chair of the M.A. in Public Relations and the M.A. in Public Affairs and Political Communication at Technological University Dublin, formerly Dublin Institute of Technology. He is the author of *Propaganda and Nation Building: Selling the Irish Free State* (Routledge, 2017), based on his doctoral research, and a primer text, *Quick Win Public Relations* (2014). A former ex officio board member of Dublin Chamber of Commerce, he is also a former member of the Green Party/Comhaontas Glas, for whom he was active in election campaign strategy and policy development. He is a member of the Public Relations Institute of Ireland, and an adjudicator on the Public Relations Consultants Association Awards for Excellence in Public Relations.

Øyvind Ihlen is Professor at the Department of Media and Communication, University of Oslo and co-director of POLKOM – Centre for the Study of Political Communication. He has over 120 publications where he applies theories of rhetoric and sociology to the study of public relations.

Melissa A. Johnson is Professor in the Department of Communication at NC State University. She holds a doctorate from the School of Media and Journalism at the University of North Carolina-Chapel Hill. Prior to joining NC State, she taught at UNC-Chapel Hill, San Diego State University and Elon University. Dr. Johnson's research explores communication concepts in international news, international public relations, ethnic media and ethnic public relations. She serves on the editorial boards of the *Journal of Public Relations Research, Howard Journal of Communications,* and *International Journal of Hispanic Media.* She is a past president of the San Diego Press Club and the Publicity Club of San Diego and a former board member of the North Carolina Public Relations Society of America chapter. Along with her academic work, Dr. Johnson has more than a dozen years of communication practitioner experience.

Amanda Kennedy is Assistant Professor of Communication Studies at St. Mary's University in San Antonio, Texas. She specialises in feminist, postmodern and critical theory and critical, qualitative and emergent methods in strategic and applied communication. Her research and teaching cover topics in public relations; disaster, crisis, risk and health communication; ethics; gender, motherhood and feminist studies; and postmodern, critical and community-centred approaches in communication studies and praxis. Kennedy enjoys teaching, mentoring and advising graduate and undergraduate students in communication and currently serves as graduate program director in her department. Kennedy is also committed to serving the discipline, maintaining active membership and leadership roles in several divisions of professional organisations including AEJMC and NCA.

Brittany Little graduated in 2016, with a Bachelor's degree in Mass Communication with a Public Relations concentration from Louisiana State University. Brittany is a native of Spring, Texas and a second-year M.A. Public Relations student at the University of Houston. Little's research interests in public relations include intersectionality, fandom and health.

David Mitchell is Assistant Professor at Trinity College Dublin. His research interests are in contemporary Northern Ireland politics, the politics of peace processes and the roles of religion and sport in transitions out of conflict. After a B.A. in History and Philosophy and M.A. in Peace and Conflict Studies, David completed a doctorate in Politics at Ulster University (Magee), where he also taught. Prior to joining ISE, David worked on projects based at the University of Aberdeen, Northern Ireland Association for Mental Health and Ulster University, carrying out qualitative and quantitative research among politicians, ex-combatants, religious activists, top-level and grassroots sports organisations, LGB, ethnic minority and transgender groups and the general public.

Camille Reyes is Assistant Professor of Public Relations at Trinity University in San Antonio, Texas. She investigates public relations in the context of social justice movements. Her work has appeared in journals such as *Public Relations Inquiry* and *Communication, Culture, and Critique*. Prior to receiving her M.A. in Media, Culture and Communication from New York University, Reyes worked in marketing and public relations for 13 years, serving a diverse range of clients from Burgerville to Microsoft. She earned her Ph.D. at the Rutgers University School of Communication and Information, where her contributions were recognised with two awards for teaching and research.

Ian Somerville is Head of the School of Media, Communication and Sociology at the University of Leicester, UK. His research has been published in a range of international communication, PR, sociology and politics journals and his most recent book is *International Public Relations: Perspectives from Deeply Divided Societies* (Routledge, 2017). He is currently a member of the editorial boards of *Public Relations Review*, *Public Relations Inquiry* and the *Journal of Media and Communication*.

Jennifer Vardeman is Associate Professor and Director of Graduate Studies at the Jack J. Valenti School of Communication at the University of Houston. Dr. Vardeman-Winter teaches courses in public relations theory and management, critical/cultural public relations and crisis communication. Her research interests include intersectionality in public relations and public health/healthcare campaigns. Prior to academia, she worked in high-tech public relations in Austin, Texas for both global electronics companies like Motorola Semiconductors and IBM Software as well as start-ups.

Dominic Wring is Professor of Political Communication at Loughborough University. He has published on the history and role of advertising and public relations within the democratic process, most notably *The Politics of Marketing the Labour Party* (2005), a study of organisational and strategic developments over the course of the twentieth century. He is also a co-editor of several books on more recent events including *Political Communication in Britain: Campaigning, Media and Polling in the 2017 General Election* (2018), and *EU Referendum Analysis 2016: Media, Voters and the Campaign* (www.referendumanalysis.eu/).

FOREWORD

Jacquie L'Etang

It is a pleasure to have been invited to write the Foreword to this collection, which takes the historical genre of public relations a step further in terms of reflective and reflexive work. Thirty-one years ago, when I started my M.A. in Public Relations, one could not have imagined critiques of corporate PR coming from *within* the discipline; critical meta-analysis of textbooks; the positioning of activism as part of PR; richly multi-layered accounts of race and gender; reflections on PR in cultural and ethnic identities or nationalism; reflections on the role of PR in sport; or engagement with political actors and propaganda – all of which appear in this volume. A generation ago PR was largely an impoverished, mechanical discipline – soulless, one might say – and as most of those teaching were ex-practitioners there was a strong sense of (misplaced) 'loyalty' to practice among those who seemed to experience conflicting identities. This resulted in a stultifying conformity blended with a rather evangelical support for instrumentalism. This collection not only offers exploratory and creative historical perspectives, but opens up public relations history to a range of disciplinary engagements.

While this volume takes a broadly historical approach, it offers great diversity in terms of subject matter presented within the critical paradigm. As the editors explain, the contributory authors reflect on the past in many different contexts in a variety of ways, thus furthering moves away from simplistic progressivist explanation initially derived from analysis of one nation-state, and instead embracing multiple readings and complexity. In so doing, the contributions begin to recover sociological, anthropological and ethnographic insights into the role of persuasion and persuaders in multiple cultural contexts, celebrating difference rather than similarity. Clearly there has already been some reconceptualisation of the boundaries of PR history and the incorporation of activism marks a major shift in the field from the 1980s, where activism was distinctly othered. Present in this collection are several chapters that engage with activism (Reyes, Hora, Vardeman et al.). The extension of public relations histories in the political arena mark constructive engagement with state actors, questions of agency, the political economy of public relations, ideological entanglements, public education and democratic practices in relation to politicians and civil servants (Wring, Garland). These contributions pleasingly blend and cross disciplines, helping to break down traditional and established silos and prejudices. Hora's discourse analysis of Swift's polemical propaganda includes issues of national identity, nation-building, the public sphere and rhetoric, while Somerville, Mitchell and Hargie provide a multi-layered account of sport promotion and Irish identity that also shows 'how history itself was deployed by the GAA as a promotional tool.'

Race, ethnicity and gender are foregrounded in societally focused contributions that implicitly challenge traditional historical approaches in PR and open up the field. Blending historical and sociological concepts, theory and data, these chapters provide fresh empirical evidence, recover important, relevant history, explore ongoing problems with representation, reconceptualise historical problems of race and gender and re-position public relations his/herstory (Fitch, Edwards, Vardeman et al., Johnson, Reyes).

The history of history in the public relations discipline is open to further analysis and theorisation, not least since much has been empirical, but lacking in historiographical thinking or historical theory to conceptualise critically, reflexively and methodologically the nature of the historical knowledge that has been produced. History is more than stories about dead people. There are key questions to be asked about the role of history in the curriculum, the purpose of PR history, and the extent to which history can and should impact theoretical developments in the field. There remains a danger that history is simply archived as a specialism, yet the questions that historical practice raises are conceptual, critical and philosophical in nature and therefore potentially transformative for the discipline. Somerville, Edwards and Ihlen encapsulate their aims for the volume thus:

> We aim to open up questions of how histories are put to use by people in different ways in order to explore how the past is constructed from the present, how the present is always historical and how both past and present can power imagined futures.

In so doing they highlight a fascinating but rather under-explored topic in public relations literature, that of time – which is interestingly alluded to at the outset of Hoffmann's contribution, in which he cites Goethe. His literary and philosophical starting point develops into a critical analysis of the politics (and paradigms) of public relations education as interpreted through an analysis of US textbooks, including their moral discourses. Similarly, Curtin's analysis opens up important questions of power and political relationships between academic disciplines and practice jurisdictions between PR, HR and industrial relations – clearly the work done by Hoffmann and Curtin could be usefully extended to other cultural contexts.

Imagination and creativity are well to the fore in this volume; Fawkes' psycho-analytic perspective continues to raise challenging questions about the relationship between the psychic elements that link individuals and society. Her contribution links PR to entertainment and celebrity and references the use of illusion. In this I have long believed there is room for further discussion of the less scientific/rational aspects of public relations and its antecedents in the pre-modern world – the myth-makers and sorcerers.

I am humbled by the intellectual gift of this book and very appreciative of the generous colleagues whose work has gone into this and the conference at which initial papers were presented at Queen Margaret University, Edinburgh in November 2017. Of course I am happy that some of my work has resonated with others and that I helped to find a space for critical and historical work in the field, uncomfortable though it was at the time – it was surely emotionally exhausting working against the tide. My particular good fortune at the outset of my academic career was to have the opportunity to work with Magda Pieczka, whose forensic scholarship and cool questioning scrutinised the limits of the field and helped me to develop my own work, not to mention that she was an ally in numerous public arguments as we attempted to develop our critical approaches to public relations in the early 1990s and to connect with others of similar ilk (in this volume: Fawkes, Somerville, Ihlen). Subsequently, I have also been fortunate to collaborate with some of the contributors to this volume (Fitch, Edwards) and I have read appreciatively all of the chapters that appear here.

I am grateful to have had the opportunity to read this volume pre-publication and am sure that other readers will also enjoy the richness of the contributions and the challenging questions raised therein for the public relations discipline. This book marks a particular moment in public relations history, but I leave it to readers to determine the nature of that moment.

INTRODUCTION

Public relations, society and the generative power of history

Ian Somerville, Lee Edwards and Øyvind Ihlen

The main theme of the book is history, defined in terms of its original meaning, which has its roots in the Greek word ἱστορία, translated by the Romans as *historia*: 'an inquiry' or 'knowledge acquired by investigation.' All contributions to this book share an approach to historical inquiry that entails using the concept generatively, as a springboard for engaging with interdisciplinary, critical and complex issues in the present as well as the past. They are united in the belief that this is a key task that public relations (PR) historical scholarship needs to address. The variety of chapters in the collection reflect upon this generative power and aim to prompt new ways of thinking about the field by unmasking and deconstructing the power relations and ideological presuppositions that mark PR histories, and remain inherent to PR practices, foregrounding topics such as gender, diversity and activism, which have been notable for their absence in other recent contributions to PR histories.

The authors here do not claim to be historiographers; as others have argued, we recognise that historiography is a neglected but important method in public relations scholarship (McKie and Xifra 2014; L'Etang 2015) but our approach in this collection has been pragmatic. There are relatively few historiographical experts in the field of public relations, and the use of history to enhance our scholarship cannot be dependent only on their work. In fact, many scholars do set out historical accounts of the profession in different contexts, and while these may not be formal historiographies, they illustrate the potential for history to enhance our understanding of the field.

This collection is situated conceptually and theoretically within this growing body of innovative historical work by both expert historiographers and others, characterised by increasingly diverse ways of drawing on history to understand the present. Until recently, histories of public relations (e.g., Cutlip 1994; Miller 1999; Ewen 1996) typically displayed a number of common intersecting and mutually reinforcing features: a tendency toward 'periodisation,' a preoccupation with 'managerialism' in the corporate/business sector, US-centrism and a concern to ignore or re-label practices considered questionable or unethical. Many books were underpinned by a (neo)liberal ideology and a focus on single-nation studies or on key historical figures (usually men). Even well-researched work that displayed robust, extensive and rigorous scholarship (Olasky 1987; Cutlip 1994, 1995; Miller 1999) documenting the role public relations played in economic, social and political affairs tended to share many of the features identified above. The advent of the annual International History of Public Relations Conference in 2010 has prompted a more international and diverse expansion of accounts of PR histories and herstories appearing in book form (notably Watson's recent edited collection of public relations histories from across the world: 2014a, 2014b, 2014c, 2014d, 2015a, 2015b) and as journal articles. While there are too many contributions to list here in full, suffice to say that this body of work has challenged mainstream corporatist and professional myths about public relations (e.g., Logan 2014; Fitch 2014; L'Etang 2004), argued for a change in emphasis from histories of practice to histories of practitioners and their agency (Miller and Lamme 2016); re-written understandings of seminal concepts such as propaganda (e.g., Myers 2015); introduced postcolonial and gendered lenses through which to view public relations histories/herstories (Munshi, Kurian and Xifra 2017); contested US-dominated models of what public relations was and is (Bıçakçı and Hürmeriç 2013; Hoy, Raaz and Wehmeier 2007; L'Etang 2004) and introduced new methods to the field (Munshi Kurian and Xifra 2017; L'Etang 2014; McKie and Xifra 2014). Moreover, some historians from outside the field add further to this increasing body of knowledge with extensive historical investigations (e.g., Marchand 1998; Anthony 2012).

The result of this work is that the specific social, cultural and political conditions that have given rise to the profession in its different forms across the globe are becoming increasingly visible, and space to challenge received wisdom about public relations is more available. There are many examples of how these challenges are emerging, but next we address four cases that exemplify the scope for critique using new ways of interrogating history: 1) the periodisation of public relations development; 2) the dominance of corporate histories; 3) the prevalence of US-centric histories; and 4) the absence of sociocultural context.

Periodisation

Public relations textbooks have tended to cast the development of the profession as a progression towards increasing sophistication, organisation and professionalisation. However, increasing numbers of scholars have rejected this narrative in recent years. Hoy et al. (2007) attributed the tendency toward periodisation to Bernays, who employed a model of progressive history in an attempt to clean up public relations' image (this is not without some irony given Bernays' (1928) own focus on the manipulative power of storytelling). Lamme and Russell (2010) also note Bernays' central importance in pushing the periodisation narrative, which was so influential in many subsequent historical accounts of the development of PR. Like L'Etang (2008), they also point out that the typology of PR practice that Grunig and Hunt (1984) outline in their highly influential textbook ultimately came to be reified into historical periodisation:

> Grunig and Hunt refined these timelines to develop a historical foundation for their four models of public relations practice. They did not seek to challenge the periodization of public relations history; instead, they integrated it into four models, which became the dominant paradigm in public relations scholarship, sparking two decades of research.
>
> *(Lamme and Russell 2010:287)*

Additionally, Lamme and Russell (2010:287) make the important point that even as interest in the Four Models paradigm waned as an accurate representation of public relations practice, 'the models became ingrained in public relations *historiography*, and they have continued to influence historical scholarship in the field.'

Given the influence of Bernays, and of Grunig, it is unsurprising that many public relations histories have deployed 'periodisation' to present a view of PR as an evolving practice on an upward trajectory towards a sophisticated, strategic and ethical activity. While it is possible to view periodisation as sometimes being helpful for cognitively managing the past, it is bound to result in descriptive abstractions that ultimately will involve some sort of arbitrariness. The progressive myth has been criticised both for doing little to develop an understanding of public relations and its history and for perpetuating an ideological message that the highest aspiration for PR is the (neo)liberal managerial corporate context typified by the United States of America (Lamme and Russell 2010; L'Etang 2015), when in practice its application elsewhere is limited (Bıçakçı and Hürmeriç 2013). As a result, in PR history scholarship more recently there have been significant departures, both from such ideological assumptions, and from the misleading notion that one can organise PR's 'evolution' into distinct time periods (see Brown 2003; Gower 2007, 2008; Hoy et al. 2007; L'Etang 2004, 2008). Our collection shares the fundamental assumption of this work: that there is important historical analysis to be done to trace transformations, changes and even evolutions but seeking to present the history of public relations as a temporal 'ethical progression' (Hoy et al. 2007:196) is not only logically impossible to sustain but also an intellectually dishonest endeavour.

Corporate dominance

Not unrelated to this tendency towards periodisation is the notion 'that the rise of public relations for big business was the culmination of all that came before, a (…) final phase of the field's development, rather than, simply, another phase in its development' (Lamme and Russell 2010:283). Lamme and Russell (2010) note that US public relations history scholarship and textbooks have traditionally overwhelmingly focused on the relationship between business and public relations in the twentieth century and that this has produced a skewed picture of the actual histories of public relations (see also Hoy et al. 2007). This tendency has of course also produced a fixation with managerial functionalism, with so-called 'Excellence' in PR practice ultimately being measured against the capacity of PR to facilitate the achievement of corporate management strategies (Grunig 1992). Other scholars have also pointed out that this corporate bias in public relations history has tended to obscure the use of public relations in other spheres (Straughan 2007; Lamme 2007). Miller's (2000:409) analysis of public relations historiography reveals the dominant presence of studies of US corporate and political (particularly presidential press relations) spheres at the expense of work in social history or 'public relations at the grass roots.' She concludes that '[p]olitical and social histories show that public relations was emerging and apparently would have emerged even if big business had not' (Miller 2000:414). Lamme and Russell (2010:283) argue that recently emerging work, freed from the big-business bias, has not only been more inclusive of women and minorities but that it also 'contradicted some of the conclusions made in the corporate public relations history studies (e.g., public relations as bottom-up grassroots persuasion versus public relations as top-down corporate suppression).'

While business/capital remains a central driver of contemporary socioeconomic formations and should therefore remain a significant focus of PR historical analysis, we concur with the view that this should not be at the expense of focusing on a much wider range of PR histories and herstories, from a range of social, political and cultural spheres. This edited collection attempts to redress the balance to an extent by including research from spheres that have hitherto been ignored or underrepresented in many historical accounts of public relations practice, including gender, race, political institutions and social movements.

US-centrism

L'Etang (2008:327) noted that a key danger in PR historical work is the 'colligation' of history, and highlights 'how one historical colligation from one culture, has come to dominate the field. The "four models" have been proselytised in an enthusiastically evangelical way, to the detriment of the field as a whole.' The global embracing of the Four Models has meant not just the dominance of a 'broad managerial paradigm that favours structural-functional management' (Pearson 1992:129) but also as, L'Etang (2008:327) notes, the primacy of 'US history's footprint on PR theory development.' More recently, however, there has been resistance to this US-centrism (Lamme and Russell 2009) and this book, while exploring the significance of US influence, is also consciously part of this resistance. L'Etang's (2004) celebrated study of British public relations history, traced from the first decade of the twentieth century, exemplifies this departure from US managerial functionalist accounts of PR and PR history. Her study emphasises the industry's roots in the trade union NALGO and locates the growth and development of the industry in British public relations agencies rather than corporations. She links the evolution of British public relations in the early twentieth century to key political, economic, social and technological developments and draws on rich empirical data to analyse some of the sociological issues relevant to the professionalisation of public relations in the second part of the twentieth century. Aside from the path forged by L'Etang there have been other significant attempts to move beyond US-centrism (Bentele 2015; Wehmeier 2015). Individual studies of public relations in different countries are now more common (e.g., Rodríguez-Salcedo and Watson 2017; Bıçakçı and Hürmeriç 2013; Theofilou and Watson 2014). A particular highlight is Watson's (2015:17) important and innovative project to draw together global histories of PR. The impressive seven-book project covers continental/regional national groups in Asia and Australasia, Eastern Europe and Russia, the Middle East and Africa, Latin America and the Caribbean, Western Europe and North America, and includes a volume on historiographical and theoretical approaches. One of the project's stated aims is to move beyond the US-centric (typified by Cutlip 1994, 1995; Marchand 1998; Olasky 1987; Pearson 1992; Tye 1998) and corporate focus and present a broader global view of the history of public relations. Nonetheless, despite the stated aim of the series, when some of the contributions are evaluated there is an unacknowledged influence of Grunigian conceptualisations of PR and the deployment of US PR as a benchmark for professionalism (Fitch and L'Etang 2017). In this volume, we follow in the footsteps of these efforts to expand the geographical 'territory' of public relations history, with chapters from a range of countries and sectors.

Sociocultural context

While Watson's series 'has taken a giant leap forward in PR's own thinking about its origins and antecedents as well as patterns of development, ruptures and conceptual and historical links to propaganda' (Fitch and L'Etang 2017:132), it also reflects other histories in having a relatively limited vision of the sociocultural context for PR beyond political and corporate environments. For example, Fitch and L'Etang (2017) note:

> [T]here is little reflexivity around the lack of recognition of women's roles in societal debates or their contributions to the development of PR in most chapters. (…) Gender is a major missing concept in the series, so evidence of female participation in PR or specialised sectors is not recorded, and, therefore, neither is historical or ongoing discrimination, stereotyping and prejudice.
>
> *(128–129)*

One result of the absence of a rich sociocultural analysis is that 'within the series, there is little if any evidence presented that shows PR practice as a negative influence within society or even playing any role in social change' (Fitch and L'Etang 2017:122–123). This lack of critical perspective on PR's impact on society has been a common feature of PR historiography. Lamme and Russell (2010) have highlighted the fact that many PR histories have simply ignored, or relabelled, practices considered questionable or unethical. They argue that:

> [T]he field cannot simply 'disown' those tactics deemed to be unethical or, at best, unsavory. (…) it is no longer acceptable – or accurate – to relegate those practices deemed 'bad PR' to another time or a different label. Instead, the field of public relations, the academy and the practice, should embrace the whole history of the field as a professional heritage
>
> *(Lamme and Russell 2010:352)*

In this collection, we respond to this and other calls to remove what can only be described as the 'spin' from public relations history. Public relations history and present must be situated and understood in social and cultural contexts (Edwards 2006; Ihlen and Verhoeven 2012). As Fitch and L'Etang (2017:123) put it, 'historical research into PR cannot be tackled without interrogation of broader scale cultural dynamics, flows and tensions. Furthermore, a sociocultural perspective potentially offers a counterbalance to dominant, organising narratives.' Like L'Etang (2015:37), we argue for 'repositioning public relations as part of wider social change and movements, rather than as a discrete story.' We aim to open up questions of how histories are put to use by people in different ways in order to explore how the past is constructed from the present, how the present is always historical and how both past and present can power imagined futures.

Structure of the book

The first section, 'Challenging corporatism and managerialism,' brings together work that examines the history of corporate PR, the centrality of the corporation in PR scholarship and the possibility of resisting corporate hegemony through PR efforts. In Chapter 1, Johanna Fawkes tracks the growing influence of public relations (PR) and other promotional industries on global culture in the past 50 years. Fawkes examines how promotion was marginalised in theorising PR practice in functionalist PR scholarship throughout the twentieth century, while at the same time media and cultural scholars increasingly identified PR almost exclusively with promotion. In taking the long view and resisting the simplistic demonisation of PR, she suggests a deeper concern emerges. To what extent has PR and its management of media and image, whether for fracking or health services, contributed to what Hedges (2009) calls 'the empire of illusion'?

In Chapter 2, Jochen Hoffmann argues in favour of a denaturalisation of what has previously been 'naturalised' by the mainstream in an academic discipline. Hoffman argues that from a communication perspective, 'naturalisation' is a strategy that equalises (normative) claims with factual realities. This kind of communicative reification is hermetic, not deliberative, because facts appear to speak for themselves. He analyses the way in which five US public relations textbooks describe the 'nature of PR' by assuming that the author's ideals of public relations reflect the reality of today's PR practices. He focuses on three 'naturalisation' strategies: 'Erasing the author as an external observer,' 'relegating problematic practices to the "dustbin of history"' and, 'incapacitating critical voices.' Hoffman argues that critical PR scholars should respond with denaturalisation by means of meta-analyses. He suggests that most mainstream PR textbooks do not support reflexive and critical thinking in higher education. Instead, they tend to be non-discursive, hermetic, promotional texts – they are public relations for public relations.

In Chapter 3, Patricia A. Curtin explores how a subset of public relations practice, employee relations, emerged historically to help construct and maintain the US corporate welfare state. It traces the historical development of the practice of employee relations and its role in negotiating and reifying public/private boundaries: who was empowered to create dominant meanings, the underlying ideologies, the counter-narratives of resistance and the creation and maintenance of a class system within a society that deemed, and still deems, itself to be classless. Taken as a whole, these trends and their implications demonstrate not only the generative power of history but highlight the implicit and explicit roles of power and resistance in current and future employee relations practices. The study highlights the competing historical narratives that continue to shape modern practice.

The theme of Part II is 'Historicising gender, ethnicity and diversity in PR work.' The focus here is on how gendered and racialised identities have been constructed and resisted both within the profession and through the result of its work. The section begins with Chapter 4, in which Kate Fitch examines the representation of women in trade media and considers more broadly the impact of second-wave feminism and societal shifts around women and the workforce in Australia. Her study highlights the need for a more historically informed position on women and public relations in order to better understand the development of an occupational and professional identity along gendered lines and the significance for the public relations industry today. She investigates the representation of women in the Australian public relations industry's trade media from 1965 to 1972, in order to understand how shifting gender dynamics in Australian society played out in the public relations industry. Fitch argues that female practitioners' restricted representation in the journal produced by the professional association points to longstanding fissures along gender lines that continue to influence understandings of professional practice and occupational identity today.

Chapter 5 engages with racialisation in the apparently post-race industry of UK public relations. Lee Edwards explores the ways in which racialisation structures discrimination and stigmatisation in the industry, based on historical constructions of the 'other' that extend back to the days of the British Empire. However, she also explores how alternative narratives of migration, resistance and community provide resources for black, Asian and minority ethnic (BAME) practitioners to resist their marginalisation and assert their right to belong in the field. She argues that interrogating the personal, professional and social histories that shape public relations can help to reveal how 'race' remains a powerful structuring factor even in an apparently post-race context.

Chapter 6 is an exploration by authors Jennifer Vardeman, Amanda Kennedy and Brittany Little assessing how PR contributed to intersectional activism in an analysis of three case studies spanning 75 years. They argue that women's status as PR agents is, in part, subjugated in these movements and bleeds into the disciplinary realm because of the act of women embracing women's interests and anti-racist agendas. This act contributes to the persistent questioning of women's status in the field of PR. The chapter examines women's use of PR to enact social change in communities that are mired in racist systems and suggests a new argument about why women practitioners and practitioners from racial minorities experience unequal workplace status. It also challenges our traditional notions of social movements as discrete, isolated and novel, as it contextualises these activisms within the tenets of intersectionality. Finally, it applies to an international audience because intersectionality theorises about power and marginalisation based on mixes of identities and contexts without privileging a single country/culture.

Chapter 7 focuses on the 'activist-turn' in public relations research. Camille Reyes discusses how scholars and practitioners alike have opportunities to push boundaries, in some cases moving scholarship towards a shared critical project of casting light on global conditions of marginalisation by demonstrating that public relations tools are not inherently oppressive; they are also used by the oppressed. Using new examples from a qualitative study of Occupy Wall Street, as well as previous scholarship on public relations work from movements past, this chapter suggests that it might be possible to dismantle the 'master's house' using the 'master's tools' (to borrow from and to question Audre Lorde). The Occupy Wall Street Press Relations Working Group (OWS PRG) practices of media relations, dubbed the 'People's PR,' bear a striking resemblance to corporate practices; however, the struggles they faced were more akin to the sort of disordered strife characteristic of many conflicts within the women's movement of the 1970s. Reyes argues it is useful to examine this case in conversation with movements past as a way of understanding to what extent practices of public relations extend and/or foreclose opportunities for social justice. Such analysis is vital in the current protest moment when #MeToo, #BalanceTonPorc ('out your pig') in France and Black Lives Matter are re-energising spaces of resistance.

In Chapter 8, Melissa Johnson analyses how public relations practitioners describe the identity histories of the cultures associated with the museums where they work, and how professionals communicate about evolving ethnic identities. Museum communication practitioners amplify identity and collective memory, transcending museum walls via digital and mobile platforms, along with other traditional communication tools. The chapter considers how public relations practitioners communicate cultural identity histories and contemporary ethnic cultures, and the challenges they face in communicating about histories and contemporary identities.

Part III engages with 'Histories of public relations in the political sphere.' In these final chapters, we bring together work on the different ways in which public relations has evolved in changing political contexts, both formally as a function within political institutions, and in the context of contributions to broader narratives of nationalism and identity. In Chapter 9, Dominic Wring explores the missing histories of media relations before the so-called 'third age,' '(post)modern' or 'mediatised' forms of political communication (Blumler and Kavanagh 1999; Norris 2000; Hjarvard 2013). The chapter explores developments in political public relations by focusing on how the once seemingly resistant Labour Party in Britain embraced rudimentary but recognisable forms of media management. The focus will be two comparable developments half-a-century apart that provide valuable insights not only into their respective eras but also as a comparative study. The cases are: the 1937 campaign to re-elect the first ever Labour-led London County Council installed three years previous, and the ultimately ill-fated but nonetheless groundbreaking attempt to 'Save the Greater London Council' during the mid-1980s.

Ruth Garland focuses on the same sphere but examines more recent historical developments. In Chapter 10 she considers the generative power of history in influencing the professional identities and purposes of media relations specialists within central governing bureaucracies, taking a UK perspective. As public servants, government press officers operate within a self-regulating system of ethical codes and proprieties, but controversies over the 2003 Iraq War (*John Williams: Statement for the Iraq Inquiry*, 2010) and the 2016 EU referendum campaign raised serious concerns among scholars and commentators that government information was becoming increasingly partisan and untrustworthy, leaving the public under-served and disillusioned (Blumler and Coleman 2015). This chapter argues that the bureaucratic culture that underpins liberal democracy has struggled to adapt to the transformation of the media environment ('mediatisation'), or to resist the drive by politicians to manage and exploit communication power.

In Chapter 11, Ian Somerville, David Mitchell and Owen Hargie analyse the Gaelic Athletic Association's (historical) promotional culture/identity construction, particularly in the period following the foundation of the Irish Republic, and argue that it was one of the most successful examples of sports PR in history because it not only ensured the dominance of newly invented/codified sports in Ireland but was also a primary element in constructing an Irish national identity for the masses. The chapter discusses the consequences that this campaign has bequeathed to today's generation, particularly in relation to issues of inclusion/exclusion in post-conflict Northern Ireland. The authors present findings from a major research project exploring the enduring legacy of a century of 'Irish' nationalist sports promotion.

Kevin Hora, in Chapter 12, makes the case for critical discourse analysis as a method of inquiry for PR historians. The chapter analyses public advocacy and nation-forming in Jonathan Dean Swift's *Drapier's Letters* (1724–1725) using Fairclough's three-dimensional framework of analysis of language texts, discourse practice and discursive events situated within their sociocultural and temporal milieu. Hora's study examines *Drapier's Letters* as a public affairs document. Using a critical discourse analysis and focusing on national identity, he examines the text in the context of the fractious Anglo–Irish relationship that transformed a dispute over coinage into a *cause célèbre*, where the printed medium was central to mobilising public opinion. It places Swift's satirical and intellectual thrust in a European Enlightenment context and challenges notions of Irish national identity.

Finally, a common feature linking the authors contributing to this volume is the intellectual debt we owe to the work of Jacquie L'Etang. Our work has been inspired by her important contribution to theorising public relations generally and in particular expanding the debate around the theory and methods of public relations historiography. Our hope is that, however imperfectly, this collection represents a testament to that inspiration and a continuation of that work.

References

Anthony, S. 2012, *Public Relations and the Making of Modern Britain*, Manchester: Manchester University Press.

Bentele, G. 2015, Problems of Public Relations Historiography and Perspectives of a Functional-Integrative Stratification Model. In Watson, T. (ed.), *Perspectives on Public Relations Historiography and Historical Theorization*, Basingstoke: Palgrave Macmillan, pp. 20–47.

Bernays, E.L. 1928, *Propaganda*, New York: Liveright.

Bıçakçı, A. and Hürmeriç, P. 2013, Milestones in Turkish Public Relations History, *Public Relations Review*, 39, pp. 91–100.

Blumler, J.G. and Coleman, S. 2015, Democracy and the Media – Revisited, *Javnost: The Public*, 22(2), pp. 111–128.

Blumler, J.G. and Kavanagh, D. 1999, The Third Age of Political Communication: Influences and Features, *Political Communication*, 16(3), pp. 209–230.

Brown, R.E. 2003, St. Paul as a Public Relations Practitioner: A Metatheoretical Speculation on Messianic Communication and Symmetry, *Public Relations Review*, 29(1), pp. 1–12.

Cutlip, S.M. 1994, *The Unseen Power. Public Relations: A History*, Hillsdale, NJ: Lawrence Erlbaum.

Cutlip. S.M. 1995, *Public Relations History: From the 17th to the 20th Century. The Antecedents*, Hillsdale, NJ: Lawrence Erlbaum.

Edwards, L. 2006, Public Relations Origins: Definitions and History. In Tench, R. and Yeomans, L. (eds), *Exploring Public Relations*, Harlow: Prentice Hall, pp. 2–16.

Ewen, S. 1996, *PR! A Social History of Spin*, New York: Basic Books.

Fitch, K. 2014, Professionalisation and Public Relations Education: Industry Accreditation of Australian University Courses in the Early 1990s, *Public Relations Review*, 40, pp. 623–631.

Fitch, K. and L'Etang, J. 2017, Other Voices? The State of Public Relations History and Historiography: Questions, Challenges and Limitations of 'National' Histories and Historiographies, *Public Relations Inquiry*, 6(1), pp. 115–136.

Gower, K.K. 2007, Preface. In Straughan, D.M. (ed.), *Women's Use of Public Relations for Progressive-Era Reform*, Lewiston, NY: Edwin Mellen Press, pp. i–iv.

Gower, K.K. 2008, US Corporate Public Relations in the Progressive Era, *Journal of Communication Management*, 12(4), pp. 305–318.

Grunig, J.E. (ed.) 1992, *Excellence in Public Relations and Communication Management*, Hillsdale, NJ: Lawrence Erlbaum.

Grunig, J.E. and Hunt, T. 1984, *Managing Public Relations*, New York: Holt, Rinehart and Winston.

Hedges, C. 2009, *Empire of Illusion: The End of Literacy and the Triumph of Spectacle*, New York: Nation Books.

Hjarvard, S. 2013, *The Mediatization of Culture and Society*, New York: Routledge.

Hoy, R, Raaz, O. and Wehmeier, S. 2007, From Facts to Stories or From Stories to Facts? Analyzing Public Relations History in Public Relations Textbooks, *Public Relations Review*, 33, pp. 191–200.

Ihlen, Ø. and Verhoeven, P. 2012, A Public Relations Identity for the 2010s, *Public Relations Inquiry*, 1(2), pp. 159–176.

L'Etang, J. 2004, *Public Relations in Britain*, Mahwah, NJ: Lawrence Erlbaum.

L'Etang, J. 2008, Writing PR History: Issues, Methods and Politics, *Journal of Communication Management*, 32(4), pp. 319–335.

L'Etang, J. 2014, Public Relations and Historical Sociology: Historiography as Reflexive Critique, *Public Relations Review*, 40, pp. 654–660.

L'Etang, J. 2015, History as a Source of Critique: Historicity and Knowledge, Societal Change, Activism and Movements. In L'Etang, J., McKie, D., Snow, N. and Xifra, J. (eds), *Routledge Handbook of Critical Public Relations*, London: Routledge, pp. 28–40.

Lamme, M.O. 2007, Alcoholic Dogs and Glory for All, *Social History of Alcohol and Drugs*, 21(2), pp. 138–159.

Lamme, M.O. and Russell, K.M. 2009, Removing the Spin: Toward a New Theory of Public Relations History, *Journalism & Communication Monographs*, 11(4), pp. 280–362.

Marchand, R. 1998, *Creating the Corporate Soul: The Rise of Public Relations and Corporate Imagery in American Big Business*, Berkeley, CA: University of California Press.

Mckie, D. and Xifra, J. 2014, Resourcing the Next Stages in PR History Research: The Case for Historiography, *Public Relations Review*, 40, pp. 669–675.

Miller, K.S. 1999, *The Voice of Business: Hill & Knowlton and Postwar Public Relations*, Chapel Hill, NC: University of North Carolina Press.

Miller, K.S. 2000, US Public Relations History: Knowledge and Limitations, *Communication Yearbook*, 23, pp. 381–420.

Miller, K.S. and Lamme, M. 2016, Theorizing Public Relations History: The Roles of Strategic Intent and Human Agency, *Public Relations Review*, 42, pp. 741–747.

Munshi, D. Kurian, P. and Xifra, J. 2017, An (Other) 'Story' in History: Challenging Colonialist Public Relations in Novels of Resistance, *Public Relations Review*, 43, pp. 366–374.

Moor, S. 2014, *Public Relations and the History of Ideas*, London: Routledge.

Myers, C. 2015, Reconsidering Propaganda in US Public Relations History: An Analysis of Propaganda in the Popular Press 1810–1918. *Public Relations Review*, 41(4), pp. 551–561.

Norris, P. 2000, *Virtuous Circle: Political Communication in Post-Industrial Societies*, Cambridge: Cambridge University Press.

Olasky, M. 1987, *Corporate Public Relations: A New Historical Perspective*, Hillsdale, NJ: Lawrence Erlbaum.

Pearson, R. 1992, Perspectives On Public Relations History. In Toth, E.L. and Heath, R.L. (eds), *Rhetorical and Critical Approaches to Public Relations*, Hillsdale, NJ: Lawrence Erlbaum, pp. 111–130.

Rodríguez-Salcedo, N. and Watson, T. 2017, The Development of Public Relations in Dictatorships – Southern and Eastern European Perspectives from 1945 to 1990, *Public Relations Review*, 43, pp. 375–381.

Straughan, D.M. (ed.) 2007, *Women's Use of Public Relations for Progressive-Era Reform*, Lewiston, NY: Edwin Mellen.

Theofilou, A. and Watson, T. 2014, The History of Public Relations in Greece from 1950 to 1980: Professionalization of the 'Art', *Public Relations Review*, 40, pp. 700–706.

Tye, L. 1998, *The Father of Spin*, New York: Crown Publishers.

Watson, T. 2014a, *Asian Perspectives on the Development of Public Relations: Other Voices*, Basingstoke: Palgrave Macmillan.

Watson, T. 2014b, *Eastern European Perspectives on the Development of Public Relations: Other Voices*, Basingstoke: Palgrave Macmillan.

Watson, T. 2014c, *Latin American and Caribbean Perspectives on the Development of Public Relations: Other Voices*, Basingstoke: Palgrave Macmillan.

Watson, T. 2014d, *Middle Eastern and African Perspectives on the Development of Public Relations: Other Voices*, Basingstoke: Palgrave Macmillan.

Watson, T. 2015a, *Perspectives on Public Relations Historiography and Historical Theorization: Other Voices*, Basingstoke: Palgrave Macmillan.

Watson, T. 2015b, *Western European Perspectives on the Development of Public Relations: Other Voices*, Basingstoke: Palgrave Macmillan.

Wehmeier, S. 2015, Historiography (and Theory) of Public Relations History. In Watson, T. (ed.), *Perspectives on Public Relations Historiography and Historical Theorization*, Basingstoke: Palgrave Macmillan, pp. 85–114.

PART I
Challenging corporatism and managerialism

1

THE CONTRIBUTION OF PUBLIC RELATIONS TO PROMOTIONAL CULTURE

Taking the long view

Johanna Fawkes

Introduction

Fitch and L'Etang (2017) argue that histories of public relations (PR) are over-directed by the influence of the Excellence approach, leading to its use an incontestable template for practice and theory in the field. Not only has it morphed from a loose description of best practice in the USA to an instruction manual for public relations, but it has also been successfully exported into curricula and professional codes globally (Parkinson 2001).

This chapter suggests that in addition to the voices that Fitch and L'Etang say are excluded from PR histories in this approach – particularly voices of gender, race and postcolonial cultures – whole areas of practice have been underexamined because the Excellence approach deemed them marginal or primarily of historical interest. The placing of persuasion in the sub-optimal, sub-ethical category has impacted scrutiny of promotion, persuasion and propaganda from within the public relations field, though these areas are heavily covered by critical and cultural scholars who see them as synonymous with public relations.

Promotional culture is now being reclaimed by public relations scholars who offer a more nuanced perspective than is often found in cultural studies literature. A less demonised, more measured view of the role of public relations in society in many ways carries a heavier ethical punch than the bogeyman caricatures. This emerging scholarship is broadly located in critical, political economy and sociological frameworks, of which more below.

However, I want to introduce a different note, employing the concepts of Persona and Shadow from Carl Jung to re-examine texts that concern public relations and promotional culture, from within and outside the field. A culture dominated by display has psychological as well as economic drivers and effects.

The chapter offers conceptual insights and the approach is broadly hermeneutic (Riceour 1981; Gadamer and Linge 1977), interpreting text against text. This values the subjective experience of text and encourages deeper reflection on commonalities and divergences. I do not claim to be an impartial observer here, but a story-teller.

The chapter is organised as follows.

- The historical impact of Grunig and Hunt's (1984) Four Models on the study of persuasion and promotion;
- Reclaiming the neglected terrain of promotional culture;
- Re-casting promotional culture in Jungian terms as collective Persona function;
- Listening to Shadow voices.

The chapter concludes with reflections and questions for further research.

The historical role of the Four Models

The starting point for this chapter is Grunig and Hunt's (1984:22) Four Models of communication, which offers a typology of public relations roles: (1) Press Agentry/Publicity, (2) Public Information, (3) Two-way Asymmetric and (4) Two-Way Symmetric. Each model is given a description of its purpose, nature, an appropriate communication model, associated research, historical figures, location and percentage of practice. Models (1) and (2) are forms of one-way communication; models (3) and (4) are two-way flows. Persuasion is seen as two-way asymmetric communication (3) and only the final model (4) is based on two-way exchanges to achieve mutual understanding.

This typology has two implications for historians. First, it is itself an historical document, produced at the earliest stages of public relations theory development, just as public relations was expanding as an educational field in search of texts (Moloney 2006; Davis 2013). As such, it is a product of its time, and in particular of its place of origin, the United States, which raises its second historical role: as an apparent summary of the historical development of the field itself. In their section on the models in history (1984:25), Grunig and Hunt offer a clear timeline from 1850 to the time of writing, with the fourth model as the apogee of the trajectory. The impression of a moral arc, culminating in the fourth model, was reinforced by the assertion (Grunig and White 1992) that the final model represents a normative ideal for public relations in most situations. This position was modified by Grunig (2001), who offered the notion of continua rather than discrete categories.

The merits of the Four Models have been argued over since publication on the grounds they are normative, functionalist and, while appearing to be a universal framework, only represent the US experience, an observation made by many critics (Pieczka 1996; L'Etang 2004; Pfau and Wan 2006; Holtzhausen 2012; McKie 2001; Davis 2013; Moloney 2000, 2006). In particular, the implication that persuasion (the third model) is inherently unethical has been widely criticised (Pearson 1989; Pfau and Wan 2006; Porter 2010; Fawkes 2015a; Brown 2015). The volume of scholarship, supportive and critical, that follows from this work and subsequent developments (Grunig et al. 1992; Grunig et al. 2002; Grunig et al. 2007; Sriramesh and Vercic 2009) has earned it the status of paradigm (Botan and Hazleton 2006), reinforcing the sense that these concepts have historical force, albeit a distorting one, as Fitch and L'Etang argue (2017).

The historical distortion is amplified by subsequent writers who have relied on Grunig and Hunt's historical overview to construct what Jansen (2017) calls a 'useful fiction,' one that emphasises the moral development of the field over time, at the expense of its failings. Another consequence, of course, is that the field came to be seen as sharing the specific US histories, ignoring what Davis (2013:24) calls 'alternative histories'; L'Etang (2004) has demonstrated the very different origins of public relations in Britain and the series edited by Tom Watson has started to include other development stories from around the world – although, as Fitch and L'Etang (2017) point out, it is still a narrow canvas.

Neglected terrains: promotional culture and public relations

The emphasis on public relations as a management function, using strategic communication to contribute to and shape organisational purpose, has, as suggested above, become the dominant narrative for public relations theory and practice (Fawkes et al. 2018). To be clear, I am not disputing the accuracy or usefulness of this description as part of the professional project, to gain social status and organisational power. Only that it is a partial image, not the whole story.

Moreover, as a result, dissenting or alternative perspectives have become marginalised. Rhetorical scholars, such as Robert Heath (2001, 2006, 2009) have maintained a strong argument for public relations as rhetoric. The engagement with advocacy as at least a potentially ethical practice offers an important counterbalance to the 'impartial' counsellor lauded in Excellence. Critical scholars have also worked for several decades to resist Excellence becoming the only available framework for public relations (L'Etang, McKie, Snow and Xifra Heras 2017; Botan and Hazleton 2006; Pfau and Wan 2006; Moloney 2006). However, this work has remained, until recently, largely invisible to those writing about public relations from outside the field, such as cultural or media scholars. While Excellence stresses best practice and the contribution of public relations to wider society, these writers excoriate its detrimental effects on democracy, social justice and human flourishing.

In a mirror-image of public relations' self-presentation, academic study has often been left to those who lump PR in with advertising and marketing as producers of promotional content, often with little understanding for the workings of the respective industries and certainly no respect for strategic functions (McKevitt 2018). Here public relations is seen as wholly malign in regard to its pernicious effect on democracy, consumer choices and collective welfare. Its operation in political and corporate propaganda is exposed, often in the context of electoral manipulation, lobbying on fossils fuels, climate change and pharmaceuticals (see Sussman 2011). This group of scholars is broadly located in the political economy approach, founded in the Frankfurt School and Herman and Chomsky's (1988) Propaganda Model (Stauber and Rampton 2004, Miller and Dinan 2008, Sussman 2011).

While most of the above treat public relations as synonymous with corporate capitalism, Sue Curry Jansen (2017) recognises that non-profit and socially responsible enterprises also require professional communication services. Unlike many of the above, she also recognises the critical scholarship undertaken by PR academics, whom she terms 'insider' critics. Nevertheless, her explorations of PR as propaganda (Jansen 2017) frame the field wholly in corporate terms. From the opposite starting point, this has the same effect as the Excellence approach: disallowing advocacy as a legitimate practice.

In a slightly different corner, other scholars of the promotional aspects of our culture, including Wernick's (1991) *Promotional Culture* and Marshall's (2014) *Celebrity and Power*, interrogate what Fairchild (2007) calls the 'attention economy.' This view conceptualises society, and particularly digital society, as a ceaseless competition for the consumer's glance, click or credit card (Wu 2017). It argues that the commodification of goods, services and institutions is a requirement of neoliberal market economics in which every provider must compete for custom by demonstrating its compliance with market standards, or at least appearing to, making promotion 'an axial principle of social life' (Wernick 1991:186). Institutions, including hospitals and universities, not only have to operate as sites of healthcare or education, but have to 'perform' these roles to secure funding and approval. All entities are can be seen as inherently promotional under this gaze, in a permanent state of self-advocacy. This summarises the broadest interpretation of promotional culture as a term and it is his approach that informs this chapter.

Davis (2013:2) defines promotional culture as the practices undertaken in the promotional industries: 'public relations, lobbying, advertising, marketing and branding – and related professions (pollsters, speechwriters etc)' (1). These in turn employ 'promotional intermediaries' who share the following characteristics: 'Their products may be ideas or objects; They access communication media; [and] They are self-organised in professions' (2). This definition is more applied than Wernick's approach, but this suits Davis' exploration of promotional practice. Like Curry Jansen, Davis (2013:7) acknowledges differences between and within promotional industries and takes an historical perspective to the competing narratives around the development of public relations and the consequent divergences in claims of the field's social value. The perspective is similar to the critics cited above, but demonstrates much closer attention to public relations as work. This subtler approach is echoed by sociologist Anne Cronin (2018), who argues that public relations deserves greater, more nuanced scrutiny because of its importance to contemporary culture, in what she calls *public relations capitalism*.

Davis, Jansen and Cronin are primarily scholars from outside the field of public relations but their insights provide a contrast to the broad amalgamation of promotional industries found elsewhere in the above-cited literature (for example, Wu's 2017 *The Attention Merchants* has only three index references to public relations, two of them concerning Bernays). This inattention is surprising, as Edwards (2018) points out. Public relations work involves shaping, reflecting and communicating identity for organisations and individuals, and is in turn shaped by the professional identity both of the field and individual public relations practitioners (Fawkes 2015b; Brown 2015; Edwards 2010; Daymon and Surma 2012; Jeffrey and Brunton 2012; Thurlow 2009). The question of appearance is central to the public relations industry, which defines itself as being about 'reputation, what you do and what people say you do' (Edwards 2018). Media and political media relations concern the 'optics,' the impressions formed in the minds of viewers and readers. Narratives and counter-narratives must be built and maintained to secure public or shareholder approval; this is where the strategist and the publicist aspects of communication management come together (McKevitt 2018).

In the past decade, public relations scholarship has increasingly engaged with cultural and social theory (Edwards and Hodges 2011; Bardhan and Weaver 2011; Curtin and Gaither 2007; Ihlen et al. 2009). This has introduced literature from those fields to public relations, including Bourdieu (Ihlen 2009), Goffman (Johansson 2009) and Du Gay (Curtin and Gaither 2005), which has enlarged the understanding of public relations as a cultural force. For example, Curtin and Gaither (2005) use Du Gay's (1997) Circuit of Culture to describe the work of public relations in each aspect of the circuit: production, regulation, consumption, representation and identity. They note the deleterious effect of separating some of the models from the whole picture:

> The dominant normative paradigm has removed propaganda and persuasion from the ranks of legitimate public relations practices, but the circuit demonstrates the need to recognize them as part of the repertoire of legitimate practices.
>
> *(2005:109)*

The most comprehensive examination of public relations as a 'circulatory mechanism for culture' (Edwards 2018:46) is Lee Edwards book, *Understanding Public Relations: Theory, Culture and Society*. As she says, 'Arguing that circulation processes deserve critical examination challenges the representation of public relations as a channel for communication that simply carries, rather than shapes, meaning' (Edwards 2018:32). Edwards explores issues of power, discourse, democracy, race and class as they operate within and through public relations as a social actor, using a vast range of theoretical frameworks, including Bourdieu, Foucault and Du Gay, with appreciation of Latour and Habermas. 'Paying attention to the promotional culture in which public relations thrives prompts ethical questions about the kind of world that we want to live in and public relations' role in constructing (or obstructing) it' (Edwards 2018:211–212).

The relocation of public relations as a contributor to promotional culture is broadly located in sociocultural and political economy theories. Public relations thus acts as an agent of capital in generating effects that benefit the specific paymasters and neoliberal, free-market ideologies in general.

There is another aspect of promotional culture that deserves closer attention but is somewhat underexplored in public relations literature – namely the promotion of individual identities, particularly those of celebrities and the effect of their combined efforts in the wider culture. In the remaining sections of the chapter I want to shift focus from the economic and political effects of promotional culture to its consequences for the interior, psychological wellbeing of the individual in the collective.

Persona and promotional culture

The first issue of the journal *Persona Studies* (Marshall and Barbour 2015) helps explain the shift from outer to inner:

> Where much of Cultural Studies has focused on collective configurations of meaning – for example, subculture – Persona Studies looks at how the individual moves into the social spaces and presents the self. As we have identified, Persona Studies is turning the approach of cultural studies on its head – not in some negation, but rather in a refocussing of critical examination of how the individual gains or articulates agency.
>
> *(2)*

Reframing promotional communication in psychological terms is not to contradict the power-based analyses cited previously but to raise slightly different questions. Specifically, I argue that the emphasis on appearance and promotion as a precondition for social acceptance conjures the archetype of Persona developed by the Swiss originator of depth psychology, Carl G. Jung (1875–1961). The concept has its origins in Greek drama and the image of the mask, a device to reveal and conceal human truths, as is explored further below. The relevance of Jung is stressed by Marshall and Barbour, who find his concept of Persona

> useful to both analyse and read the contemporary condition (…) Persona can be seen as something that needs to be managed and, from this perspective, to be understood as a personal practice that is performed in order to enter the social world in some particular way.
>
> *(4)*

For Jung, Persona is a complicated system of relations between individual consciousness and society, a kind of mask designed to 'impress and conceal' and to meet societal demands (Jung 1953:paras 305–309). As the ego gravitates to the public 'approved' view, unconscious activity starts to compensate. The personal unconscious is structured around archetypal images, the templates of which are located in the collective unconscious (Jung's concept of shared human experience). Archetypes are organised in binary opposites in what can be either a creative or destructive tension, for example, in the twins of Persona and Shadow, the former containing conscious, 'approved' elements of the personality, the latter the repository for all that is feared or despised in the individual. Jung describes the two sources of the Persona as 'on the one hand the expectations and demands of society and on the other the social aims and aspirations of the individual' (Jung CW6/798[1]). The Persona has the task of navigating the individual's relationship with their society and needs 'to both relate to objects and protect the subject' (Stein 1998:119). Thus Persona is essential for developing a foundation for adulthood, through acquisition of status in family, organisation and/or wider society. However, in mid-life, Jung found that unexpressed parts of patients' psyches became disruptive if unheeded. In his clinical work Jung noted that those who placed excessive emphasis on external aspects (such as their appearance, how they were perceived by others, as opposed to their internal experience of the world) and others experienced psychological, even existential, distress and social disconnection. This he attributes to lack of internal communication, particularly with the Shadow aspects, which Jung treats as potentially benign. The Shadow includes those elements of the personal unconscious that are not considered acceptable to consciousness (JungCW11/130–4). While Jung's concepts have been applied to organisational dynamics (Feldman 2004; Hede 2007; Corlett and Pearson 2003; Singer and Kimbles 2004), the emphasis here is on their relevance to promotional culture.

Marshall and Barbour (2015) conclude that

> Persona-making as a practice, in short, is pandemic. And Persona Studies must necessarily be a discipline that is transdisciplinary, drawing on and cultivating a series of new connections to reveal insights into the contemporary self and the volatile world of the fabricated publics these collective selves conjure.
>
> *(9)*

This 'transdisciplinary space' is certainly capacious enough to include public relations scholars re-framing celebrity (e.g., Fitch 2017), branding, promotion and the digital self. For example, rich meta-theoretical insights are offered by Robert E. Brown (2015) in his concept of PR*e*, the public relations of everything. Drawing on literature, Greek drama and sociologists like Goffman, he revisits, *inter alia*, notions of face and reputation as central both to contemporary culture and to the practice of public relations. Importantly, he locates public relations not as a social science but in the humanities, rooted in dramaturgy, crisis, conflict, creativity and interpretation. The ubiquity of public relations is a point worth repeating – this approach moves away from examining discrete acts of promotion and suggests the locus is non-temporal, more like a state of consciousness.

In a hyper-promotional culture, therefore, I suggest that the collective is manifesting the symptoms Jung describes, in the intense idealisation of some public selves and the demonisation of others. A fascinating collection of essays by Jungian scholars (Cruz and Buser 2016), written during the Trump candidacy, frames his appearance in the political arena not in terms of the narcissism of the central character, but by asking what unmet needs in the US psyche Trump (and by extension the UK Brexit debate) answered.

Self-promotion is not new, but the amplification resulting from global digital connectivity is (Wu 2017). Public relations is, as suggested above, centrally involved in the management and presentation of both corporate and individual personae (St. John 2017). Persona is a term widely used in public relations practice (a Google search yielded thousands of PR agencies with the term in the title or running a campaign purporting to create and manage personae for clients). However, the Jungian use of the term has a dark side as the Shadow is inextricable from Persona and a balance between the two must be maintained for psychic health (Stein 1998).

The next section explores a strand of writing from the USA over the past half-century that, I suggest, can be framed as a stream of commentary from the Shadow side of the collective consciousness.

Shadow voices

Historian Roland Marchand (1998) demonstrates that US corporations in the late nineteenth and early twentieth centuries explicitly debated the degree to which they gained or lost their 'souls.' He makes it clear that public relations practitioners were intimately involved in this debate and the idea of US corporations as moral agents, with PR people as their ethical guides, goes back to the late nineteenth century. Echoes of this are found in contemporary writers on public relations' ethics, such as Bowen (2008) and the wider discussion of PR's role as ethical guardian or conscience of the organisation. The issue of whether this is a particularly American phenomenon is outside the scope of this chapter and in any event I want to move outside the organisation and suggest that, if public relations is centrally engaged with the production and maintenance of Persona roles for individuals, organisations and nations, it should also be paying attention to the Shadow voices that represent the unexpressed or hidden aspects of such entities.

This is the context for revisiting three books published in the USA across a 50-year period (1961–2011). They are selected because they relate to the work of public relations and what Davis (2013) calls the promotional industries, and because the writers reflect deeply on the effect of these industries on US culture. (While European writers like Baudrillard and Debord have written powerfully on themes of hyperreality and spectacle, they are not considered here, other than to note that Boorstin has been credited as an influence on both, and to ask why the tone of the US books is so much more anguished than the wry observations of the French philosophers.)

It is the tone of these texts that indicate a Shadow role; as outlined above, there are plenty of critics of promotional culture and the role of public relations within it. However, the Shadow voice comes with a particular urgency and Cassandra-like despair that it will not be heard.

The texts are:

- Daniel Boorstin's (2012 [1961]) *The Image: A Guide to Pseudo-Events in America* (first published in 1961);

- Christopher Lasch (1979), *The Culture Of Narcissism: American Life in an Age of Diminishing Expectations*;
- Chris Hedges (2010), *Empire of Illusion: The End of Literacy and the Triumph of Spectacle*.

It is worth noting that Boorstin (1914–2004) was a historian and Lasch (1932–1994) a historian and cultural commentator. Hedges (1956–) is a journalist and ordained minister. They have disparate political positions and have variously been championed and condemned by opposing causes.

Writing at the start of mass consumerism, Boorstin references PT Barnum and Edward Bernays as foundational to American culture – unlike Grunig and Hunt's (1984) Four Models, which relegate Barnum to an historical embarrassment, and distance public relations from Bernays' propaganda. Boorstin recognises Barnum's genius in understanding not just that people could be fooled, but that, in fact, *they* wanted *to* be fooled: 'Contrary to popular belief, Barnum's great discovery was not how easy it was to deceive the public but rather how much the public enjoyed being deceived' (209).

Boorstin is most well known for his identification of the manufacture, by public relations personnel, of events primarily for media consumption, which he defined as pseudo-events (2012/1961:11). As he noted, their relationship 'to the underlying reality of the situation is ambiguous.' The consequences, for Boorstin (2012:240), are profound: 'We risk being the first people in history to have been able to make their illusions to vivid, so persuasive, so "realistic" that they can live in them.' He sees PR activity as part of the machinery for the generation of illusion, but notes (260) that 'illusory solutions will not cure our illusions (…) Each of us must disenchant himself, must moderate his expectations, must prepare himself to receive messages coming in from outside.' In a pre-smart phone era, Boorstin talks of Narcissus and describes a dystopian society saturated with manufactured images and distractions, adrift in a sea of promotional communication.

Lasch saw no improvements to this situation when he wrote his book on the Narcissistic tendencies in American culture in 1979. He too is intrigued by the power of promotional industries across the social sphere: 'Madison Avenue packages politicians and markets them as if there were cereals or deodorants; but the art of public relations penetrates even more deeply into political life, transforming policy-making itself' (60). Like Boorstin, Lasch (1979:56) cites Barnum as precedence, as a pioneer of the monetisation of self-promotion: 'Barnum valued the good opinion of others not as a sign of one's usefulness but as a means of getting credit.' Discussion of Barnum raises issues of false claims and intentional deception, practices that were amplified in the twentieth century with the growth of mass communication, but Lasch (74) sees this as misguided: 'the rise of mass media makes the categories of truth and falsehood irrelevant to an evaluation of their influence. Truth has given way to credibility, facts to statements.'

Concern about illusion and self-illusion is brought into the twenty-first century by journalist Chris Hedges, who shares interests with Boorstin and Lasch and a tone approaching heartbreak, witnessing the collapse of US culture into staged, self-obsessed, dishonest discourse. He studies a range of cultural institutions, including wrestling, pornography, education and corporations, not merely as service providers of various types, but performers of service providers and generators of false narratives. As he puts it (45), 'The culture of illusion thrives by robbing us of the intellectual and linguistic tools to separate illusion from truth (…) Pseudo-events destabilise truth.'

He identifies the engines of this collapse:

> Pseudo events, dramatic productions orchestrated by publicists, political machines, television, Hollywood or advertisers (…) have the capacity to appear real, even though we know they are staged. They are capable because they can evoke a powerful emotional response of overwhelming reality and replace it with a fictional narrative that often becomes accepted as truth.
>
> *(50)*

The consequences are clear, and relate closely to both Boorstin's and Lasch's (both frequently cited) foreboding:

> A public that can no longer distinguish between truth and fiction is left to interpret reality through illusion (…)when the most important skill is the ability to entertain, the world becomes a place where lies become true, where people can believe what they want to believe.
>
> *(51)*

There is a clear thread running through these selected texts: the promotional industries have moved out of the commercial arena of marketing goods and colonised the wider culture, so that political and personal life is shaped by notions of presentation and framing. The amplification provided by social media has globalised this development. In the cacophony of commercialised communication, it is impossible to navigate between fictions.

In summary, these three authors, writing over half-a-century, come to remarkably similar conclusions about the toxic effects not of publicity itself – they are more amused than horrified by Barnum – but by the social structures that support the normalisation of this mode of communication, almost to the exclusion of all else. As cultural commentators, rather than the propaganda scholars cited above, they note the impact on society and attribute it to something in the American psyche rather than the industrial–military complex.

Conclusion and implications for public relations

I suggest these writers offer a counter-narrative to the dominant story in public relations with which this chapter opened. Far from progressing from circus tent to boardroom as the Four Models indicate, the spirit of P.T. Barnum and the promotion of illusions is thriving in the digital age. Listening to the commentary from

Boorstin, Lasch and Hedges could prompt deeper reflection on public relations' negative contribution to society than is found in much PR literature. The insights from Jung and others remind us that integration of such material need not be an exercise in self-flagellation but the opportunity to evolve a more mature sense of the field's role in the wider world.

This chapter has argued that the marginalisation of promotion and persuasion in the Excellence approach to public relations has left those aspects to critics outside the field, who demonstrate little understanding of the complexities and sometimes contradictory nature of public relations in either theory or practice. In the past decade or so that has begun to shift, with cultural and media scholars like Davis (2013) and Jansen (2017) and sociologists like Cronin (2018) engaging more thoughtfully with the field, even if their conclusions remain hostile. At the same time, scholars from within public relations, particularly Edwards (2018) and Brown (2015), show how social theory and dramaturgical theory, respectively, broaden and deepen understanding of public relations as a cultural practice.

In this context, I have introduced the archetypes of Persona and Shadow from Jung's understanding of the psyche and reframed promotion as a Persona function, valuing the outer world of appearances over inner experience and reflection. The dangers of neglecting the latter aspects were illustrated by finding texts that seem to express the Shadow aspects of this imbalance.

Moreover, they generate questions entirely suitable for consideration in public relations literature. For example, public relations has certainly benefitted from the social and corporate obsession with appearance (Jansen 2017); has it also contributed to the loss of value in substance? Given PR's role as a means of cultural circulation, as an agent, not just a channel (Edwards 2018), what responsibility must the profession bear for the present state of global culture? Is PR a power in its own right, or the servant of power? Can critics and defenders of public relations find common ground?

These questions merit further discussion and indicate why notions of publicity, promotion and propaganda need to be rescued from the historical margins of Grunig and Hunt's Four Models. While the research focus of PR academics has primarily been into the function and operations of professional communication inside and around organisations, it may be that the real impact of public relations has escaped our full attention.

Note

1 Unless otherwise stated, all Jung citations refer to the *Collected Works*, edited by H. Read, M. Fordham and G. Adler and published in London by Routledge, Kogan Page. Citations are to paragraphs, not page numbers.

References

Bardhan, N. and Weaver, C.K. 2011, *Public Relations in Global Cultural Contexts: Multi-Paradigmatic Perspectives*, New York; London: Routledge.

Boorstin, D.J. 2012 [1961], *The Image: A Guide to Pseudo-Events in America*, New York: Vintage Books.

Botan, C.H. and Hazleton, V. 2006, *Public Relations Theory II*, Mahwah, NJ; London: Lawrence Erlbaum.

Brown, R.E. 2015, *The Public Relations of Everything: The Ancient, Modern and Postmodern Dramatic History of an Idea*, London; New York: Routledge.

Bowen, S.A. 2008, A State of Neglect: Public Relations as 'Corporate Conscience' or Ethics Counsel, *Journal of Public Relations Research*, 20(3), pp. 271–296.

Corlett, J.G. and Pearson, C. 2003, *Mapping the Organizational Psyche: A Jungian Theory of Organizational Dynamics and Change*, Gainesville, FL: Center for Applications of Psychological Type.

Cronin, A.M. 2018, *Public Relations Capitalism: Promotional Culture, Publics and Commercial Democracy*, [S.l.], Palgrave Macmillan.

Cruz, L. and Buser, S. 2016, *A Clear and Present Danger: Narcissism in the Era of Donald Trump*, Asheville, NC: Chiron Publications.

Curtin, P.A. and Gaither, T.K. 2005, Privileging Identity, Difference and Power: The Circuit of Culture as a Basis for Public Relations Theory, *Journal of Public Relations Research*, 17(2), pp. 91–115.

Curtin, P.A. and Gaither, T.K. 2007, *International Public Relations: Negotiating Culture, Identity and Power*, Thousand Oaks, CA: Sage.

Davis, A. 2013, *Promotional Cultures: The Rise and Spread of Advertising, Public Relations, Marketing and Branding*, Cambridge; Malden, MA: Polity.

Daymon, C. and Surma, A. 2012, The Mutable Identities of Women in Public Relations, *Public Relations Inquiry Public Relations Inquiry*, 1(2), pp. 177–196.

Du Gay, P., Hall, S., Janes, L., Mackay, H. and Negus, K. 1997, *Doing Cultural Studies: The Story of the Sony Walkman*, London: Sage.

Edwards, L. 2010, *An Exploratory Study of the Experiences of 'BAME' PR Practitioners in the UK Industry*, Leeds: ESRC/Leeds Metropolitan University.

Edwards, L. 2018, Understanding Public Relations: Theory, Culture and Society, Thousand Oaks, CA: Sage.

Edwards, L. and Hodges, C.E.M. 2011, *Public Relations, Society and Culture: Theoretical and Empirical Explorations*, 1st edn. Abingdon; New York: Routledge.

Fairchild, C. 2007, Building the Authentic Celebrity: The Idol Phenomenon in the Attention Economy, *Popular Music and Society*, 30(3), pp. 355–375.

Fawkes, J. 2015a, *Public Relations Ethics and Professionalism: The Shadow of Excellence*, London; New York: Routledge.

Fawkes, J. 2015b, Performance and Persona: Goffman and Jung's Approaches to Professional Identity Applied to Public Relations, *Public Relations Review*, 41(0), pp. 675–680.

Fawkes, J., Gregory, A., Falkheimer, J., Gutierrez-Garcia, E., Rensburg, R., Sadi, G., Sevigny, A., Sison, M. D., Thurlow, A., Tsetsura, K. and Wolf, K. 2018, *Building a Global Capability Framework for the Public Relations and Communication Management Profession*, Huddersfield: University of Huddersfield.

Feldman, B. 2004, Towards a Theory of Organizational Culture: Integrating the 'Other' from a Post-Jungian Perspective. In Singer, T. and Kimbles, S.L. (eds), *The Cultural Complex: Contemporary Jungian Perspectives on Psyche and Society*, New York: Brunner-Routledge, pp. 251–261.

Fitch, K. 2017, Seeing the Unseen Hand: Celebrity, Promotion and Public Relations, Public Relations Inquiry, 6(2), pp. 157–169.

Fitch, K. and L'Etang, J. 2017, Other Voices? The State of Public Relations History and Historiography: Questions, Challenges and Limitations of National Histories and Historiographies (Review), *Public Relations Inquiry*, 6(1), pp. 115–136.

Gadamer, H.-G. and Linge, D.E. 1977, *Philosophical Hermeneutics*, Berkeley, CA; London: University of California Press.

Grunig, J.E. 2001. Two-Way Symmetrical Public Relations: Past, Present and Future. In Heath, R.L. (ed.), *The Handbook of Public Relations*, Thousands Oaks, CA: Sage, pp. 11–30.

Grunig, J.E., Dozier, D.M., Ehling, W.P., Grunig, L.A., Repper, F.C. and White, J. 1992, *Excellence in Public Relations and Communication Management*, Hillsdale, NJ: Lawrence Erlbaum.

Grunig, J.E., Grunig, L.A. and Toth, E.L. 2007, *The Future of Excellence in Public Relations and Communication Management: Challenges for the Next Generation. LEA's Communication Series*, London: Lawrence Erlbaum.

Grunig, J.E. and Hunt, T. 1984, Managing Public Relations, New York; London: Holt, Rinehart and Winston.

Grunig, J.E. and White, J. 1992, The Effect of Worldviews on Public Relations Theory and Practice. In Grunig, J.E. (ed.), *Excellence in Public Relations and Communication Management*, Hillsdale, NJ: Lawrence Erlbaum, pp. 31–64.

Grunig, L.A., Grunig, J.E. and Dozier, D.M. 2002, *Excellent Public Relations and Effective Organizations: A Study of Communication Management in Three Countries. LEA's Communication Series*, Mahwah, NJ; London: Lawrence Erlbaum.

Heath, R.L. 2001, A Rhetorical Enactment Rationale for Public Relations: The Good Organisation Communicating Well. In Heath, R.L. and Vasquez, G. (eds), *Handbook of Public Relations*, Thousand Oaks, CA: Sage, pp. 31–50.

Heath, R.L. 2006, Onward Into More Fog: Thoughts on Public Relations' Research Directions, *Journal of Public Relations Research*, 18(2), pp. 93–114.

Heath, R.L. 2009, The Rhetorical Tradition: Wrangle in the Marketplace. In Heath, R.L., Toth, E.L. and Waymer, D. (eds), *Rhetorical and Critical Approaches to Public Relations II*, New York: Routledge, pp. 17–47.

Hede, A. 2007, The Shadow Group, Towards an Explanation of Interpersonal Conflict in Work Groups, *Journal of Managerial Psychology*, 22(1), pp. 25–39.

Hedges, C. 2010, *Empire of Illusion: The End of Literacy and the Triumph of Spectacle*, Toronto: Vintage Canada.

Herman, E.S. and Chomsky, N. 1988, *Manufacturing Consent: The Political Economy of the Mass Media*, New York: Pantheon Books.

Holtzhausen, D. 2012, *Public Relations as Activisim: Postmodern Approaches to Theory and Practice*, New York: Routledge.

Ihlen, Ø. 2009, On Bourdieu: Public Relations in Field Struggles. In Ihlen, Ø., Fredriksson, M. and Ruler, B.v. (eds), *Public Relations and Social Theory: Key Figures and Concepts*, New York; London: Routledge, pp. 62–82.

Ihlen, Ø ., Fredrikson, M. and Van Ruler, B. (eds) 2009, *Public Relations and Social Theory: Key Figures and Concepts*, New York; London: Routledge.

Jansen, S.C. 2017, *Stealth Communications: The Spectacular Rise of Public Relations*, Cambridge: Polity Press.

Jeffrey, L. and Brunton, M. 2012, Professional Identity: How Communication Management Practitioners Identify with their Industry, *Public Relations Review*, 38(1), pp. 156–158.

Johansson, C. 2009, On Goffman: Researching Relations with Erving Goffman as Pathfinder. In Ihlen, Ø., van Ruler, B. and Fredriksson, M. (eds), *Public Relations and Social Theory, Key Figures and Concepts*, New York: Routledge, pp. 119–140.

Jung, C.G. 1953, *Two essays on Analytical Psychology*, New York: Pantheon Books.

Jung, C.G. Psychology and Religion: West and East, in *Collected Works, Volume 11*, London: Routledge and Kegan Paul.

Jung, C.G. Psychological Types. *Collected Works, Volume 6*, London: Routledge & Kegan Paul.

L'Etang, J. 2004, *Public Relations in Britain: A History of Professional Practice in the Twentieth Century*, Mahwah, NJ; London: Lawrence Erlbaum.

L'Etang, J., McKie, D., Snow, N. and Xifra Heras, J. 2017, The Routledge Handbook of Critical Public Relations, London; New York: Routledge.

Lasch, C. 1979, *The Culture of Narcissism: American Life in an Age of Diminishing Expectations*, New York: Warner Books.

Marchand, R. 1998, *Creating the Corporate Soul: The Rise of Public Relations and Corporate Imagery in American Big Business*, Berkeley, CA: University of California Press.

Marshall, P.D. 2014, *Celebrity and Power: Fame in Contemporary Culture; with a New Introduction*, Minneapolis, MN: University of Minnesota Press.

Marshall, P.D. and Barbour, K. 2015, Making Intellectual Room for Persona Studies: a New Consciousness and a Shifted Perspective, online journal, Deakin University. Retrieved from https://digital.library.adelaide.edu.au/dspace/bitstream/2440/95362/3/hdl_ 95362.pdf.

McKevitt, S. 2018, *The Persuasion Industries: The Making of Modern Britain*, Oxford: Oxford University Press.

McKie, D. 2001. Updating Public Relations: 'New Science' Research Paradigms and Uneven Developments. In Heath, R.L. (ed.), *The Handbook of Public Relations*, Thousand Oaks, CA: Sage, pp. 75–91.

Miller, D. and Dinan, W. 2008, *A Century Of Spin: How Public Relations Became the Cutting Edge of Corporate Power*, London: Pluto.

Moloney, K. 2000, *Rethinking Public Relations: The Spin and the Substance*, London: Routledge.

Moloney, K. 2006, *Rethinking Public Relations: PR Propaganda and Democracy*, 2nd edn. London: Routledge.

Parkinson, M. 2001, The PRSA Code of Professional Standards and Member Code of Ethics: Why they are Neither Professional nor Ethical, *Public Relations Quarterly*, 46(3), pp. 27–31.

Pearson, R. 1989, Beyond Ethical Relativism in Public Relations: Co Orientation, Rules and the Ideal of Communication Symmetry. In Grunig, J.E. and Grunig, L.A. (eds), *Public Relations Research Annual, vol. 1*, Hillside, NJ: Lawrence Erlbaum Associates, pp. 67–87.

Pfau, M. and Wan, H. 2006, Persuasion: An Intrinsic Function in Public Relations. In Botan, C.H. and Hazleton, V. (eds), *Public Relations Theory II*, Mahwah, NJ: Lawrence Erlbaum, pp. 101–136.

Pieczka, M. 1996, Paradigms, Systems Theory and Public Relations. In L'Etang, J. and Pieczka, M. (eds), *Critical Perspectives in Public Relations*, London: International Thomson Business Press, pp. 124–156.

Porter, L. 2010, Communicating for the Good of the State: A Post-Symmetrical Polemic on Persuasion in Ethical Public Relations, *Public Relations Review*, 36, pp. 127–133.

Riceour, P. 1981, *Hermeneutics and the Human Sciences: Essays on Language, Action and Interpretation*, Cambridge: Cambridge University Press.

Singer, T. and Kimbles, S.L. (eds) 2004, *The Cultural Complex: Contemporary Jungian Perspectives on Psyche and Society*, New York: Brunner-Routledge.

Sriramesh, K. and Vercic, D. 2009, *The Global Public Relations Handbook: Theory, Research, and Practice*, expanded and revised edn. London: Routledge.

St. John, B. 2017, *Public Relations and the Corporate Persona: The Rise of the Affinitive Organization*, London; New York: Routledge.

Stauber, J.C. and Rampton, S. 2004, *Toxic Sludge is Good for You: Lies, Damn Lies and the Public Relations Industry*, London: Robinson.

Stein, M. 1998, *Jung's Map of The Soul: An Introduction*, Chicago, IL: Open Court.

Sussman, G. 2011, *The Propaganda Society: Promotional Culture and Politics in Global Context*, New York: Peter Lang.

Thurlow, A. 2009, 'I Just Say I'm in Advertising': A Public Relations Identity Crisis, *Canadian Journal of Communication*, 34(2), pp. 245–264.

Wernick, A. 1991, *Promotional Culture: Advertising, Ideology and Symbolic Expression*, London: Sage Publications.

Wu, T. 2017, *The Attention Merchants: How our Time and Attention are Gathered and Sold*, London: Atlantic Books.

2
'PRESENCING' AND 'ABSENCING'

A deconstruction of US-based public relations textbooks

Jochen Hoffmann

> When, to the Moment then, I say:
> 'Ah, stay a while! You are so lovely!'
> Then you can grasp me: then you may,
> Then, to my ruin, I'll go gladly!
> Then they can ring the passing bell,
> Then from your service you are free,
> The clocks may halt, the hands be still,
> And time be past and done, for me!
> *(Goethe 1808)*

I was baffled the first time I came across US-based public relations textbooks. They seemed to succeed where Goethe's Faust had failed: holding on to the one 'lovely' moment by painting a timeless picture-perfect version of public relations. Faust, however, knew that a 'lovely' moment cannot be captured and that Mephisto's 'passing bell' is always sure to follow. Is it not until then that time is 'past and done'?

This chapter will describe how US-based public relations textbooks enter a pact with the devil. I will outline their failed aspiration to create the eternal moment of a utopic PR, while ignoring the 'passing bell.' My approach was inspired primarily by Duffy's (2000:213) deconstruction of the 'imposing, totalizing and prescriptive' character of PR textbooks. The books she analysed present assumptions of the dominant US-based functionalist paradigm as the only possible way of looking at PR, where a diversity of perspectives is reduced to the factuality of one idealised mainstream (Myers 1992). The textbooks paint a picture of professional practitioners who contribute to the 'effectiveness' of organisations, while being truthful and engaged in symmetric communication. Research on social psychology and management textbooks point in a similar direction. Billig (2015:703–704) argues 'that social psychology textbooks typically fulfil a conservative function by training students to accept the dominant assumptions of the discipline' (see also Lubek 1993). The same is true of managerial textbooks, which have increasingly adapted to the writing style of 'pop' management gurus, with academic substance and critical thinking replaced with prescriptive step-by-step toolboxes and fancy diagrams (Cummings, Bridgman and Brown 2016).

All of this affects the ways in which histories of disciplines and practices are constructed. For example, research on social psychology and management textbooks reveal how authors simplify and ultimately abuse the legacy of Kurt Lewin in order to legitimise the positivistic, experimental and prescriptive mainstream of today (Delouvée, Kalampalikis and Pétard 2011; Billig 2015; Cummings, Bridgman and Brown 2016). PR textbooks use temporality in a similar way. Hoy, Raaz and Wehmeier (2007) show how the history of public relations is conceptualised as a process of maturation. It is a modernistic understanding of 'evolution' as a linear progression over time (see also Raaz and Wehmeier 2011). What drives the construction of such a history is its instrumental value for the legitimation of current hegemonic discourses (Foucault 1965). Narratives of the past are 'written as anticipation: viewed in terms of making sense of the present's great "heights"' (Cummings, Bridgman and Brown 2016:39). Thus, analysing constructions of PR history is not an end in itself. It helps us to understand how ideologies of the present are created and supported.

Overall, there is some critical research on textbooks, particularly in the field of social psychology and management. There are also a few impressive studies on PR textbooks, which expose the totalizing ontology behind the promoted PR ideology. However, what I will challenge in this chapter is the often implicit assumption that the telling of an authorial story necessitates the 'silencing' of alternative stories (Clair 1998). The historiography of textbooks points in a different direction: anyone claiming the current existence of a mature and professionalised PR necessarily requires an immature and unprofessional PR in the past as a point of reference. Thus, I created the theoretical item pair 'presencing' and 'absencing,' which will guide my analysis: whenever textbooks *presence* utopia, they *absence* dystopia. Absencing should not be equated with silencing – it is a very active communication process that banishes problematic PR practices into other spaces or times. This chapter will reveal the self-deconstructive nature of PR textbooks by looking at both presencing and absencing communication. I will show how every attempt to present an ever-lasting 'lovely' PR moment here and now is under threat of a 'passing bell.'

Differánce and deconstruction

The phenomenologist Edmund Husserl (1893–1917; 1936) believed in the achievability of the Faustian moment as an immediate true presence here and now, the self not confused by the other, the moment not confused by the past or the future. His metaphysics of presence was challenged by post-structuralist philosopher Jacques Derrida (1962; 1967). Derrida argued that otherness is required to create the self, that the untruthed is constitutive for the declaration of truth, and that every attempt to preserve a pure presence of being is foredoomed. The true moment cannot 'stay a while,' because it cannot be isolated. Thus, it is not identity but difference that constitutes texts, spaces and times. It is the difference between self and other, between here and there. Similarly, the 'now' is not a state either, but the difference between 'before' and 'then' (Bernet 1986).

Overall, theories of identity in the tradition of Husserl have been contested increasingly often by theories of difference (Raaz and Wehmeier 2016). Derrida's neologism *différánce* highlights not only the spatial dimension of *difference* – the 'here' contaminated by a 'there' – but also the temporal dimension of *deferral* – the 'now' permeated by a 'before' and a 'then.' Derrida refers to this as deconstruction. Every claim in a text deconstructs itself, because it cannot avoid marking a difference from what it might prefer to silence. In consequence, deconstruction is neither a theory nor a method (Burman and MacLure 2005). Deconstruction happens without intervention: we simply cannot hold on to the true moment. The researcher makes use of the temporality of deconstruction by deferring a now-meaning of the analysed text to a then-meaning of the analysing text. A first-order signification of present elements proceeds into a second-order observation of the difference between presence and absence.

The strategic rejection of second-order observations has been explained using terms such as essentialism, factuality, reification, objectivation or naturalisation. From a communication perspective, such 'being-realism' (Chia 1996) transforms into a power resource. It is tempting to let a constructed reality appear 'natural,' because deconstruction and denaturalisation then appear as a radical, almost insane move (Fournier and Grey 2000). Facts appear to speak for themselves and those who question them can be said to have lost contact with reality. Thus, deciding what is presenced as superior and absenced as inferior is ultimately a question of inclusion and exclusion (Fuery 1995). Raaz and Wehmeier (2016:175) argue that a first-order observation constitutes 'a well-structured, morally integrated world, and thus promotes the notion of an identity-centred account of society.' It is a world at peace with itself. Claimed ideals are equalised with a reality here and now in order to legitimise a contingent status quo of hegemonial power structures. Presencing as commodified communication refuses to distinguish between the description of a world as it is and the promotion of a world as it ought to be. As a result, we are deprived of the option to discuss alternative worlds (Horkheimer and Adorno 1944).

The theoretical interplay of *différánce* and deconstruction facilitates the development of a research design that is sensitive to the constitutive and legitimizing power of textbook communication, while concurrently revealing its vulnerability. Three differences – (a) presencing and absencing, (b) utopia and dystopia, (c) spatiality and temporality – are combined into an analytical scheme (see Table 2.1). It allows me to observe the textbooks' self-deconstruction by asking: (1) How does presencing work? How do textbooks talk a utopic PR into existence (here and now)? (2) How does ontological absencing work? How do textbooks talk a dystopic PR into non-existence (neither here nor now)? (3) How does spatial absencing of dystopic PR

TABLE 2.1 The spatial and temporal dimensions of presencing utopia and absencing dystopia

	Now	*Not now*
Here	Presencing of utopic PR	Temporal absencing of dystopic PR
Not here	Spatial absencing of dystopic PR	Ontological absencing of dystopic PR

work (now, but not here)? (4) How does temporal absencing of dystopic PR work (here, but not now)?

Method

The globally pervasive mainstream of PR functionalism originates primarily from the United States (L'Etang 2008b; Macnamara 2012). Therefore, I decided to focus on US-based textbooks when analysing presencing and absencing strategies. The following selection criteria were applied to the textbooks I found in library databases and online sources.

- The authors teach at, or have in the past regularly taught at, US universities.
- If there is both a US and an international edition, the international edition will be chosen.
- The book explicitly (but not necessarily exclusively) targets students.
- The book is (at least officially) written solely by the authors. It is not an edited volume.
- The book is available as a hardcover or paperback (not just sewn binding).
- The book is labelled as a general introduction to public relations.

Qualitative research is time consuming. Therefore, I had to limit the amount of text. I included the latest editions of the five most current textbooks (see Table 2.2). Books published after June 2017 could not be taken into consideration. Furthermore, I analysed only the introductory chapters of the five books selected. These are most instructive, because they set the foundation for the more specific content that follows. It is here that a basic understanding of PR and its spatial and temporal positioning is communicated.

As a first inductive move, I let the data speak for itself, which resulted in three broad categories: (1) any excerpts claiming a 'natural' state of current PR, (2) any excerpts referring to a potential PR critique, (3) any excerpts discussing changes in PR over time. I then looked for suitable theories and found Derrida's ideas on difference and deconstruction most useful as a way of reorganising these categories and reallocating the codes to the more systematic four dimensions presented in Table 2.1. The following sections will provide an in-depth analysis of each of the four dimensions, before I go on to discuss some specifics of TB5, which – at least in parts – marches to a different beat.

TABLE 2.2 Selected textbook chapters

Acronym	Authors	Publication year	Edition	Title, place of publication, publisher	Introductory chapter title	Pages
TB1	Broom, G.M. and Sha, B.-L.	2013	11	*Cutlip and Center's Effective Public Relations*, Essex: Pearson.	Introduction to Contemporary Public Relations	26–47
TB2	Lattimore, D.L., Baskin, O., Heiman, S.T. and Toth, E.L.	2013	4	*Public Relations: The Profession and the Practice*, New York: McGraw-Hill.	The Nature of Public Relations	2–23
TB3	Newsom, D., VanSlyke Turk, J. and Kruckeberg, D.	2013	11	*This is PR. The Realities of Public Relations*, Boston, MA: Cengage Learning.	PR Roles and Responsibilities	1–21
TB4	Smith, R.	2014	1	*Public Relations: The Basics*, New York: Routledge.	A First Look at Public Relations	3–35
TB5	Wilcox, D.L., Cameron, G.T. and Reber, B.H.	2015	11	*Public Relations. Strategies and Tactics*, Essex: Pearson.	Defining Public Relations	27–64

Analysis

The presencing of utopic PR

'This is PR. The realities of public relations' – the title of TB3 gets straight to the point of what presencing is about. As TB2:2 puts it, the claim is to describe the 'nature of public relations.' The authors position themselves as authoritative voices with privileged access to the ultimate truth of public relations, as it exists here and now: 'What it is. What it isn't' (TB4:3). As such, definitions play a key role for the authors' presencing strategies. TB1:29 expects a PR definition to describe 'what public relations is and does,' which surprisingly results in the following: 'Public relations is a management function that establishes and maintains mutually beneficial relationships between an organization and the publics on whom its success or failure depends' (TB1:29).

The definition illustrates the key purpose of presencing as a communication strategy: the authors transform normative claims, ambitions or expectations concerning public relations into a factual reality here and now. They talk utopia into existence: PR *is* a strategic management function, it *is* oriented towards consensus by promoting a transparent dialogue with all of its stakeholders. Since the organisation *is* dependent on these stakeholders, the main activity of PR *is* an adaptation to the environment. In consequence, PR *is* serving the public interest (in detail: Hoffmann 2019).

Instead of asking when and under which conditions these ambitions may be realised, they are simply presented as facts. Such a presencing of utopic practices requires a kind of relaxed creativity when it comes to the selection and treatment of sources that are supposed to provide empirical evidence. All textbooks work with references, but many claims about what 'PR is and does' simply stand alone, without referring to any research. Overall, practitioner quotes dominate. Other heavily used sources are publications by PR associations and 'research' initiated and funded by the industry and its associations. Texts authored, supported or promoted by the Public Relations Society of America (PRSA) play a key role for referencing. TB1:28 and TB2:5 devote half a page to quoting its 'Official Statement of Public Relations' dating from 1982. That definition includes all of the aforementioned key elements of presenced PR and most likely served as an ideological nucleus from which the textbooks over the years developed their more detailed presencing strategies. Industry associations set the tone; textbook authors follow. There is barely a contextualisation, nor any critique of these sources. TB4:10, for instance, lists a number of PR definitions issued by PR associations and concludes:

> There isn't a single definition because the profession is still evolving. But nowhere in these definitions do you find room for untruth or propaganda, exaggerations or stonewalling, publicity stunts or media gimmicks. Rather, the definitions of public relations, as they are articulated by the leading professional organizations in the field, all focus on strategic management, organizational goals, mutual understanding, goodwill and public interest.

In other words, if PR associations claim that certain PR practices are true, then they must be true. This renders empirical research obsolete. The totality of presencing leaves no room for academic observers who are able to draw a line between themselves and the subject of their research. Instead, the textbooks are transformed into materialised dummies ventriloquised by PR practitioners and their associations: 'To get a real look at anything, it's always a good idea to go straight to the source. Here's what public relations people say about their profession' (TB4:9).

The analysis of presencing strategies confirms what critical studies have already established about one-sided and hegemonic reality constructions in textbooks. The next step will go beyond these studies and look at absencing strategies. As Derrida argued, you cannot properly observe presencing without absencing. Dystopic practices are not merely silenced, they need actively to be talked into nonexistence (Hoffmann 2018). Textbooks do this by applying: (a) an ontological binary code – not in reality, but in fiction; (b) a spatial binary code – not here, but elsewhere; and (c) a temporal binary code – not now, but in the past.

The ontological absencing of dystopic PR

> Delusions or misconceptions? Or untruths and lies? We'll use a term with more neutral nuance and call these erroneous statements fallacies. These simply are false, no blame implied. It may seems unusual to begin a book with a list of criticisms, but by airing these fallacies we can actually glimpse a bit of the positive side of public relations.
>
> *(TB4:4)*

TB4 affords the juxtaposition of 'fallacies' of PR with its 'realities' five pages. For example: 'Fallacy: PR equates to lying, hype and exaggeration. Reality: Truth is a foundation of public relations. (…) Public relations is about accuracy, honesty and information in context' (TB4:4–5). The construction of 'fallacies' is an ontological absencing that attempts to convince by linking 'false' statements on PR with sources that *a priori* appear to be sensationalist and untrustworthy.

> Movies and television programs featuring public relations practitioners often do not present accurate portrayals. Media coverage seldom associates public relations with positive stories of organizations and their accomplishments. Books such as 'PR! A Social History of Spin and Toxic Sludge Is Good for You' sensationalize accounts of press agentry and advocacy on behalf of clients and causes later proven to be of dubious merit.
>
> *(TB1:43)*

Opposing voices are even primed in the context of conspiracy theories (TB4:8). The term 'confusion' is used repeatedly (TB1:29, TB1:35–36, TB1:42, TB2:7, TB3:8, TB4:8). It allows for the circumvention of any harsh critique of critics ('no blame implied'). Instead, the reader is encouraged to pity these disoriented individuals. They are positioned as immature children whose 'confusion' needs to be remedied with some thorough education about the great true 'nature' of PR. Accordingly, the establishment of such a patronizing relationship between 'those who know' and 'those who need to be educated' leaves no room for the acknowledgement of critical PR research on a level playing field.

However, ontological absencing is a vulnerable persuasion strategy, since the absenced is made present in the texts. Simply mentioning dystopic PR practices – despite their claimed nonexistence – facilitates reflexive second-order observations. The authors do not appear to have much choice in the matter, since they are aware of the salience of negative PR images and must therefore make reference to them: 'Many people wrongly assume that public relations means image-making in the sense of creating a false front, a cover-up or "spinning" facts' (TB3:18–19). Students may be influenced by these images. The result is a strategic dilemma: something potentially present in the mindset of the reader needs to be absenced by making it present in the textbooks.

The spatial absencing of dystopic PR

Ontological absencing is the negation of a social reality in an absolute sense: something is communicated into a 'nowhere' and 'never.' It is fiction. Spatial absencing instead acknowledges the existence of contested social practices 'somewhere,' but not within the realm of public relations. Thus, spatiality is understood here in its social dimension. The 'not here, but somewhere else' should be translated into a 'not us, but somebody else.' Distancing in social spaces can occur between professions and between organisations, but also within a single organisation.

Spatial absencing constitutes a difference 'between a real public relations practitioner and someone with communication or persuasive skills merely pretending to do public relations work' (TB4:33). Readers may then ask: if it is not PR, what is it instead? And who are these people 'pretending' to do PR? TB3:14 laments 'lawyers,' 'former media personnel' and 'management-trained executives' doing something only 'under the name of public relations.' TB1 and TB4 are more concrete about what that something might be.

> For example, many do product publicity, because that is what they are paid to do under the rubric of public relations. Others see it as getting 'ink' or 'hits' (exposure in the mass media or on the website), because that is their experience as former journalists now working in public relations.
>
> *(TB1:43)*

> A company advertises for a PR representative, only to have the job turn out to be a sales rep or a telemarketing caller. A restaurant has a job in PR, but only for young women with great bodies willing to wear sexy outfits. A politician wants a PR person to do opposition research to distort another candidate's record. That's definitely not public relations.
>
> *(TB4:8)*

PR 'pretenders' might be career changers without any appropriate PR education. They engage in practices that are rather technical and/or unethical – perhaps something like 'opposition research' 'with a sexy outfit.' The quotes reflect in a crude way the professionalisation debate within the discipline (including some gendered stereotyping). However, the textbooks do not distinguish between more and less professional PR practices. The logic of spatial absencing turns everything upside down: PR is by definition a profession and if we observe a practice that is not professional, then it is not PR. Who knows, perhaps it is marketing?

> For example, the Coca-Cola company had to weigh the value of relationship building with the educational community against the cost of pursuing a marketing strategy involving exclusive arrangements in schools to ensure only its products would be sold on campus. Coca-Cola came down on the side of preserving its long-term reputation and franchise by concluding that it needed to support nonexclusive agreements in schools, allowing a range of beverages and brands to be available to students. As a result, there was no crisis with national education associations or parent-teacher groups, because the soft drink company listened, assessed the facts, and made a decision.
>
> *(TB2:12)*

> For every cereal manufacturer advertising sugary food to kids, dozens of nonprofit groups use public relations to educate parents on childhood nutrition, to expose the false claims of the marketers, and sometimes to advocate for effective public oversight on marketing practices.
>
> *(TB4:6)*

In these statements, marketing-driven approaches appear narrow-minded and unethical. PR instead cares about the concerns of parents and teachers; its purpose is education carried out primarily by non-profit groups serving the public interest. Utopic practices are reserved for public relations, whereas marketing is burdened with dystopic practices. Besides marketing, the senior management are also frequently instrumentalised as scapegoats.

> Although PR people cannot be a conscience to an organization whose leadership has none, their role is to raise issues and concerns and remind management of ethical responsibilities.
>
> *(TB3:15)*

> Sometimes public relations is asked to clean up the mess caused by others, usually managers who made bad decisions with even worse consequences, often because they failed to consider public relations perspectives before they acted.
>
> *(TB4:7)*

Overall, spatial absencing involves creating a social distance between PR professionals engaged in utopic practices and 'outsiders' who are blamed for the existence of dystopic practices. They might be career changers, they might be narrow-minded marketers and, particularly if something goes wrong, equally narrow-minded members of senior management can be held accountable. PR, meanwhile, is by definition always great and always right. Thus, even though spatial absencing acknowledges the existence of potentially problematic practices, the utopic nature of PR is never challenged.

The textbooks claim to be about 'true' public relations. This is the social space they define, so there appears to be no need to refer to anything that merely pretends to be PR. However, this is exactly what happens. Once again, the texts deconstruct themselves by making the absenced present. They destroy the 'lovely' PR moment each time they desperately attempt to hold on to it.

The temporal absencing of dystopic PR

Like spatial absencing, temporal absencing acknowledges the existence of dystopic practices. However, instead of communicating those practices out of the common social space, they are pushed into the past. Constructing the history of PR as a process of maturation from dystopic to utopic practices has been a key finding of the few existing analyses of PR textbooks referred to above. The relationship with the past is more than a minor issue. Conceptualizing PR as a process of progression over time is a key element of functionalist PR ideologies. Grunig and Hunt's (1984) 'Four Models' are probably the most popular example of a trivial modernistic understanding of PR history.

The textbooks follow the 'Four Models' ideology and ignore alternative academic approaches (e.g., L'Etang 2008b). After assuming a massive quantitative growth in PR over time (TB1:26, TB2:19, TB3:15, TB4:13, TB5:29) they leave the impression that this growth in numbers goes hand-in-hand with a qualitative improvement in PR skills: 'More than at any time in the past, today's public relations practitioner is better educated, better paid, and more prepared to take on a range of strategic planning and communication functions for organisations of all kinds' (TB2:20). PR is even credited with achieving ethical progress both within the individual organisation and in society as a whole. TB1:43 observes 'a heightened attention to public accountability and social responsibility among government administrators and business executives.' The authors present as evidence the popular 'best practice' Tylenol poisoning case from 1982. Johnson & Johnson, the pharmaceutical company that manufactures the painkiller Tylenol, is praised for its effective and ethical crisis communication – despite the fact that it is still unclear what happened and who was responsible for the deaths of seven people.

The temporal presencing of well-educated, effective and ethical professionals requires the banishing of the opposite to history: 'Old school PR has been shuffled off to the retirement home' (TB1:27; see also TB1:38). The textbook takes this quote from an advertisement for a communication agency. It shows a cigar-chomping older man wearing a gold chain and smirking into the camera while enjoying his retirement in a swimming pool.[1] The rise of the Internet and globalisation (TB2:14–17; TB3:6; TB:5:31) are used as the primary argument as to why 'Old School PR' has ended up in the retirement home: 'One fortunate outcome of the instant international communication on the Internet is the shift in a balance of power to those outside the organization' (TB3:15). Transparency, responsiveness and adaptation to the powerful (who could be anybody except the organisation's own leaders) would be the consequence. Once more, providing empirical evidence is not a strength of the textbooks. Obscure sources dominate and narratives of practitioners are taken at face value.

> Clarke, Torie. Lipstick on a pig. Winning in the No-Spin Era by someone who knows the game, New York: Free Press/Simon & Schuster, 2006. Former Pentagon spokeswoman and assistant secretary of defense for public affairs outlines why the concept of spin is both not possible and irrelevant in the Internet age.
>
> *(TB1:47)*

The textbooks' relaxed and creative use of sources allows utopic PR to be positioned as the 'lovely' response to the promises of a utopic global Internet world. One is left wondering how future editions will refer to recent discourses on fake news and the post-truth society. Will they insist on a great global Internet society that allows a transparent, responsive and symmetric PR to flourish in the here and now?

The value of temporal absencing is its capacity to legitimate an asserted pure and true presence. The textbooks are cleaning up, they are 'relegating bad practices to the dustbin of history' (TB4:8). The mere existence of PR today is proof enough of its greatness: 'If public relations was so negative, it couldn't last' (TB4:4). The author here utilises the naturalizing power of circular arguments (Alvesson, Bridgman and Willmott 2011): PR exists here and now, because it is great, otherwise it could not exist here and now. History functions as a 'dustbin' in order to let the present shine even brighter – and it will shine forever. As soon as history is conceptualised as a linear progression and the PR of today is presented as the highest possible stage of this progress in terms of effective and ethically responsible communication, there is nothing left to explore. The reality of PR is a never-ending utopia. Thus, what these authors implicitly postulate is the end of history (Fukuyama 1992). Equipped with the 'dustbin of history,' PR enters an eternal presence, free from any future challenges.

It doesn't have to be this way

The deconstruction thus far might leave the impression that all five of the textbook chapters analysed write more or less the same thing. While I did indeed observe a high degree of standardization sustained by commodified products that promote the ideology of the industry, there is one noteworthy exception. TB5, at least in parts, stands out from the rest. It conceptualises PR as an intentional activity with 'the ultimate purpose of ensuring an organization's success and economic survival'

(TB5:44). The authors do not presence PR as a kind of non-profit activity directed solely towards the public interest. The harmonious society set up as the scenery for utopic PR is contested by an understanding of PR as the 'strategic management of competition and conflict for the benefit of one's own organization and – when possible – also for the mutual benefit of the organization and its various stakeholders or publics' (TB5:33). Trade-offs between organisational and public interest are not ruled out by definition. The establishment of mutually beneficial relations is not the very 'nature' of PR, it is 'only' a normative ambition: 'Public relations activity *should be* mutually beneficial to the organization and the public' (TB5:33, emphasis added). Simply writing 'should be' here instead of 'is' signifies a fundamental renunciation of presencing as a persuasive communication strategy that advances PR ideals into factual realities. PR remains PR, even if it does not contribute to symmetric relations and the public interest. TB5 builds here on ideas that Cameron, one of the co-authors, has developed together with his colleagues. The PR contingency theory (Cancel et al. 1997) aims to overcome the intentional confusion of descriptive and normative categories that has guided functionalist PR writing since Grunig and Hunt first published their 'Four Models.'

Consequently, issues of power and persuasion do not disappear behind harmonistic win-win ideologies (see also Fawkes, Chapter 1, this volume). Instead of permanently adapting to expectations of publics, the authors dare to assert that it is also an objective of PR 'to change people's attitudes and behaviors in order to further an organization's goals and objectives' (TB5:41). It is even acknowledged that PR persuasion may, at times, be unethical. The authors present a case brought by Burson-Marsteller on behalf of Facebook in the form of a whisper campaign against Google (TB5:37). The other textbooks would consign such a case to spatial absencing; if that did indeed happen, then Burson-Marsteller must have been taken over by aliens that were merely pretending to do PR…

Overall, TB5 comprises some remarkable examples of a less biased way of teaching the complex and conflicting realities of public relations. Most importantly, it avoids the risks of replacing the PRSA ideology with a critical ideology that would have the same effect as the mainstream – only in reverse: presencing dystopic practices and absencing utopic practices. PR does not by its very definition either influence or adapt. It is not by definition either powerful or powerless, nor is it by definition either unethical or ethical (TB5:32). It is therefore up to empirical research to find out how the interplay between persuasion and responsiveness works in different contexts (Sarcinelli and Hoffmann 1997). Admittedly, other parts of TB5 still read like a promotional PRSA text, but the authors generally reflect to a greater degree on the complexities, dynamics and inconsistencies of a multitude of PR activities. While such an approach might confuse some students (Stringer 1990), confusing students is better than manipulating them.

Conclusion

When I embarked on this research, I believed that what I was going to do would be a meta-analysis; my intention was to analyse scholarly texts that themselves analyse and present public relations as an object of teaching and research. However, as it turned out, this is not the positioning of the textbook authors. Instead, their motto is: we are public relations and we invite the reader to become part of our great community. In other words, the authors do not follow a difference-oriented approach, but an identity-oriented approach. They do not preserve an intellectual domain that would allow to look from the outside at PR as a social practice (Dozier and Lauzen 2000). Instead, the textbooks themselves are public relations and they carry out *public relations for public relations.*

Their key PR strategy is presencing. This involves the conversion of normative claims into statements of fact. Utopic images of PR are presented as if they were the very nature of the practice here and now. Presencing as a communication strategy is self-immunizing, but not symmetrical. Critical stakeholders are not respected but are instead disqualified as 'confused' minds who have lost touch with reality. The presencing of the textbooks serves the ideology of the PR industry, but not the interests of students as key stakeholders. It conceals its dependency on associations instead of being transparent and reflexive about it. In other words, the textbooks are engaged in precisely the type of PR that they seek to deny the existence of. The textbooks employ dystopic PR practices to prove the nonexistence of dystopic PR practices.

I have to admit that it was an intellectual pleasure to observe how the textbooks deconstruct themselves. They cannot silence dystopic practices as they represent these very practices, making them present with every new attempt to talk them into nonexistence. This is good news for every second-order observer – be it an independent academic or a student committed to critical thinking (Schoenberger-Orgad and Spiller 2014). The dominant research and teaching ideology is not as persistent as it appears. In consequence, it would be most instructive for future research to analyse how editions of established PR textbooks have changed over time and when and why publishers decide to launch a different type of textbook. One of the textbooks analysed is markedly different and offers more than a glimmer of hope. I conclude that every form of *PR for PR* that is tempted by the promises of 'lovely' totality will ultimately fail, and so too will the textbooks' pact with the devil.

This book is dedicated to Jacquie L'Etang, who also published a public relations textbook that stands out from the commodified mainstream. Let us take the hope she formulates in her preface as a calling not to end history, but to write history: 'I hope this "textbook" will not only introduce readers to the PR establishment but also to its dis-establishment. Rock on!' (L'Etang 2008a:xi).

Note

1 I contacted US-based agency Carmichael Lynch Spong several times asking for permission to reprint their ad for this chapter. They ignored my enquiries. First-hand experiences like these reveal far more about the responsiveness of so-called professional communicators than any number of self-promotional industry-funded surveys ever will.

References

Alvesson, M., Bridgman, T. and Willmott, H. 2011, Introduction. In Alvesson, M. and Willmott, H. (eds), *The Oxford Handbook of Critical Management Studies*, Oxford: Oxford University Press, pp. 1–28.

Bernet, R. 1986, Differenz und Anwesenheit. Derridas und Husserls Phänomenologie der Sprache, der Zeit, der Geschichte, der wissenschaftlichen Rationalität, *Phänonemenologische Forschungen*, 18, pp. 51–112.

Billig, M. 2015, The Myth of Kurt Lewin and the Rhetoric of Collective Memory in Social Psychology Textbooks, *Theory & Psychology*, 25(6), pp. 703–718.

Burman, E. and MacLure, M. 2005, Deconstruction as a Method of Research. In Somekh, B. and Lewin, C. (eds), *Research Methods in the Social Sciences*, London: Sage, pp. 284–292.

Cancel, A.E., Cameron, G.T., Sallot, L.M. and Mitrook, M.A. 1997, It Depends: A Contingency Theory of Accommodation in Public Relations, *Journal of Public Relations Research*, 9(1), pp. 31–63.

Chia, R. 1996. The Problem of Reflexivity in Organizational Research: Towards a Postmodern Science of Organization, *Organization*, 3(1), pp. 31–59.

Clair, R.P. 1998, *Organizing Silence: A World of* Possibilities, New York: State University Press of New York.

Cummings, S., Bridgman, T. and Brown, K.G. 2016, Unfreezing Change as Three Steps: Rethinking Kurt Lewin's Legacy for Change Management, *Human Relations*, 69(1), pp. 33–60.

Delouvée, S., Kalampalikis, N. and Pétard, J.-P. 2011, There is Nothing So Practical as a Good… History: Kurt Lewin's Place in the Historical Chapters of French Language Social Psychology Textbooks, *Estudios de Psicología*, 32(2), pp. 243–255.

Derrida, J. 1962, *Edmund Husserl's "Origin Of Geometry": An Introduction*, translated from French by D. Carr, Reprint 1989, Lincoln, NE: University of Nebraska Press.

Derrida, J. 1967, *Voice and Phenomenon: Introduction to the Problem of the Sign in Husserl's Phenomenology*, translated from French by L. Lawlor, Reprint 2010. Evanston, IL: Northwestern University Press.

Dozier, D.M. and Lauzen M.M. 2000, Liberating the Intellectual Domain from the Practice: Public Relations, Activism, and the Role of the Scholar, *Journal of Public Relations Research*, 12(1), pp. 3–22.

Duffy, M.E. 2000, There's No Two-Way Symmetric About It: A Postmodern Examination of Public Relations Textbooks, *Critical Studies in Media Communication*, 17(3), pp. 294–315.

Foucault, M. 1965, *Madness and Civilization: A History of Insanity in the Age of Reason*, translated from French by R. Howard, New York: Random House.

Fournier, V. and Grey, C. 2000, At the Critical Moment: Conditions and Prospects for Critical Management Studies, *Human Relations*, 53(1), pp. 7–32.

Fuery, P. 1995, *The Theory Of Absence: Subjectivity, Signification, and Desire*, Santa Barbara, CA: Greenwood Press.

Fukuyama, F. 1992, *The End of History and the Last Man*, reprint 2012, London: Penguin Books.

Goethe, J.W. von 1808, *Faust*, Part I, Scenes IV to VI, Translated from German by A.S. Kline [online]. Available at: www.poetryintranslation.com/PITBR/German/FaustIScenesIVtoVI.php (accessed 9 May 2018).

Grunig, J.E. and Hunt, T. 1984, *Managing Public Relations*, Belmont, CA: Wadsworth.

Hoffmann, J. 2018, Talking Into (Non)Existence: Denying or Constituting Paradoxes of Corporate Social Responsibility, *Human Relations*, 71(5), pp. 668–691.

Hoffmann, J. 2019, Harmonious Public Relations: A Deconstruction of US-Based Public Relations Textbooks, *Critical Studies in Media Communication*, 36 (3), pp. 289–303.

Horkheimer, M. and Adorno, T.W. 1944, The Culture Industry: Enlightenment as Mass Deception, translated from German by E. Jephcott. In Durham, M.G. and Kellner, D.M. (eds), *Media and Cultural Studies*, Oxford: Blackwell, pp. 41–72.

Hoy, P., Raaz, O. and Wehmeier, S. 2007, From Facts to Stories or from Stories to Facts? Analyzing Public Relations History in Public Relations Textbooks, *Public Relations Review*, 33(2), pp. 191–200.

Husserl E. 1893–1917, *On the Phenomenology of the Consciousness of Internal Time*, reprint 1964, translated from German by J.B. Brough, Bloomington, IN: Indiana University Press.

Husserl, E. 1936, *The Crisis of European Sciences and Transcendental Phenomenology: An Introduction to Phenomenological Philosophy*, translated from German by D Carr, reprint 1970, Evanston, IL: Northwestern University Press.

L'Etang, J. 2008a, *Public Relations: Concepts, Practice and Critique*, London: Sage.

L'Etang, J. 2008b, Writing PR History: Issues, Methods and Politics, *Journal of Communication Management*, 12(4), pp. 319–333.

Lubek, I. 1993, Social Psychology Textbooks: An Historical and Social Psychological Analysis of Conceptual Filtering, Consensus Formation, Career Gatekeeping and Conservativism In Science. In Stam, H.J. et al. (eds), *Recent Trends in Theoretical Psychology*, 3, New York: Springer, pp. 359–378.

Macnamara, J. 2012, The Global Shadow of Functionalism and Excellence Theory: An Analysis of Australasian PR, *Public Relations Inquiry*, 1(3), pp. 367–402.

Myers, G.A. 1992, Textbooks and the Sociology of Scientific Knowledge, *English for Specific Purposes*, 11(1), pp. 3–17.

Raaz, O. and Wehmeier, S. 2011, Histories of Public Relations: Comparing the Historiography of British, German and US Public Relations, *Journal of Communication Management*, 15(3), pp. 256–275.

Raaz, O. and Wehmeier, S. 2016, Double Deconstruction: Transparency, Dialogue and Social Media from a Critical Post-Structuralist Perspective. In L'Etang, J. et al. (eds), *The Routledge Handbook of Critical Public Relations*, Abingdon: Routledge, pp. 173–185.

Sarcinelli, U. and Hoffmann, J. 1997, Öffentlichkeitsarbeit zwischen Ideal und Ideologie: Wieviel Moral verträgt PR und wieviel PR verträgt Moral. In Röttger, U. (ed.), *PR-Kampagnen: Über die Inszenierung von Öffentlichkeit*. Wiesbaden: VS-Verlag, pp. 35–51.

Schoenberger-Orgad, M. and Spiller, D. 2014, Critical Thinkers and Capable Practitioners: Preparing Public Relations Students for the 21st Century, *Journal of Communication Management*, 18(3), pp. 210–221.

Stringer, P. 1990, Prefacing Social Psychology: A Textbook Example. In: Parker, I. and Shotter, J. (eds), *Deconstructing Social Psychology*, New York: Routledge, pp. 17–32.

3

HOW EMPLOYEE RELATIONS SHAPED AND MAINTAINED US CORPORATE WELFARE

A historical overview

Patricia A. Curtin

Among the many contributions Jacquie L'Etang has made to public relations scholarship is encouraging public relations historians to move beyond a US corporate, progressive narrative and integrate public relations history into its broader sociocultural context (L'Etang 2014a). She has urged scholars to take a more critical stance toward the role of public relations in society, addressing issues of power and hegemony, of class, gender, and race (Fitch and L'Etang 2017).

This study, although grounded in US corporate practice, situates the development of employee relations within the larger sociocultural and political-economic environment, using cross-disciplinary sources. My research interest is driven in part by having worked in corporate employee relations and served as a union steward. The latter makes me part of the just 10.7 percent of US citizens with personal knowledge of organized labor (BLS 2018:1).

The chapter reviews the scant received history that addresses employee relations. It then places the early development of personnel policies within the context of gender, race, and class, demonstrating how employee relations developed from within multiple disciplines, public relations among them, to address social norms and concerns. The legislative reforms of the New Deal helped propel employee relations into a more purely public relations function, separate from the related field of industrial relations. As such, the employee relations functions of public relations practice morphed from a general publicity role to that of employee education, selling the benefits of corporate welfare versus those of the state. This work contends that contrary to what scholars such as Marchand (1998) have proposed, corporate welfare programs designed to prevent government social welfare initiatives didn't disappear in the 1930s but instead evolved into new forms, maintained in large part by what have become modern employee relations practices.

Received history: employee relations

US public relations histories often date the start of the profession to the Progressive Era (roughly 1890 to 1920), emerging as a corporate response to muckrakers (Ross 1959) or more generally as a way to harness the growing power of public opinion to affect business interests (Tedlow 1979). Among those public opinion issues was 'the labor problem,' characterized by numerous strikes (4,450 in 1917 alone; Taft 1976:171) and the increasing use of violence against labor (Domhoff 2013). According to prominent accounts, Ivy Lee's skill in resolving labor violence helped establish public relations as a profession and marked its progression from publicity to a management advisory function (Cutlip 1994:58; Hiebert 1966).

The development of employee relations as a specialized area of practice is often ignored. Cutlip's comprehensive history (1994:110) only briefly mentions employee relations as an established area of practice by 1927 and notes that Hill & Knowlton used employee relations to circumvent dealing with organized labor (1994:472). He makes no mention of Progressive Era corporate welfare initiatives, although Pearson (2009) suggests they may have played a formative role in employee relations practice. Marchand's (1998) more complete accounting of public relations' role in corporate welfare provides a sociocultural perspective. He argues that the corporate welfare structure died in the wake of New Deal reforms designed to address the effects of the Depression. Mention of employee relations post-Second World War is rare, despite the fact it is an active interest section within the Public Relations Society of America.

If the received view is relatively silent concerning employee relations, it is mute about the related field of industrial relations. Conversely, industrial relations texts are either silent or dismissive of the role of public relations in labor relations (Miller 1995:306). A key US industrial relations history text, for example, makes no mention of public relations, although similar to histories of public relations it traces the birth of the field to the Progressive Era and defines it as 'the relationship between employers and workers and the labor problems that grow out of this relationship' (Kaufman 1993:11).

Ivy Lee's work for John D. Rockefeller engendered rare interdisciplinary scholarship, with Hallahan concluding it was the industrial relations work of Mackenzie King, and not the public relations work of Ivy Lee, that 'ultimately had the greater influence on employee relations' (2002:300). Gitelman (1988), a labor historian, less generously concludes that Lee was incapable of advising management concerning labor relations, whereas King provided sound policy and practice. These more inclusive perspectives contradict Hiebert's (1966) glowing portrait of Lee's employee relations work. The little recorded history that tries to parse the two fields and their respective contributions to labor relations, then, provides competing narratives based on one instance in time.

Miller (1999), one of the few public relations historians to highlight the formative role of labor issues in the development of the field, provides a comprehensive examination of how the Hill & Knowlton agency used public relations to defend laissez-faire capitalism from government interference during the 1940s and 1950s. She suggests that, 'Although companies and practitioners often describe the motive for PR as putting forth industry's voice in the marketplace of ideas, the real motive may be market *control* of ideas, particularly relating to labor' (Miller 2000:392).

This study builds on Miller's proposition while focusing on the development of employee relations, in tandem with the concomitantly developing, and related, field of industrial relations. It draws on primary and secondary sources from industrial relations, labor economics, business, public relations, and politics, including textbooks, trade publications, speeches, media coverage, corporate archives, legal decisions, and government reports, to provide a contextualized perspective on the development of employee relations as a distinct branch of public relations. The historical record, however, is of necessity incomplete, fractured, and often recorded by those in power and privileged to do so. What follows, then, is an origin tale of one branch of public relations practice in the US – but it is hardly the only tale, nor a definitive account.

The formative role of gender, class and race

Received PR and industrial relations histories point to the rapid growth of factory workforces during the Progressive Era as creating a need for formalized worker relations. The Firestone Tire & Rubber Company, for example, grew from 12 workers in 1902 to 10,000 in 1917 (Brandes 1976:14). Harlow (1981:34) went so far as to suggest that PR practice arose as a

> substitute for the loss of the owner-employer intimacy once enjoyed by small concerns (…) No longer could management be safe in carrying on activities involving thousands of employees (…) without some cement to bind them together and give them a feeling of belonging to a single family.

Lee (1907:163) credited the rise of large-scale industry with providing better provisions for workers, resulting in 'harmony between the employer and employe.'

Women's work

While a desire to restore family feeling and create harmony engenders a romantic picture of early employee relations practices as the domain of public relations, historical records suggest gender, race, and geography played more formative roles in a field that was not yet clearly defined by disciplinary boundaries. As early as 1840, for example, the Lowell, Massachusetts textile mill complex employed almost 8,000 workers, the vast majority of whom were young, single women off the farm. Women were preferred because weaving was 'women's work'; women could be hired for about 30 percent of what men were paid, and they were deemed more compliant than men (Dray 2010:20–21).

At the time, no federal laws protected workers, but social norms concerning women pressured employers to adopt protective policies. Lowell management prescribed boarding houses run by carefully screened Christian matrons who ensured the Sabbath was kept and good manners cultivated. Management justified the 14-hour workdays by claiming hard work, not leisure, would lead to good character and keep the women from indulging in debauchery, presenting factory work as a form of moral improvement (Pessen 1976:66). By mid-century the long hours and poor work conditions led to worker unrest and strikes, but a government commission concluded no regulations were warranted because they might harm any competitive business advantage (Dray 2010:55).

The need to protect the morality of a female workforce engendered other personnel policies that were similar in form but differed in particulars. The smaller Fred Harvey Company began hiring young, single women in 1883 as serving staff for remote railway restaurants as a way to establish a culture of gentility not usually found in such places. Similar to Lowell, management provided housing, and carefully selected house mothers strictly enforced house rules and behavior in line with company policy. In contrast to the mills, however, Harvey ensured good working conditions, fairly generous pay, and advancement opportunities, earning worker loyalty (Poling-Kempes 1991).

In 1875, the family-owned H. J. Heinz Co. hired a 'social secretary' who served as a mother figure for its mainly female, urban-based workforce (Brandes 1976) and oversaw its recreation and dining facilities designed to attract workers in a competitive market (Butko 2012). A common factor in these early efforts was that the work women performed was of relatively low status compared to professions such as teaching or nursing (Poling-Kempes 1991:53), but gender trumped class in terms of the need to formulate employee policies because 'What employer can escape the responsibility to protect the maligned "factory girl," as chary of her reputation as her sister in the so-called upper world?' (Beeks 1903:2517).

Formalized employee policies and functions, then, predated the Progressive Era, but they varied according to the particular owners' business philosophies and location. What the Progressive Era added to these early practices was an increased social reform sensibility, resulting in the establishment of usually female-run women's welfare departments in the corporate structures of urban factories and retail stores (Brandes 1976:117). Many companies would hire only single women, making the average tenure for a female factory worker just shy of two years (Tone 1997:141). With the workplace perceived as a short-term finishing school prior to a woman's 'real' work of marriage and motherhood, many companies offered instruction in home economics, including cooking, sewing, and hygiene. Short-term employment was cast as a way to turn lower-class factory girls into middle-class housewives.

The women's departments of the Progressive Era demonstrated a growing institutionalization of the employee relations function (Mandell 2002:69), but they were closely related to a nascent form of industrial relations (Brody 1993:12) and operated separately from most publicity and public relations functions (Tone 1997:173). Management soon realized, however, the value of publicizing its efforts to 'improve' the lives of female workers in an age of social reform. Publicists deflected criticism of women in the workforce by casting these employment arenas as creating opportunities for class mobility.

Americanizing the workforce

National Cash Register's Woman's Department made extensive use of a press bureau to publicize its efforts (Morris 1921:120). The workers who appeared in NCR's publicity materials shared one important characteristic besides gender – they were US-born and therefore classified as 'white.' NCR management scorned immigrants, no matter their race, because they were 'wholly uneducated. These we do not want' (Tone 1997:158). Others, like the Lowell mills, had an almost wholly immigrant female workforce by 1900 to keep labor costs down and profit margins up. Between 1882 and 1903 the US passed three comprehensive immigration acts targeted not so much at the number of immigrants as where they came from because 'serious problems have arisen as a result of the influx of many thousands of unskilled laborers from southern and eastern Europe, belonging to nationalities less easily assimilated and Americanized than the English, Irish, and Germans' (Cowdrick 1923:151).

Personnel programs addressing these 'less desirable' immigrants arose not because society thought they needed protection but because society viewed them as a threat. In 1881 the Colorado Fuel & Iron Company established medical facilities to serve its distant mine camps. With the influx of Eastern and Central Europeans and growing labor unrest, CFI reorganized the medical facilities into a Sociological Department, which provided English lessons and Christian-based recreation activities. In 1923, CFI owner John D. Rockefeller, Jr., who hired both public relations practitioner Ivy Lee and industrial relations practitioner Mackenzie King to advise him, declared the program a success, noting that the workers 'were only yearning to be taught how to be Americans,' and the program represented 'an overwhelming achievement of remaking the miners in our image' (Henry 2014:96).

In 1913, the Ford Motor Company formed its Sociological Department, which oversaw a 71-percent foreign-born male workforce, representing 22 nationalities (Meyer 1981). Believing that 'good home conditions beget the qualities most desirable for productive factory labor' (Lee 1916:308), the Sociological Department trained 400 employees to become home inspectors to ensure only Christian men of 'proven thrifty habits' received benefits (Lee 1916:302). Ford's employment department provided English and civics lessons because doing so was 'perhaps the wisest course that any employer of labor can take to sift and solve the many of the problems that daily confront us' (Lee 1916:306). Ford's English School for Foreigners graduated 16,000 employees over the course of its first six years (Morris 1921:70), with graduates descending into a large 'Melting Pot,' dressed in their native garb, and emerging from the other side wearing US clothes and waving American flags (Marquis 1923). Large and small companies offered 'Americanization' courses, with English-language classes as their core. Other coursework included personal hygiene, thriftiness, and the capitalist system; some offered Bible classes as well (Brandes 1976:15).

Key to the development of early employee and industrial relations programs, then, were social and cultural norms surrounding gender, race, and class. Employee relations developed in large part to address issues surrounding marginalized members of society who constituted a cheaper labor pool. The personal values and beliefs of corporate owners shaped how these programs were instigated and administered, and no clear professional boundaries were in place that defined this work as the purview of public relations only.

Centralizing the employee function

Over the course of the Progressive Era, as the scale and scope of industrialization grew, women's welfare departments and sociological departments often gave way to centralized employee units (Mandell 2002:2), bringing employee relations out of the margins and into the mainstream. Many factors contributed to this move, but two appear pivotal. One was the rise of scientific management, commonly known as Taylorism, designed to increase worker efficiency, and therefore profits, through large-scale manufacturing and assembly-line approaches (Taylor 1911). The result, ironically, was often repetitive, dehumanizing work, leading to rapid employee turnover, which in turn increased costs. The Ford Motor Company, for example, experienced a 370-percent turnover rate in 1913 (Brandes 1976:135). However, many companies turned to centralized personnel functions to enact scientific management principles.

The second was an increase in union membership. Most US businessmen opposed unionization as contrary to individual freedom and the rights of business leaders to do as they wished. A national trade association resolution succinctly stated, 'It is the privilege of the employee to leave our employ whenever he sees fit and it is the privilege of the employer to discharge any workman he sees fit' (Action of the National Metal Trades Association 1901:678). A major railroad president expressed the divine capitalist noblesse oblige of the day:

> The rights and interests of the laboring man will be protected and cared for –
> not by the labor agitators, but by the Christian men to whom God in His
> infinite wisdom has given the control of the property interests of the country,
> and upon the successful Management of which so much depends.
>
> *(Baer 1902:1)*

An ambitious social experiment

Although Taylorism and union organizing may have contributed to the centralization of personnel functions, such centralization took a variety of forms. All formats, however, shared a common goal of providing employees with a service, improvement, or benefit beyond that required by law in order to produce 'sound and harmonious relationships between men and management' similar to the 'sound and harmonious relationship between a man and his wife' (US Steel company executive, quoted in Domhoff 2013:24). In 1929 a labor economist called these programs

> one of the most ambitious social experiments of the age, because they aim, among other things, to counteract the effect of modern technique upon the mind of the worker, to prevent him from becoming class conscious and from organizing trade unions.
>
> *(Brody 1993:57)*

It wasn't difficult to provide more than the law required, given that so few laws existed. President Theodore Roosevelt (1908) observed that 'It is a reproach to us as a Nation that in both Federal and State legislation we have afforded less protection to public and private employees than any other industrial country in the world.'

Benefits introduced included profit sharing, which it was claimed would erase class differences, and stock ownership, designed 'to bridge the gap between capital and labor' (Brandes 1976:87). Pension plans and medical and life insurance were instituted, although a number of plans excluded women, blacks, and union members, favoring the compliant Northern European male breadwinner (Klein 2003:13). Companies could withhold or withdraw these benefits at any time because US courts declared them a gift not legally owed to employees (Tone 1997:212), causing one socialist to warn that talk about how good these programs were was 'just so much haywire put out by publicity boys' (Dunn 1927:19).

Industrial relations takes charge

Administering personnel programs became a centralized function in at least half of all organizations by 1920 (Jacoby 1997:18). What job title or department was associated with that function, however, varied. Kaufman (1993:46) states that industrial relations took off as a field around 1920, defined as using personnel management to avoid conflict and achieve harmony through education and persuasion. This description of industrial relations is so similar to that of the employee relations aspects of public relations practice as to be indistinguishable; Ivy Lee (1907:163) described his work as designed to achieve harmony between employers and employees.

Both *public relations* and *industrial relations* were in the common business lexicon, and the term *employee relations* appears to have been gaining currency as well. A well-read 1921 text states that training was being offered in industrial relations, which included employee relations (Morris 1921:59). In 1922, industrial relations became a field of study at Princeton University; that same year, Edward L. Bernays taught the first class in public relations at New York University.

One distinction may be that industrial relations was acquiring a scientific veneer, encompassing natural and behavioral sciences, but was not inclusive of communication (Bernstein 1969:175; Kaufman 1993:16–17). In 1919, John D. Rockefeller, Jr., formed the Special Conference Committee to solve labor issues (Jacoby 1997:21). The group became known as Industrial Relations Counselors (IRC) in 1921, characterized as a business-to-business research and consulting group designed 'to promote improved relations between employers and employees' (Kaufman 1993:7). Ivy Lee, still in Rockefeller's employ, was conspicuously absent from the group. The IRC produced 15 major research studies between 1930 and 1939, based on the scientific research of the day (Kaufman 1993:57).

Conversely, public relations had strong ties to mass communication, but it lacked scientific standing. In most instances, public relations appears on the periphery of centralized personnel offices, publicizing the benefits programs run by industrial relations departments and producing employee magazines (i.e., company organs). With the relative prosperity of the 1920s came less labor unrest, and keeping employees contented by publicizing benefits was key to reducing turnover. About 50 percent of manufacturers had employee magazines at this time (Raucher 1968:69), which did not deal directly with labor discontent but instead stressed worker satisfaction and family feel (Tone 1997:102; Marchand 1998:110). A common theme was a story highlighting the humble beginnings of the CEO, stressing how through hard work he had gained the necessary knowledge of economics and business to lead the company, resulting in a rags-to-riches American Dream tale (Brandes 1976:63–64).

It was an era of relatively peaceful employee relations that required more administrative prowess than it did relationship building. A visiting Australian scholar noted in 1928 that 'Labour organization exists only by the tolerance of employers (…) It has no real part in determining industrial conditions' (Bernstein 1969:83). A government report concluded that US laborers did not like to feel dependent on the state, making corporate welfare efforts more palatable that those of the state (Tone 1997:39), thus legislation was unwarranted.

The New Deal, a new role for public relations

The common pattern of centralized industrial relations departments and peripheral public relations efforts may have continued unabated were it not for the Great Depression and resulting New Deal legislation. The Depression marked the cessation of most corporate welfare programs (Marchand 1998), and President Franklin Roosevelt introduced legislation to address resulting labor and social welfare issues. The 1935 National Labor Relations Act (commonly known as the Wagner Act) and the 1935 Social Security Act particularly galled US business leaders, for they seriously curtailed owners' perceived divine right to manage their property as they saw fit and violated the US ethos of rugged individualism.

Although the Social Security Act was modeled after the private system and only supplemented, not supplanted, it, business owners loudly protested the government's 'socializing tendencies' (Griswold 1937:129). They viewed the Wagner Act as even more pernicious because it guaranteed workers' rights to engage in collective bargaining and strikes. The Act also created the National Labor Relations Board, which had the authority to adjudicate labor disputes and actions, creating what public relations practitioner John Hill termed 'the unholy alliance between labor and the administration' (Miller 1999:93). Industry complained to any who listened that 'Business is distrusted by the public and mistreated by the government' (Belden 1944:97).

For business, employees became a crucial public (Griswold 1939:708) in need of persuasion, rather than simply a variable in a labor efficiency equation, bringing public relations to the fore: 'In the present disturbed structure of industrial management, the problem of employer and employee relationships in relation to unions, the government, and the like, has come to occupy the central place in public relations' (Harlow 1942:28). Industry turned to public relations to educate employees concerning the benefits of the free enterprise system, viewing it as a necessary expense, even in tight financial times (Walker and Sklar 1938:8–15; Griswold 1937:126). The National Association of Manufacturers' public relations department produced materials specifically for employees and labor markets, such as the *Uncle Abner Says* cartoon series, which used folksy characters to denigrate government interference in business, and the 'I Knew Him When' ads, which portrayed the American Dream in action, demonstrating that everyone could succeed if they just worked hard enough (Walker and Sklar 1938:46, 54).

Employee relations personnel began using readability scales for employee communications (Whyte 1952:67) to ensure financial information was 'presented in an elementary manner' so employees could appreciate the finer points of capitalism (Cole 1940:500). Business owners optimistically believed that 'Once they understand a business's objectives and how those objectives involve the greater good for all employees (…) people will lend willing and warm support to their realization' (Day 1966:18). Some employees were required to attend in-house economics education programs, and new job titles, such as *Manager of Economics Training*, appeared on organizational charts (Fones-Wolf 1994:81–83).

By 1940 public relations executives were claiming that industrial relations was a specialized subset of public relations practice (Griswold 1940:487), with business owners increasingly considering communication key to their personnel programs (Jacoby 1997:179). A few suggested the two fields were melding: 'Both efforts seem to be more rationally and more effectively expressed in the merged form' (Walker and Sklar 1938:69). Public relations seminars for business leaders stressed labor and industrial relations as major themes and provided pointers in 'The Solid Basis of Laissez Faire' (Fine 1941:111).

The new corporate welfare state

Following the Second World War and the 'miracle of American production,' credited with winning the war, the last vestiges of the Depression cleared, and many Americans experienced growing economic prosperity and a growing fear of communism. In this new economic and political climate Congress passed the 1947 Labor Management Relations Act, better known as the Taft-Hartley Act, effectively gutting the labor-friendly reforms of the Wagner Act. It required union leaders to sign anti-communist affidavits, it allowed businesses to take a vocal anti-union stance in the workplace, and it made the passage of 'right-to-work' laws possible (Domhoff 2013:52). The legislation opened the door for a resurgence of laissez-faire capitalism.

Eisenhower's election in 1953 cemented the political shift to a pro-business stance, continuing the rollback of government regulation of business (Jacoby 1997:200–201). A *New York Times* article, under a picture of a line of workers, asked, 'Denizens of tomorrow's welfare state? No, employees of Sears, Roebuck & Company and participants in one of the most fabulous pension plans on the present-day business scene' (Rutter 1956:34). Articles in *PR News* (St. John 2014:325) and *Public Relations Quarterly* (Day 1966:17) touted the role of public relations in changing public opinion concerning labor legislation and setting corporate employee welfare back on track.

Despite the rollback of New Deal-era labor protections, business continued to fear possible government encroachment. An article in *Public Relations Quarterly*, 'PR Man: Industry's New Bosom Buddy,' warned that 'Government, more and more, is interrelating with economic life. Business increasingly is operating in a goldfish bowl; and its management must account to government, unions, customers, employees and the public at large' (Heady 1969:35). Employee relations remained a centralized function in most large companies to help convince employees of the value of company-provided benefits and free enterprise, which expanded to include not just medical and life insurance, pension plans, and stock-sharing programs, but also child and eldercare, in-house spas and gym facilities, and educational benefits.

Corporate welfare, then, far from dying during the Depression as Marchand (1998) has suggested, merely took new forms, making 'the present seem less like a break than a rerun' (Jacoby 1997:9). As a result, a 1990 study found that of the top 18 industrialized nations, the US provided the fewest state benefits and relied most on the private sector, resulting in what one critic called 'corporate serfdom' (Esping-Andersen 1990:97). Employee relations, as a branch of public relations practice, emerged in the post-Second World War era as US business' tool of choice in selling that ideology to workers. Industrial relations, conversely, has mainly disappeared from view (Kaufman 1993), and human relations departments are now tasked with overseeing relations with unions for the few US workers who are unionized (10.7 percent; BLS 2018:1).

Conclusion

Although Harlow (1981) suggested employee relations propelled the development of public relations practice as a whole, the evidence does not support his conclusion. The evidence also doesn't support the received 'truth' that public relations arose solely as a response to the muckrakers, although it suggests that social reform initiatives may have served as one of many contributing factors. What this study adds is *a* narrative, not *the* narrative, of a strand of practice within an ill-defined profession struggling to establish itself and to which many formative factors contributed. As L'Etang (2014b:655) observed, 'History thinking and writing is interpretive and rhetorical, an argumentative process, not a catalogue. Archives may be sources, but without broader level theoretical interpretation they are simply partial fragments of past human activities.'

This study suggests that industrialization drove a need for better employee relations as workers became distanced from management on the organization chart as well as increasingly distant in terms of gender, ethnicity, and/or class. Early employee relations efforts began as individualized actions, outside of disciplinary bounds, that varied widely. As they proliferated in an environment of Progressive Era reforms, they often appeared under the purview of industrial relations, with public relations providing a supplementary publicity function. Employee relations as a more wholly public relations function did not become institutionalized until business, threatened by restrictive legislation, deemed employee communication and education necessary to retain 'market *control* of ideas, particularly relating to labor,' as Miller (2000:392) noted. It was in the ideological arena that employee relations as a public relations practice came into its own.

Employee relations has helped maintain that control by promoting corporate welfare as the American way, and it emerged from 'a distinctive American environment composed of large firms, weak unions, and small government' (Jacoby 1997:4). This US emphasis on individual rights and responsibilities has informed government policy and social norms, creating a distinct US form of employee relations that supports and maintains laissez-faire capitalism, keeping corporate welfare efforts at the forefront of US policy at the expense of the state.

References

Action of the National Metal Trades Association 1901, *American Machinist*, vol. 24, pp. 678–679.

Baer, G.F. 1902, *Letter to Mr. Clarke*, The Clarence Darrow Digital Collectio. Available at http://moses.law.umn.edu/darrow/trials.php?tid=12 [accessed 12 April 2018].

Beeks, G. 1903, Employees' Welfare Work, *The Independent*, vol. 55, pp. 2515–2518.

Bernstein, I. 1969, *The Lean Years: A History of the American Worker, 1920–1933*, New York: Houghton Mifflin.

BLS, 2018, *Union Members—2017. Bureau of Labor Statistics News Release*, Washington, DC: US Department of Labor.

Brandes, S.D. 1976, *American Welfare Capitalism, 1880–1940*, Chicago, IL: University of Chicago Press.

Brody, D. 1993, *Workers in Industrial America: Essays on the Twentieth Century Struggle*, 2nd edn. New York: Oxford University Press.

Butko, B. 2012, Heinz: Much More than 57 Varieties, *Pennsylvania Heritage Magazine*, 38(2). Available at www.phmc.state.pa.us/portal/communities/pa-heritage/heinz-much-more-than-57-varieties.html [accessed 27 June 2017].

Cole, R.J. 1940, A Survey of Employer Attitudes, *Public Opinion Quarterly*, 4(3), pp. 497–506.

Cowdrick, E.S. 1923, *Industrial History of the United States*, New York: The Ronald Press Company.

Cutlip, S.M. 1994, *The Unseen Power: Public Relations. A History*, Hillsdale, NJ: Erlbaum.

Day, V.B. 1966, Communication in Labor Relations, *Public Relations Quarterly*, summer, pp. 15–23.

Domhoff, G.W. 2013, *The Rise and Fall of Labor Unions in the U.S.*, Who rules America.net. Available at www2.ucsc.edu/whorulesamerica/power/ history_of_labor_unions. html [accessed 2 February 2015].

Dunn, R. 1927, The Class War is Still On. *New Masses*, April, p. 19.

Dray, P 2010, *There is Power in a Union: The Epic Story of Labor in America*, New York: Anchor Books.

Esping-Andersen, G. 1990, *The Three Worlds of Welfare Capitalism*, Princeton, NJ: Princeton University Press.

Fine, B. 1941, New York Course on Public Relations, *Public Opinion Quarterly*, 5(1), pp. 111–113.

Fitch, K. and L'Etang, J. 2017, Other Voices? The State of Public Relations History and Historiography: Questions, Challenges and Limitations of 'National' Histories and Historiographies, *Public Relations Inquiry*, 6(1), pp. 115–136.

Fones-Wolf, E.A. 1994, *Selling Free Enterprise: The Business Assault on Labor and Liberalism 1945–1960*, Urbana, IL: University of Illinois Press.

Gitelman, H.M. 1988, *Legacy of the Ludlow Massacre: A Chapter in American Industrial Relations*, Philadelphia, PA: University of Pennsylvania Press.

Griswold, G. 1937, Public Relations: Some Misconceptions, *Public Opinion Quarterly*, 1(3), pp. 126–131.

Griswold, G. 1939, The McGraw-Hill Public Relations Forums, *Public Opinion Quarterly*, 3(4), pp. 704–709.

Griswold, G. 1940, Humanized Employee Relations: Studebaker, an Example, *Public Opinion Quarterly*, 4(3), pp. 487–496.

Hallahan, K. 2002, Ivy Lee and the Rockefellers' Response to the 1913–1914 Colorado Coal Strike, *Journal of Public Relations Research*, 14(4), pp. 265–315.

Harlow, R. 1942, Public Relations and Social Action, *Journal of Higher Education*, 13(1), pp. 25–29.

Harlow, R. 1981, A Timeline of Public Relations Development, *Public Relations Review*, 7(2), pp. 33–42.

Heady, R.K. 1969, PR Man: Industry's New Bosom Buddy, *Public Relations Quarterly*, 14(2), pp. 5, 35–38.

Henry, R.C. 2014, In Order to Form a More Perfect Worker, in F.-A. Montoya (ed.), *Making an American Workforce: The Rockefellers and the Legacy of Ludlow*, Boulder, CO: University of Colorado Press, pp. 81–101.

Hiebert, R.E. 1966, *Courtier to the Crowd: The Story of Ivy Lee and the Development of Public Relations*, Ames, IA: Iowa State University Press.

Jacoby, S.M. 1997, *Modern Manors: Welfare Capitalism since the New Deal*, Princeton, NJ: Princeton University Press.

Kaufman, B.E. 1993, *The Origins and Evolution of the Field of Industrial Relations in the United States*, Ithaca, NY: ILR Press.

Klein, J. 2003, *For All These Rights: Business, Labor, and the Shaping of America's Public-Private Welfare State*, Princeton, NJ: Princeton University Press.

Lee, I.L. 1907, An Open and Aboveboard 'Trust', *Moody's Magazine*, July, pp. 158–164.

Lee, J.R. 1916, The So-Called Profit Sharing System in the Ford Plant, *Annals of the American Academy of Political and Social Science*, 65, pp. 297–301.

L'Etang, J. 2014a, Foreword, in B. St. John III, M.O. Lamme, and J. L'Etang (eds), *Pathways to Public Relations: Histories of Practice and Profession*, New York: Routledge, pp. xii–xviii.

L'Etang, J. 2014b, Public Relations and Historical Sociology: Historiography as Reflexive Critique. *Public Relations Review*, 40, pp. 654–660.

Mandell, N. 2002, *The Corporation as Family: The Gendering of Corporate Welfare 1899–1930*, Chapel Hill, NC: University of North Carolina Press.

Marchand, R. 1998, *Creating the Corporate Soul: The Rise of Public Relations and Corporate Imagery in American Big Business*, Berkeley, CA: University of California Press.

Marquis, S.S. 1923, *Henry Ford: An Interpretation*, Boston, MA: Little, Brown, and Company.

Meyer, III, S. 1981, *The Five Dollar Day: Labor Management and Social Control in the Ford Motor Company, 1908–1921*, Albany, NY: State University of New York Press.

Miller, K.S. 1995, National and Local Public Relations Campaigns during the 1946 Steel Strike, *Public Relations Review*, 21(4), pp. 305–323.

Miller, K.S. 1999, *The Voice of Business: Hill & Knowlton and Postwar Public Relations*, Chapel Hill, NC: University of North Carolina Press.

Miller, K.S. 2000, US Public Relations History: Knowledge and Limitations. In M.E. Roloff (ed.), *Communication Yearbook*, vol. 23, Thousand Oaks, CA: Sage, pp. 381–420.

Morris, J.V.L. 1921, *Employee Training: A Study of Education and Training Departments in Various Corporations*, New York: McGraw-Hill Book Company, Inc..

Pearson, R. 2009, Perspectives on Public Relations History. In R. Heath, E.L. Toth, and D. Waymer (eds), *Rhetorical and Critical Approaches to Public Relations II*, New York: Routledge, pp. 92–109.

Pessen, E. 1976, Builders of the Young Republic. In R.B. Morris (ed.), *The American Worker*, Washington, DC: US Department of Labor, pp. 56–80.

Poling-Kempes, L. 1991, *The Harvey Girls: Women Who Opened the West*, New York: Marlowe & Company.

Raucher, A.R. 1968, *Public Relations and Business (1900–1929)*, Baltimore, MD: Johns Hopkins Press.

Roosevelt, T. 1908, Special Message to Congress on Labor. Available online www.presidency. ucsb.edu/ws/ index.php?pid=69676 [accessed 11 November 2017].

Ross, I. 1959, *The Image Merchants: The Fabulous World of Public Relations*, Garden City, NY: Doubleday.

Rutter, R. 1956, Sears' Pension Fund Provides Good Protection for 'Rainy Day', *New York Times*, May 21, pp. 34, 37.

St. John III, B. 2014, The Good Reason of Public Relations: PR News and the Selling of a Field. In B. St. John III, M.O. Lamme, and J. L'Etang (eds), *Pathways to Public Relations: Histories of Practice and Profession*, New York: Routledge, pp. 321–339.

Taft, P. 1976, Workers of a New Century. In R.B. Morris (ed.), *The American Worker*, Washington, DC: US Department of Labor, pp. 152–176.

Taylor, F.W. 1911, *Principles of Scientific Management*. New York: Harper & Brothers.

Tedlow, R.S. 1979, *Keeping the Corporate Image: Public Relations and Business 1900–1950*, Greenwich, CT: JAI Press.

Tone, A. 1997, *The Business of Benevolence: Industrial Paternalism in Progressive America*, Ithaca, NY: Cornell University Press.

Walker, S.H. and Sklar, P. 1938, *Business Finds its Voice: Management's Effort to Sell the Business Idea to the Public*, New York: Harper & Brothers.

Whyte, Jr., W.H. 1952, *Is Anybody Listening? How and Why U.S. Business Fumbles when it Talks with Human Beings*, New York: Simon and Schuster.

PART II

Historicising gender, ethnicity and diversity in PR work

4

WIVES, SECRETARIES AND BODIES

Representations of women in an Australian public relations journal, 1965–1972

Kate Fitch

Introduction

Despite growing interest in the history of public relations (PR), relatively little attention has been paid to the changing role of women in the field even though women were employed in PR and related industries throughout the twentieth century. Few histories challenge the exclusion of women from historical narratives. This chapter examines the representation of women in trade media and considers more broadly the impact of second-wave feminism and societal shifts around women and the workforce. It highlights the need for a more historically informed position on women and PR in order to better understand the development of an occupational and professional identity along gendered lines and the significance for the PR industry today.

This study investigates the representation of women in the Australian PR industry's trade media from 1965 to 1972 in order to understand how shifting gender dynamics in Australian society played out in the PR industry. This is a relatively short but arguably pivotal period in terms of women and work, as these years coincided with the rise of the women's liberation movement in Australia and the publication of Germaine Greer's *The Female Eunuch* in 1970, and culminated in the 1972 Equal Pay Decision. There is almost no research regarding women working in PR in Australia in the period immediately prior to the 1970s and 1980s, when the PR occupation underwent a sustained period of feminisation.

My chapter begins with a brief overview of the postwar history of women and work in Australia, in order to understand the broader social context in which I locate this study, and of feminised work in media industries. I also discuss the marginalisation of women in PR historiography and identify the need to understand the changing significance of gender for PR. I then present the findings of my analysis of the representation of women in the journal produced by the state-based Public

Relations Institutes of Australia from 1965 to 1972. *Public Relations Journal* was renamed *Public Relations Australia* in 1968, as it aspired to be a national journal; it did not represent the Tasmanian institute until 1968 nor the Western Australian institute until 1971 but nevertheless aimed to represent all members throughout Australia (Fitch 2016b). The New South Wales institute initially produced the journal until it moved to Victoria in 1966. I analyse the ways in which women are represented in the journal: as wives, secretaries, consumers, practitioners and as 'body parts' in art and design. The representation of expert female practitioners is limited, despite evidence of established senior women in the industry and an increase in female members, particularly in entry-level positions. Finally, I discuss the only explicit reference to women's rights in the journal along with a book written by a high-profile institute member that addressed women's careers. I conclude by considering how a historically informed position on women and PR contributes to a better understanding of the gendering of the contemporary occupational identity.

Women and work in Australia

Although the journal examined in this chapter only spanned a few years, they are arguably pivotal years in the broader context of women and the Australian labour force and the emergence of the women's liberation movement. The twentieth century saw increasing participation of women in paid work in Australia. Postwar industrialisation and economic growth between 1948 and 1968 offered new employment opportunities in white-collar occupations and for middle-class and married women (Aveling and Damousi 1991; Curthoys 1987; O'Donnell and Hall 1988). In 1966, just over one-third of women were employed and employment was highest among younger women (ABS 2017). Women's participation in paid work increased from one-fifth to one-third of the total workforce between 1945 and 1975, and while only 32 per cent of women were in paid employment in 1961, by 1976 it was 50 per cent (Fox 1991). In 1950 only 12 per cent of married women were employed but by 1974 this figure had increased to 40 per cent (Aveling and Damousi 1991).

Despite the increasing participation of women in paid work, their career paths were often limited; for example, men entered roles in the public sector with significant opportunities for advancement while women were confined to clerical work (Curthoys 1987). This gendered segregation was confirmed in interview-based research I conducted with female PR practitioners about their experiences in the 1970s and 1980s (Fitch and Third 2014) and is mirrored in the experiences of women working as radio and television producers for the Australian public broadcaster in the 1950s and 1960s (Andrews 2016).

Campaigns for equal pay for men and women had begun as early as the 1930s and occurred again from the early 1960s, spearheaded by the union movement (Curthoys 1975, 1987). The 1972 Equal Pay Decision confirmed equal pay for work of equal value would be introduced in stages by June 1975. Yet, as Curthoys argues, the equal pay principle resulted in the further segregation of work along gender lines. The PR industry, unlike journalism, was not unionised and PR consultants often fell into the groups such as employers, self-employed, managerial and professional staff not covered by federal and state awards (O'Donnell and Hall 1988). Writing on women in Australian advertising, Dickenson (2016) notes that the equal pay debates of the 1960s and 1970s simply did not apply to that non-unionised industry and nor was equal pay a concern for the professional body. Indeed, as Edwards (2014) later notes, in service industries such as PR, there is considerable flexibility even to this day around the negotiation of individual workers' salaries.

Low pay, precarity and service roles are typical of feminised work (Adkins and Dever 2016). Given the widespread recognition of the feminisation of PR, and the corresponding devaluing of 'women's work,' and related issues such as the gender pay gap and the glass ceiling, it is important to recognise such devaluing in its historical context. The feminisation of the Australian PR industry in the 1980s provoked considerable anxiety among industry leaders (Fitch and Third 2014). This anxiety persists today. To offer just one example, PRIA (2016) released a diversity and inclusion policy in late 2016; their primary strategy to address the industry's gender imbalance was to recruit more men. The response in the 1980s was to establish more professional structures, yet the very processes of professionalisation marginalise women's work (Davies 1996; Fitch and Third 2010; Witz 1992). As I discuss in the following section, women have always worked in PR, even if various histories erase their participation and suggest their entry into the occupation was relatively recent. The historical shifts around women and PR are worth studying to better understand how gender continues to structure both the field's occupational identity and PR work.

Women in public relations history and historiography

In recent years, historical research on the role of women in Australian media and promotional industries has flourished. There are studies of women working in press photography (Darian-Smith 2016); war reporting; (Baker 2015); journalism (Lloyd 2014); public broadcasting (Andrews 2016); and advertising (Dickenson 2016). Baker and Lloyd refer to histories of gendered media labour as 'previously invisible histories' (2016:12). The value of such research is in offering new perspectives on gender and media work, including the feminisation of particular practices and sectors. Yet, other than a couple of studies (see Fitch 2016a, 2016b; Fitch and Third 2014), few media historians have researched the highly feminised Australian PR industry. In part, this may be due to longstanding tensions between PR and journalism and media studies in the academy as well as competing disciplinarity between advertising and PR. That said, advertising and PR were not always separate functions in the twentieth century, but professionalisation demanded the establishment of 'unique' fields of expertise (Dickenson 2016; Fitch 2016a, L'Etang 2004). It is worth noting experience in almost any kind of media work – in advertising, radio, journalism, television, magazines and newspapers – allowed women and men into PR roles from the mid-twentieth century (Fitch 2016a).

Few PR histories focus on women in the industry. Gender was 'a major missing concept' in the first major book series on PR history (Fitch and L'Etang 2017:129). Even when chapter authors in that series acknowledge women in relation to national histories, the information tends to be presented uncritically, for example, noting the number of women working in the industry, their dominance in certain sectors and that historically PR was perceived as event management performed by attractive women. The lack of attention to women in PR history can partly be attributed to a poor understanding of historiography within the discipline. The dominance of practitioner and industry perspectives, which historically have shaped the curriculum, framed the field and even influenced the scope of research, have resulted in histories that tend to lack criticality and evidence (Fitch 2015). Such histories structure the development of the PR industry in terms of an evolution towards the modern profession (Fitch and L'Etang 2017). This poses a number of challenges, not least the failure to consider broader societal changes around women and work, the masculine coding of professions, and the ways in which feminisation is entangled with processes of professionalisation.

Researching the role of women is therefore fraught. In the last two decades, a small number of scholars have begun to pay attention to the role of women. These histories include biographies of individual practitioners, such as Doris Fleischman (Lamme 2001, 2007) and Jane Stewart in the USA (Miller 1997), and Teresa Dorn in Spain (Rodríguez-Salcedo and Gómez-Baceiredo 2017); interview-based investigations of the lived experiences of female practitioners in earlier decades (Fitch and Third 2014; Yaxley 2013); and investigations of women in the PR industry through analysis of trade media and publications in the USA (Gower 2001; Horsley 2009); trade media combined with oral history interviews in the UK (L'Etang 2015); and of trade media and digitised newspaper archives in Australia (Fitch 2016a, 2016b). These latter studies offer convincing evidence that women participated in the Australian PR industry throughout the second half of the twentieth century and yet are poorly represented in contemporary histories.

Investigating public relations' trade media

Given the challenges of understanding the historical shifts around gender in the PR industry, studying an occupation's media can offer important insights. A journal produced by the professional association is significant for its 'disciplining effect' as it constructs 'a relatively coordinated and consistent understanding across the field of what PR is, where it belongs, and how it should be practised' (Edwards and Pieczka 2013:20). Studying trade media therefore can reveal the construction of institutional norms and, assuming a historical approach, changing dynamics and discursive shifts.

Gower (2001) found significant shifts in the representation of women in the years 1945–1972 in the *Public Relations Journal* produced by the Public Relations Society of America, and identified their almost complete absence in the late

1950s. The industry was represented almost exclusively as a male profession, despite the fact that by 1960, women made up one-quarter of all practitioners. Female practitioners were increasingly concerned in the 1960s about their lack of representation, and Gower notes the impact of women's liberation saw three articles focusing on women in PR between 1966 and 1972 as well as a letter to the editor complaining about the continuing use of 'PR men' to represent practitioners (2001:18). An analysis of practitioner biographies in a 1970 communication directory confirms that women actively participated in the US PR industry, including at relatively senior levels, and yet were systematically excluded from other industry publications (Horsley 2009).

L'Etang (2015) investigated the impact of gender on the professional project through an analysis of *Public Relations*, the UK's Institute of Public Relations journal, from 1948–1970 along with practitioner interviews. The industry was clearly segregated along gender lines with different entry points, careers paths and roles for men and women. Like Gower, she noted the profile of women in the journal diminished in the 1950s and 1960s. L'Etang also notes the relative 'invisibility' of women in the journal and yet, somewhat paradoxically, they remained the object of the 'male gaze' with an emphasis on physical attractiveness and certain kinds of feminised labour, demanding interpersonal and communication skills and organisational ability (2015:366). L'Etang concluded 'the public relations occupational body presented men as performers and women as decorative backstage labour, only allowed to perform in domesticated zones' (2015:366). Women made minimal contributions to the journal's discourse and the lower-paid, technical, feminised work of PR was mostly absent.

Representing women

Based on analysis of the representation of women through articles, reports, committee memberships, conference programs, photographs, illustrations and advertisements, it appears women were marginalised from the institutional norms constructed in *Public Relations Journal/Public Relations Australia*. There are whole issues without a single image or acknowledgement that women exist. My analysis of the few mentions of women can be broken down thematically: wives, secretaries, consumers, practitioners and bodies. I discuss the representation of female practitioners in the following section.

Women as wives

Wives of practitioners feature at social events such as Christmas parties that welcomed 'members, wives and friends' (Social Gathering 1966) and special rates were offered for wives at national conferences, as both L'Etang (2015) and Gower (2001) found in their analysis of UK and US trade media. Eric White Associates employee and former Victorian councillor Fay Douglas was farewelled in her new role as Mrs John Molyneux, where she would live on her husband's rural property 'far away from PR' (People in PR 1966). The journal also features a wedding photo of prominent South Australian practitioner, Don Dyer, marrying Silvia Birdsey (Wedding Bells 1967). Although Sylvia Dyer was never a member of the Public Relations Institute of Australia (PRIA), her contributions through 'fund-raising, community care and organisational support roles at state and national levels' were later honoured with a PRIA Life Membership (PRIA 2010). Professional wives made a valuable contribution to their husbands' PR careers, as recognised by Sylvia Dyer's life membership and this was not unique to public relations. A 1971 ABC news story features a paid training course for 'company wives' and the acknowledgement by recruitment consultants that a wife 'can make or break a husband's career' to the extent that meeting wives in social settings was often part of the recruitment process (Jones 1971).

Women's bodies and body parts

There are more representations of the female body or body parts in the journal than there are images of expert female practitioners. This theme emerged primarily through analysis of the visual elements in advertisements, photography or graphic design, particularly as freelance designers, photographers and illustrators were able to showcase their work by providing artwork for the cover when the journal began to be produced by the Victorian institute in 1966. It also includes a model posing in front of a camera to illustrate an article about the use of films (Bodinnar 1967). One 1971 cover was an award-winning photograph of a female nude 'based on a man-woman encounter idea' (Photos Win 1971). A woman's breast illustrated an article about Milton Schuman's criticism of television, which he calls the electronic nipple and likens to 'a sinister and vicious mother' (Electronic Nipple 1972). Other body parts (mostly fingers and heads) feature in advertisements aimed at secretarial staff or offering secretarial services. These bodily illustrations are significant given feminised labour is often considered 'a natural extension of the body' (Mayer 2013:51), and sexualisation, where, as L'Etang (2015) found, women in PR were perceived as dolly-birds and 'Eve.'

Women as secretaries, administrative support and service roles

The most prominent references to women are in service roles: as secretaries, stenographers, airhostesses, telephonists, receptionists and even a nurse (see Figures 4.2 and 4.3). There is a clear distinction between PR officers and their support staff. L'Etang (2015) noted that women working in PR often functioned as the 'office wife' in terms of feminised, administrative labour. A case study of the 'the Gold Coast's public relations team (a P.R.O. and two stenographer assistants)' responded to widespread news stories about the destruction of Gold Coast beaches following a cyclone (To the Rescue 1968). The male PR officer spearheaded a successful campaign to protect regional tourism, which included sending buckets of sand to journalists. Although L'Etang (2015) found that this

FIGURE 4.1 'Wanted PR Men' (advertisement for commercial photography service, The Studios of Gordon De'Lisle and Associates), *Public Relations Journal*, April 1966, p. 6. Source: State Library of Victoria. Reproduced with the permission of the Public Relations Institute of Australia.

FIGURE 4.2 'Dial a Secretary' (advertisement), Riddells, The Staff People, *Public Relations Journal*, March/April, 1967, p. 10. Source: State Library of Victoria. Reproduced with the permission of the Public Relations Institute of Australia.

'invisible labour' in the form of technical, lower-paid, administrative work such as that performed by 'Girl Fridays' was absent from the UK trade journal, it features in the Australian journal, often through paid advertising for secretarial services. However, feminised 'support' work was excluded from conceptualisations of professional practice.

Women as consumers

Women were recognised as a growing and significant market for PR activity, as illustrated by the inclusion of 'women's media' in the curriculum for a new diploma course featured in the journal (Outline of Mitchell College 1971). Contrasting bank advertisements in the journal show a husband looking after the family finances with a woman looking on (see Figure 4.4) (Pocketbank 1968) and a young, sole woman with cropped hair and wearing badges with pithy slogans such as 'have a groove house,' 'show more interest,' and 'save, don't rave' (Everything in Banking 1969). This latter image addresses the independent career woman managing her own finances. The recognition of women as a specialised market sector offered significant career opportunities for female practitioners, as information about their new appointments often specified responsibility for 'women's interest accounts.'

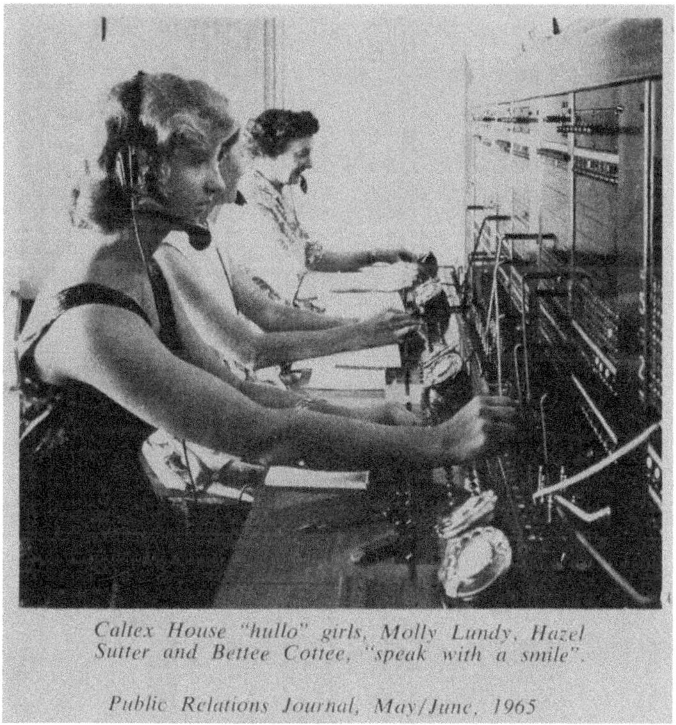

Caltex House "hullo" girls, Molly Lundy, Hazel
Sutter and Bettee Cottee, "speak with a smile".

Public Relations Journal, May/June, 1965

FIGURE 4.3 'Meeting the Public': Caltex House 'hullo' Girls, Molly Lundy, Hazel
Sutter and Bettee Cottee, 'speak with a smile' (photographs provided by Caltex
Public Relations), *Public Relations Journal*, May/June, 1965, p. 9. Source: State Library
of NSW. Reproduced with the permission of the Public Relations Institute of
Australia.

Representing female practitioners

Despite evidence of women's participation in the Australian PR industry during
the years of the journal, female practitioners are often poorly represented in its
pages. In 1968, there were 56 female members (almost 12 per cent of the membership), with most employed in Sydney and Melbourne (Fitch 2016b). Half of
the female members were married, suggesting PR offered better employment for
married women in comparison with the labour market. By 1970, women made up
one-quarter of members in Victoria. Despite this growth, some issues of the journal
have no reference to female practitioners and male pronouns are widely used in
accounts of industry events and articles refer to 'the public relations man' (Bodinnar
1967) and 'The New Breed of PR Man' (1967). Photographs of industry events
show all or almost all men. Reports of annual state and national council elections
demonstrate, in contrast to the early years of state institutes in the 1950s, the almost
complete absence of women other than in the state of Tasmania (Fitch 2016b).

Public Relations Australia, Aug./Sept., 1968

FIGURE 4.4 'Pocketbank!' (National Bank Advertisement), *Public Relations Australia*, August/September, 1968, p. 2. Source: State Library of Victoria. Reproduced with the permission of the Public Relations Institute of Australia.

The four-day national conventions in 1969 and 1971 featured no female speakers other than Penny Cresswell at the informal dinner dance to close the convention in 1971 (Fitch 2016b); Cresswell was the only speaker not to have their photograph included in the programme.

Women worked in diverse roles and sectors but this diversity is not always reflected in the journal. The 1968 membership list shows female PRIA members worked in: hospitality (primarily hotels); travel (airlines and cruise ships); manufacturing (textile and chemical industries); retail (department stores); the public sector (the post office and the ABC); and the charity and community sector (ranging from youth groups to the Red Cross) (PRIA Membership List 1968). Women also worked in consultancies, and sometimes established their own or were self-employed. Industry news in the journal often announced new appointments and these were not restricted to 'women's interest accounts'; for example, senior consultant Olive Kellie specialised in machinery, engineering and construction (Appointments 1968; Fitch 2016b). Gower (2001) made similar findings regarding the diversity of women's practice.

More than half of female members in 1968 were full professional-grade members. However, from 1965 to 1972, the journal features only a few images of senior female practitioners. These images include Esta Handfield, a Victorian council member in the 1950s, former state president and the only female PRIA Fellow on the 1968 membership list who chaired a session on graphic arts and spoke in the consultants' session at the second national convention in 1966; Jessie Fawsitt, who worked for airlines from the late 1940s and was a member of the New South Wales council from the 1950s and the national council in 1965, at a luncheon in London for BOAC PR officers; Cresswell, a Tasmanian council member, state president and national councillor, depicted in an illustrated cover as the sole woman in a room full of men at the national council meeting in 1970 (see Figure 4.5). Kay Brownbill (see Figure 4.6), vice-president of the South Australian institute and PR officer for the Adelaide newspaper, *The Advertiser*, who was elected to the House of Representatives as a member for the Liberal Party of Australia; Mandie Eckersley, who transferred to Sydney to manage Handfield's Image Australia office there; and Pauline McGrath, a former Image Australia employee who had set up her own PR company, 'Etcetera' (1969).

Similarly, women's contributions to the journal remain limited. Jean Stanger collated an industry news column, 'People in PR,' in the early years of the journal, and in late 1971 and 1972, Esther Morrish and Judy Tierney were identified as state-based correspondents for New South Wales and Tasmania respectively. One of the few articles that positioned a woman as an 'expert' reported on the only female speaker at a workshop: Mary Elliott, editor of the *Australian Post Office* magazine (see Figure 4.7); the photograph reveals, in contrast to other images, a number of women in the audience (Contents – A Case Study 1965; Workshop in Pictures 1965). Between 1965 and 1972, I identified only four articles written by women. One was not by a practitioner but by a building trade magazine editor, Marjorie McNeece (1966), who had presented at a Hobart symposium organised

FIGURE 4.5 Illustrator Bob Young, Independent Arts Studio, attended a lunch for National delegates in Melbourne and even inserted the Victorian president (centre foreground), who was unable to attend. Penny Cresswell, the Tasmanian delegate, is the only woman. Cover page, *Public Relations Australia*, June/July 1968. Source: State Library of Victoria. Reproduced with permission of the Public Relations Institute of Australia.

FIGURE 4.6 Miss Kay Brownbill takes delivery of two oil paintings by His Excellency the Governor of SA, Sir Edrich Bastyan, from an aide-de-camp during preparation for '*The Advertiser*' Open Air Art Exhibition, *Public Relations Journal*, March 1966, p. 7. Source: State Library of NSW. Reproduced with permission of the Public Relations Institute of Australia.

FIGURE 4.7 'Workshop in Pictures,' Miss Mary Elliott, B.E.M. Editor of the *Australia Post Office* magazine, *Public Relations Journal*, May/June 1965, p. 5. Source: State Library of NSW. Reproduced with permission of the Public Relations Institute of Australia.

by Cresswell. Two articles were written by Morrish (1971a, 1971b): a case study of the Israeli Government's tourist campaigns in Australia (she managed their account from 1962 to 1969) and an analysis of the Australian Institute of Management' annual report awards. Morrish also produced a 52-page members' directory for New South Wales (NSW Expanded 1972). The fourth article is a book review by a former journalist. McIndoe (1970) identifies her status as a PR novice, noting 'there were sections that I, as a complete stranger to public relations, found a little confusing, perhaps even rather frightening!'

Feminism and public relations

There is almost no mention of women's liberation, equal pay campaigns or feminism in the journal in the years of study. This does not mean that these were not issues of concern for women working in the industry, but rather such concerns were not represented in the journal. The only references to women's rights are reports of guest speakers at Victorian functions. In 1967, the first female Melbourne City Councillor Clare Cascarett discussed her experience of being a woman in politics (Aware of PR 1967). Cascarett had received widespread publicity for not attending the Lord Mayor's dinner and, in explaining her decision, Cascarett distanced herself from the women's movement:

> Much as I admired the suffragette of pre-war days, I don't wish to emulate them. I rather believe in the motto, Hasten Slowly, which brings me to the subject of the Lord Mayor's dinner. (…) I declined for the very simple reason it was a man's 'do' and I do not wish to bring about that sort of radical change.
>
> *(Aware of PR 1967)*

That decision appears somewhat out of step with the changing sexual politics of the late 1960s and early 1970s. In contrast, an American marketing lecturer from Fordham University, Dr Claire Corbin, speaking at an institute event, praised the number of women in the room as evidence of their widespread participation in the Australian industry (Changing Mores of the Marketplace 1970). Two other reports of guest speakers are worth noting, one because of its sexist language and the other because the speaker was a high-profile activist for abortion. The first featured the ABC's 'Miss Diana Ward', described as a '"dish" in anyone's language' and 'who did not put a tiny foot wrong' (A.B.C. Girl Charms 1965). In the second, Dr Bertram Wainer alleged widespread police corruption in the protection of backyard abortionists (Stanley 1970).

Given broader societal concerns in Australia at that time around women's liberation and equal pay, the lack of attention to these issues in the PR trade media is curious. Unlike the American *Public Relations Journal*, there appears to be little backlash against the inadequate representation of women. Writing on the Australian advertising industry, Dickenson (2016) notes that women grew more confident in 1960s and 1970s but were mostly confined to feminised roles and accounts as men moved more into more authoritative work such as creative direction and planning. Susan Chadwick wrote to the editor of *B&T*, the advertising industry magazine: 'wait until Women's Liberation hits your agency baby – the flak hasn't even started yet' (1973, cited in Crawford 2008:163). It may be that similar changes were about to occur in the PR industry, although there is no evidence in the journal up until 1972.

Only four years later, Handfield (1976), who maintained a high profile as co-owner of a PR consultancy in Melbourne, wrote *Double Bed and Separate Bank Account*. Handfield identifies herself as a PRIA Fellow and former state president in the book and acknowledges how the relative 'openness' of PR allows women to 'quickly [move] from clerical to public relations work' and advises women to dress so that 'nobody is going to take you for a stenographer' (1976:30, 53). Handfield's observations on occupational fit and career paths confirm the relatively informal structures of PR work offered opportunities for individual women. The publication of this book only a few years after the end of the journal suggests feminism was not absent from the PR industry.

Implications and conclusions

This chapter does more than make visible the historical contributions of women to the Australian PR industry. It highlights the marginalisation, and sometimes the erasure, of women from trade media in the years of study. Along with conferences, state councils and professional-grade memberships (from which women were also underrepresented or absent), these are important cognitive and normative mechanisms of professionalisation identified by Noordegraaf (2011) that contribute to disciplinary norms, construct PR knowledge and support claims for professional status. This marginalisation occurred in the context of increasing participation of women in the Australian workforce and widespread demands for equal pay and recognition. However, the increasing professionalisation of PR actively excluded women, as the institutional norms constructed in the journal helped define industry understandings of PR (Edwards and Pieczka 2013), and offered a gendered dimension in terms of who should practise it. Ironically, women were better represented in trade media in the early 1950s by serving on editorial boards and writing regular columns and industry news (Fitch 2016b), echoing Gower's (2001) finding that the professional development of the PR industry increased institutional barriers for women.

The marginalisation of women as senior practitioners and experts in the journal reveals the significance of gender in attempts to establish a professional identity for PR. The concept of a profession hinges on the ways in which women's 'inclusion … is masked' or curtailed to ensure the profession is not threatened (Witz 1992:63). Women's representation in the journal, as wives, secretaries and (novice) practitioners, highlights how their contributions are primarily confined to supporting roles and feminised labour is erased from conceptualisations of professional practice, despite evidence that women worked in relatively senior roles in the industry. Similarly, L'Etang (2015) found that representations of women in UK PR trade media were limited to domesticated, service and administrative roles. Further, the use of photographic models, female body parts and even naked bodies for illustrative purposes points to the objectification and sexualisation of women (see Figure 4.1) and are typical of the framing of feminised labour as an extension of the body (Mayer 2013).

The value of studying trade media is that it offers insights into the complex operation of gender on the occupational identity of PR. There are of course limitations. Trade media can be insular and subject to the concerns of the publisher, in this case the professional, state-based institutes, and tend to adopt, rather than challenge, institutional norms (Edwards and Pieczka 2013). Yet, they offer some evidence of the priorities and expectations of the professional institutes in their selective reporting of industry activity and potentially challenge histories that lack evidence and uncritically narrate a steady – and ostensibly ungendered – development towards the modern profession. I have argued in this chapter that the ways women are included in the journal informs an historical understanding of PR and of the impact of gender. A more intersectional approach would consider the significance of race and class and other sources might offer additional insights into lived experiences. Future research should investigate historical sources other than industry publications to understand the broader social context in which the historical development of PR occurs.

Concerns about the gender pay gap and the poor representation of women at senior levels in the Australian industry remain prominent and the ongoing exclusion of publicity and promotional work from conceptualisations of professional practice offer further evidence of the marginalisation of feminised labour. Given that women have always been employed in PR and related industries, and in high-profile roles, their absence from Australian PR history prior to the 1980s deserves further examination. This chapter argues their restricted representation between 1965 and 1972 in the journal produced by the professional association points to longstanding fissures along gender lines that continue to influence understandings of professional practice and occupational identity today.

Acknowledgement

An early version of this paper was presented at the Public Relations: Critical Perspectives, Edgework and Creative Futures conference at Queen Margaret University, Edinburgh on 24–25 August 2015.

References

A.B.C. Girl Charms Sydney Audience 1965, *Public Relations Journal*, November/December, p. 5.

Adkins, L. and Dever, M. 2016, *The Post-Fordist Sexual Contract: Working and Living In Contingency*, Basingstoke: Palgrave Macmillan.

Andrews, K. 2016, Don't Tell Them I Can Type: Negotiating Women's Work in Production in the Post-War ABC, *Media International Australia*, 161(1), pp. 28–37.

Australian Bureau of Statistics 2017, *2071.0 – Census of Population and Housing: Reflecting Australia – Stories from the Census, 2016: Employment In Australia*. Available online www.abs.gov.au/ausstats/abs@.nsf/Lookup/by%20Subject/2071.0~2016~Main%20Features~Employment%20Data%20Summary~67 [accessed 4 December 2018].

Appointments 1968, *Public Relations Australia*, November/December, p. 11.

Aveling, M. and Damousi, J. (eds) 1991, *Stepping Out of History: Documents of Women at Work in Australia*, North Sydney: Allen & Unwin.

Aware of PR 1967, *Public Relations Journal*, November/December, p. 5.

Baker, J. 2015, *Australian Women War Reporters: Boer War to Vietnam*, Sydney: New South Wales Press.

Baker, J. and Lloyd, J. 2016, Gendered Labour and Media: Histories and Continuities. *Media International Australia*, 161(1), pp. 6–7.

Bondinnar, J.W. 1967, Examining the Film Medium, *Public Relations Journal*, September/October, pp. 1, 3, 15.

Changing Mores of the Market Place 1970, *Public Relations Australia*, November/December, p. 9.

Contents – A Case Study 1965, *Public Relations Journal*, May/June, p. 4.

Crawford, R. 2008. *But Wait, There's More … A History of Australian Advertising, 1900–2000*, Carlton: Melbourne University Press.

Curthoys, A. 1975, Towards a Feminist Labour History. In Curthoys, A., Eade, S. and Spearritt, P. (eds), *Women at Work*, Canberra: Australian Society for the Study of Labour History, pp. 88–95.

Curthoys, A. 1987, *Women and Work*, Woden: The Curriculum Development Council.

Darian-Smith, K. 2016, The 'Girls': Women Press Photographers and the Representation of Women in Australian Newspapers, *Media International Australia*, 161(1), pp. 48–58.

Davies, C. 1996, The Sociology of the Professions and the Profession of Gender, *Sociology*, 30, pp. 661–678.

Dickenson, J. 2016, *Australian Women in Advertising in the Twentieth Century*, Basingstoke: Palgrave Macmillan.

Edwards, L. 2014, Discourse, Credentialism and Occupational Closure in the Communications Industries: The Case of Public Relations in the UK, *European Journal of Communication*, 29, pp. 319–334.

Edwards, L. and Pieczka, M. 2013, Public Relations and 'Its' Media: Exploring the Role of Trade Media in the Enactment of Public Relations' Professional Project, *Public Relations Inquiry*, 2(1), pp. 5–25.

Electronic Nipple, The 1972, *Public Relations Australia*, February/March, p. 1.

Etcetera 1969, *Public Relations Australia*, July/August, p. 7.

Everything in Banking for Everyone [Advertisement] 1969, *Public Relations Australia*, March/April, p. 14.

Fitch, K. 2015, Making History: Reflections on Memory and Elite Interviews in Public Relations Research, *Public Relations Inquiry*, 4(2), pp. 13–144.

Fitch, K. 2016a, Rethinking Australian Public Relations History in the Mid-20th Century, *Media International Australia*, 160(1), pp. 9–19.

Fitch, K. 2016b, *Professionalizing Public Relations: History, Gender and Education*, London: Palgrave Macmillan.

Fitch, K. and L'Etang, J. 2017, Other Voices? The State of Public Relations History and Historiography: Questions, Challenges and Limitations of 'National' Histories and Historiographies, *Public Relations Inquiry*, 6(1), pp. 115–136.

Fitch, K. and Third, A. 2010, Working Girls: Revisiting the Gendering of Public Relations, *Prism*, 7(4). Available online www.prismjournal.org.

Fitch, K. and Third, A. 2014, Ex-Journos and Promo Girls: Feminization and Professionalization in the Australian Public Relations Industry. In Daymon, C. and Demetrious, K. (eds), *Gender and Public Relations: Critical Perspectives on Voice, Image and Identity*, Abingdon: Routledge, pp. 247–267.

Fox, C. 1991, *Working Australia*, North Sydney: Allen & Unwin.

Gower, K. 2001, Rediscovering Women in Public Relations: Women in the *Public Relations Journal*, 1945–1972, *Journalism History*, 27(1), pp. 14–21.

Handfield, E. 1976, *Double Bed and Separate Bank Account*, Carlton: Platypus Press.

Horsley, S.J. 2009, Women's Contributions to American Public Relations, 1940–1970, *Journal of Communication Management*, 13, pp. 100–115.

Jones, C. 1971, August 21. Finishing School for Wives of Aspiring Executives, *This Day Tonight*, Sydney: ABC News. Available online www.youtube.com/watch?v=hK6JyRyCS9whttp://www.abc.net.au/news/about/backstory/television/2018-07-26/retrofocus-shares-abc-archive-with-digital-audience/10037720 [accessed 4 December 2018].

Lamme, M.O. 2001, Furious Desires and Victorious Careers: Doris E. Fleischman, Counsel on Public Relations and Advocate for Working Women, *American Journalism*, 18(3), pp. 13–33.

Lamme, M.O. 2007, Outside the Prickly Nest: Revisiting Doris Fleischman, *American Journalism*, 24(3), pp. 85–107.

L'Etang J. 2004, *Public Relations in Britain: A History of Professional Practice in the 20th Century*, Mahwah, NJ: Lawrence Erlbaum.

L'Etang, J. 2015, 'It's Always Been a Sexless Trade'; 'It's Clean Work'; 'There's Very Little Velvet Curtain': Gender and PR in Post-Second World War Britain, *Journal of Communication Management*, 19(4), pp. 354–370.

Lloyd, J. 2014, Women's Pages in Australian Print Media from the 1850s, *Media International Australia*, 150(1), pp. 61–66.

Mayer, V. 2013, To Communicate is Human; To Chat is Female: The Feminization of US Media Work. In Carter, C., Steiner, L. and McLaughlin, L. (eds), *The Routledge Companion to Media and Gender*, Abingdon: Routledge, pp. 51–60.

McIndoe, L. 1970, Communication is Easy, or Is It?, *Public Relations Australia*, February/March, p. 11.

McNeece, M. 1966, Publicity Material and the Editor, *Public Relations Journal*, June, p. 7.

Miller, K.S. 1997, Woman, Man, Lady, Horse: Jane Stewart, Public Relations Executive, *Public Relations Review*, 23, pp. 249–269.

Morrish, E. 1971a, Case History: Israel's Tourist Promotion, *Public Relations Australia*, April/May, p. 7.

Morrish, E. 1971b, The Art of the Annual Report, *Public Relations Australia*, October/November, pp. 1, 4, 12.

New Breed of PR Man, The 1967, *Public Relations Journal*, March/April, p. 1.

NSW Expanded Membership Directory 1972, *Public Relations Australia*, April/May, p. 5.

Noordegraaf, M. 2011, Remaking Professionals? How Associations and Professional Education Connect Professionalism and Organizations. *Current Sociology*, 59, pp. 465–488.

O'Donnell, C. and Hall, P. 1988, *Getting Equal: Labour Market Regulation and Women's Work*, North Sydney: Allen & Unwin.

Outline of Mitchell College PR Course 1971, *Public Relations Australia*, June/July, pp. 10–11.

People in PR 1966, *Public Relations Journal*, January/February, p. 4.

Photos Win World Trip 1971, *Public Relations Australia*, October/November, p. 3.

Pocketbank [Advertisement] 1968, *Public Relations Australia*, November/December, n. p.

PRIA Membership List 1968, *Public Relations Australia*, April/May [Supplement].

PRIA 2010, October 19. Donald and Sylvia Dyer. Available online www.pria.com.au/aboutus/in-honour/donald-and-sylvia-dyer [accessed 25 May 2015].

PRIA 2016, Diversity and Inclusion Policy. Available online www.pria.com.au/documents/item/7045 [accessed 4 December 2018].

Rodríguez-Salcedo, N. and Gómez-Baceiredo, B. 2017, A Herstory of Public Relations: Teresa Dorn, from Scott Cutlip to Burson-Marsteller Europe (1974–1995), *Public Relations Review*, 29(1), pp. 16–37.
Social Gathering 1966, *Public Relations Journal*, January/February, p. 6.
Stanley, L.G. 1970, Dr Wainer Speaks Out, *Public Relations Australia*, July/August, p. 12.
To the Rescue 1968, *Public Relations Australia*, February/March, p. 7.
Wedding Bells 1967, *Public Relations Journal*, July/August, p. 10.
Witz, A. 1992, *Professions and Patriarchy*, London: Routledge.
Workshop in Pictures 1965, *Public Relations Journal*, May/June, p. 5.
Yaxley, H. 2013, Career Experiences of Women in British Public Relations (1970–1989), *Public Relations Review*, 39(2), pp. 156–165.

5
HISTORY, RACIALISATION AND RESISTANCE IN 'POST-RACE' PUBLIC RELATIONS

Lee Edwards

In this chapter, I consider the importance of history in the construction of UK public relations as a professional field underpinned by racial structures. In a 'post-race' environment, racism is apparently overcome and discrimination outlawed (Bonilla-Silva 2015). Arguably, the widespread recognition among industry bodies of the importance of diversity in public relations suggests that in professional environments, too, a 'post-racial' world has emerged. Yet, in the UK and US at least, statistics show that Black, Asian and minority ethnic (BAME) groups are under-represented, and little has changed in the dominance of Whiteness in the field for over a decade (Chartered Institute of Public Relations 2018; Ford and Brown 2016; Public Relations and Communications Association 2016). There is clearly a need to interrogate how 'race'[1] continues to influence the professional environment.

Race is: 'neither an event nor a specific series of events (…) (it) is a process of structured events which over time demonstrate a system whereby groups and individuals are racialized' (Coates 2008:209). Systems persist, and understanding race as a systemic process therefore prompts the need to historicise its contemporary appearance, as well as to move away from a focus on racism as individual actions and towards racism as embedded in the social context. I begin the chapter with a brief overview of the origins and current manifestation of post-racism, before considering the historical racial hierarchies that underpin discrimination and stigmatisation in public relations; I conclude by reflecting on alternative histories that provide BAME practitioners with the capacity to resist racism and assert their right to belong.

Post-racism

The idea of a post-racial state first emerged in American scholarship, reflecting the fact that the claims of civil rights and anti-racism movements have been accommodated in contemporary social, political and legal systems that now officially outlaw racism. Because race is no longer a locus of official discrimination, claims of systemic discrimination are no longer valid – in this way, equal opportunities legislation performs a powerful erasure of racism (Ahmed 2007). The idea of a 'post-race' society is further strengthened by the growth of the middle-class in Black and other ethnic minority communities, suggesting that race is no longer an impediment to social mobility, and that individual effort is all that is required to be successful in a post-race world.

In reality, of course, race and racism contribute to multiple forms of disadvantages in the lives of minority communities in countries across the world. In the UK, ethnic minority groups tend to do less well than White communities on educational outcomes, are more likely to live in poverty, have poorer health outcomes, earn less than their White colleagues in equivalent roles and remain underrepresented in white-collar occupations. In work, they are slower to be promoted and are discriminated against in recruitment processes (The Cabinet Office 2018). In public relations, for example, discrimination remains an uncomfortable reality and practitioners of colour are significantly underrepresented in the field, despite ongoing industry attempts to address 'diversity.' For those living the experience of racialisation in the UK, the idea of a post-race society is problematic, to say the least.

The key to understanding racism in a post-race society is to seek out its manifestation as a social structure, a system of differentiation rather than a set of episodic events driven by individual prejudice (Bonilla-Silva 2015). Indeed, to argue that racism is a matter of individual prejudice ignores the multiple forms it takes *despite* the increasingly liberal attitudes among contemporary societies that disapprove of, or at least disavow, racism (manifest in organisational or industry-wide statements about valuing diversity or encouraging wider representation). Resolving this conundrum requires recognition that the racial structure, as 'a network of social relations at social, political, economic, and ideological levels that shapes the life chances of the various races' (Bonilla-Silva 2015:1360), categorises people into different groups in a way that fosters perceptions of opposition and otherness rather than commonality, ultimately generating disadvantage for some and privilege for others.

Racial structures are deeply embedded in institutional life and need no incidence of individual prejudice to sustain their existence. On the contrary, their history justifies their present form – in the UK, the ideology that sustains contemporary racial structures can be traced back to colonial histories where the purpose of official discourse was to communicate the superiority of Whiteness[2] as a form of property that could be put to work in ways that generated sustained economic, political and social advantages for those who could claim it (Harris 1993). In other words, racial structures have always been fundamental to accumulating a range of advantages through the continual growth and circulation of capital, in ways that serve White privilege (Baptist 2014; Saha 2016).

In post-race societies, the ideologies that sustain racial structures must remain hidden because they have no judicial legitimacy, public policy overtly rejects them and popular support for them is hotly contested and marginalised by activists. Yet, racial disadvantage persists, suggesting that racist ideologies continue to structure people's lives, naturalised as part of the ways we see the world, and all the more powerful and difficult to resist because of their contemporary invisibility. In professional contexts, both discrimination – experiencing disadvantage in access to material resources (Imoagene 2018) – and stigmatization – experiencing a 'defilement of the self' (Lamont et al. 2016:403) through disrespect, dishonour or a denial of status – affect the lives of racialised individuals.[3] Justifications of racial discrimination in 'post-race' professional contexts take the form of 'colour-blind' racism, where the reasons for disadvantage deny the existence of race. Thus, unsuccessful promotion applications are ascribed to a lack of skill or experience; exclusion is put down to personality or a lack of common interests.

The historical roots of racism in the UK are elided by these techniques of obscuring racial structures, the ideologies that underpin them and the consequences they have, through discourses that exclude the language of racialisation. This discursive exclusion is crucial – it silences the collective memories of British communities with roots in the colonial era and postcolonial waves of migration to the UK, memories that are replete with painful episodes of overt racism, exclusion, denigration and slaughter, and reverberate in the contemporary lives of second- and third-generation community members (see, e.g., BBC 2018; Hughes 2018; Waymer and Street 2015). To silence such memories is to refuse to acknowledge the events that gave rise to them. Thus, silencing is perhaps an ultimate act of violence, since our humanity depends on our ability to appear to others as ourselves, with our own stories and experiences to tell (Couldry 2010). If we are forced to accept the experiences of others as our own, denying our visceral reality, our very existence is challenged.

Histories in/of public relations

In UK public relations, the social, cultural, political and economic dimensions of Britain's history, and the role played by PR in helping to create them, contribute to the ways in which Whiteness is realised, and BAME practitioners. The occupation's roots lie in colonial trade, politics and historically accepted racism sponsored by state and commerce and communicated through 'civilising' discourses that were (and are) dependent on definitions of the 'other' (the colonial subject, the enemy within). I argue that these 'conditions of arrival' for BAME PR practitioners entering the field constitute a racialised, gendered and classed legacy (Skeggs 1994) that they must negotiate.

During the British Empire, maintaining the superiority of Britain over its colonial territories depended on the construction of indigenous populations as inferior, uncivilised and uneducated, and therefore a justifiable focus for Britain's 'civilising' influence (McClintock 1995; Ramamurthy 2012; Ramdin 1999; Said 1995). This was no moral mission; colonial territories provided a vital supply of labour and markets for the Empire, through which Britain reaped enormous profits until the abolition of the African slave trade in 1807, and the abolition of slavery in India (where approximately 16 million Indians were enslaved) in 1841 (Ramdin 1999). Some migration to Britain from its colonies did occur, so that by the end of the eighteenth century a vibrant, active African and Caribbean community numbered over 10,000, and Indian communities became well-established during the nineteenth century, across a range of social classes (Ramdin 1999).

While communicating White British superiority was fundamental throughout the years of Empire, the use of public relations was formalised particularly in its latter stages. The founding of the Empire Marketing Board in 1926 was important, since it was a state-sponsored institution charged with the specific mission of promoting trade and consumption across and between British territories (L'Etang 2004). In a context where resistance and decolonisation movements were increasingly vocal, the EMB's communication strategies were based on an idealised narrative of the British Empire as a unified space where the benefits of trade were available to all, where imperialist ideology was presented as a preferred option over socialism and where Britain's paternalistic support could help to civilise 'backward' nations (Aitken 1990:94). They confirmed White, Western and specifically British identities as more valuable than indigenous colonial citizens or ethnic minority communities in Britain.

Thus, a significant driver for the emergence of the UK PR industry was to serve a racist agenda for the British state that included 'others' only insofar as they served the interests of the state. 'Other' economic, social, cultural and political identities and activities were ignored or denigrated in the process (Anthony 2012; Tallents 1932). The 'other' was placed unequivocally outside, and in opposition to, the superior British establishment. As decolonisation proceeded during the second half of the twentieth century, the same principles applied, this time in the context of the need to protect Britain's trading partnerships in newly independent nations. Commercial companies and the state both used public relations to justify the benevolent act of granting independence to domestic audiences and to frame resistance to a continuing British presence as pathological. For postcolonial audiences, the narrative was one of Britain as a source of valuable expertise, necessary for a robust independent economy and polity (L'Etang 2004). British intellectual, moral and economic superiority was protected through these narratives, while the voices and identities of 'other' populations were obscured.

A growing number of migrants from Britain's former colonies joined the already existing communities of colour in the UK during the 1950s and 1960s. Their arrival prompted a differently-inflected type of racist narrative, where the 'uncivilised other' – most often referring to African or Caribbean groups who had arrived in the UK to help with Britain's labour shortage in the 1950s – was recast as an enemy within, ungovernable, violent and incapable of stable family life (Gilroy 1987; S. Hall, Critcher, Jefferson, Clarke and Roberts 2013; Lawrence 1982; Yuval-Davis, Anthias and Kofman 2005). Racial structures thus influenced narratives of British identity long after the demise of the Empire; however, at the same time, the growth of BAME communities led to their increasing presence in politics, education, commerce and as a new cultural presence (Solomos 2003; Solomos and Back 1995). Their empowered voices and narratives of identity countered state and media representations and provided communities with an alternative, more positive reading of their history and place in the UK. In 1976, the Race Relations Act was introduced, outlawing racial discrimination for the first time and multiculturalism became the favoured approach to managing migration. The Notting Hill Carnival (first run in 1965) became a more popular and accepted cultural event (Gilroy 1993) and the number of ethnic media started to grow significantly (Syedain 1993). Public sector communication started to emphasise the importance of 'equal opportunities' as an attempt to ameliorate racial tensions – although race was still presented in dualistic, essentialist terms of 'Black' and 'White' (Hesse 2000).

In summary, the professional history of UK public relations is embedded within support for racist narratives against colonial populations and ethnic minority communities in Britain, based on 'a residual set of attitudes accumulated during the imperial period around the idea of child/savage' (Lawrence 1982:70). The impact of this is visible in the remarkably intransigent whiteness of the professional field, its preference for recruits from elite institutions and the ongoing links between those in the higher echelons of the occupation and leaders of the British Establishment (Chartered Institute of Public Relations 2018; Davis 2018; Leveson 2012; Public Relations and Communications Association 2016). Arguably, the profession's history of promoting the idea of the 'other' has had material effects on the profession itself, constructing it as a place where whiteness is located at the top of the racial structures that underpin its hierarchies. Because the 'other' was judged as inferior to white British subjects in the areas that matter most to occupational fields (intelligence, reliability, rationality, cultural sophistication), 'common sense' dictates that white practitioners from the middle and upper classes are more suitable professionals. The cultural capital associated with the profession may make this kind of 'common sense' seem even more plausible: research in the UK suggests that practitioners still share very similar tastes and preferences, and constitute a relatively homogeneous group in terms of their class and educational background (Edwards 2008).

Reproducing oppression? The contemporary public relations profession

How do histories of racialisation and discrimination continue to affect a 'post-race' public relations industry, where professional structures are ostensibly neutral and 'race' is excluded from professional discourse (Edwards 2014)? Certainly, the lived experience of being a person of colour in the UK industry suggests that discrimination is alive and well, and a systemic problem. As Goldberg notes, '[e]xperiential racism – the personal and collective experience of racist expression or action – will be a function, then, of underlying structural conditions' (Goldberg 2015:31), and so it is in the normative, *professional* structures of the field that we will rediscover how *racial* structures are operationalised. In fact, the post-race neutrality of professional structures (e.g., recruitment and promotion based only on talent and merit) belies the fact that *racial* structures are embedded in professional life. Their historical legitimacy forms part of the logic we use to make sense of contemporary organisational and occupational decisions, processes and hierarchies. They make discrimination both acceptable and invisible because discrimination appears *as neutrality*, given the 'knowledge' we have about the capabilities, skills and attributes of 'others.'

In public relations, the professional habitus has fostered racialisation of BAME practitioners and established white identity as the occupational norm. While the habitus has many different aspects (see Edwards 2014), one of the most powerful disciplinary influences on practitioners is the discourse of the client, which is used to justify certain forms of embodiment and character in the occupational field. The assumptions of whiteness that are embedded in client discourses are, however, constantly challenged by BAME practitioners. In the remainder of this chapter, I draw on two empirical studies to explain how racial structures are manifest and challenged in the ostensibly 'post-race' environment of UK public relations.

The client as benchmark: 'competence' and 'fit'

In public relations, competence is framed in terms of the figure of the client, which appears in discourses that circulate through industry association websites, trade press and in publicity for major consultancies. The client is a market-related construction, universally applicable (all in-house and consultancy practitioners, working in any sector, have 'clients') and unequivocally powerful, because without clients public relations has neither legitimacy nor territory. The disciplinary power of the client is framed in terms of their strategic requirements of communication, which PR purports to solve. However, as a professional service occupation, public relations' offering extends beyond the provision of skills to being a trusted advisor, who accompanies the client through their complex business journey, providing objective expertise along the way (Anderson-Gough et al. 2000). The promise of a personal relationship produces a demand for homology, a consultant that is similar to the client, prompting a feeling of comfort and security that provides the foundation for a long-term relationship founded on mutual trust (Hanlon 1999). The happiness of the client becomes the measure of a good practitioner (Du Gay and Salaman 1992).

Delivering effective service to a client also depends on the right mix of rationality and managed emotion. Rationality is the normative mode of operation for those who assume a strategic identity – in 'modern-masculinist' organisations (Brewis and Grey 1994:69), emotion is only permissible if is marketable – for example, as enthusiastic commitment to the job, or as emotional labour, where care and attention is paid to clients' well-being (Hesmondhalgh and Baker 2011; Hochschild 1983; Korczynski 2003). Thus, one major consultancy website promises rationality:

> An impartial perspective is crucial (…) We give frank and constructive advice to ensure that the positive messages come across clearly.
>
> *(Fishburn Hedges 2010)*

Another promises emotional commitment that will lead to success:

> We are passionate about your business but also about our industry. Passion makes us determined to say yes (Even when the safe answer should be no). (…) Passion's made us ambitious, challenging and honest (We think you're paying for the right response for you, not the easy one for us). (…) Enthusiasm drives you to think the unthinkable, passion drives us to do the un-doable.
>
> *(Freud Communications 2010)*

The need to demonstrate rationality, managed emotion and homology are post-racial disciplinary mechanisms, in the sense that they call on market rationalities for their legitimacy (securing and keeping clients is a natural thing for PR practitioners to do in a competitive market for their services), and thereby mask the racial structures that underpin them and systematically disadvantage BAME practitioners. For example, while BAME practitioners may be able to draw on some aspects of their identity, such as class or gender, to establish commonality with the client, their bodies, as signifiers of difference (Hall 1996; Puwar 2004) are more likely to disturb the perceptions of a neatly aligned client/practitioner partnership, at least in the initial stages of a relationship. For white colleagues, as Carbado and Gulati (2003:1778) argue, the problem is not the same.

> In the context of workplaces that are structured around cooperative work, whites do not have to, in terms of race, think about being the same. They have a limited need to strategize about how and when to signal an integrational capacity to work within teams without causing grit. Whiteness is presumptively grease.

Racial stereotypes also mitigate against BAME practitioners being seen as naturally rational and able to manage their emotions. The position of the 'other' is frequently associated with uncontrollable emotion, irrationality, a lack of self-discipline and a tendency to the unpredictable (Hall 1997), while stereotypes of Black women in particular emphasise their sexuality and promiscuity, as well as their availability for White men (bell hooks 1994; Ladson-Billings 2009). These sedimented identities, while originating in a colonial era very different to the professional context of PR, nonetheless undermine claims to professionalism made by BAME practitioners.

The impact of these norms on perceptions of practitioner suitability is illustrated by the ways in which the principle of 'fit' sits alongside skills and experience as the basis for PR recruitment, essential to professional identity.[4] As the following quotes from recruiters to the PR industry illustrate, identifying suitable candidates includes defining the 'preferred personality' in a process that is compared to 'dating,' or 'matchmaking':

> What we want to find out from [the client] is what kind of personality fits. (…) What things went well with the person that was in the role before? What things didn't work so well?
>
> *(Interview LSD20387)*

Once the candidates are chosen, various interviews are conducted, but the final stage is frequently an interview with the potential PR agency or in-house team, where personality and character are assessed for 'fit.' If this final hurdle is not overcome, the position may not be offered.

> We will whittle it down to two or three and then it's chemistry interviews with the person who they're going to be working most closely with.
>
> *(Interview IN-1)*

The idea of 'fit' also extends beyond the individual client or team, to the client brand. Here, market logic once again acts as a structuring mechanism for professional hierarchy, and embodiment frequently plays a role, where to fit is to look 'appropriate' (in terms of size, shape, looks) for the brand identity.

In an environment where the vast majority of practitioners and clients enjoy the invisible privileges of Whiteness (McIntosh 1997; Owen 2007), and take the normativity of their identity for granted, having a vague, arbitrary and subjective idea of 'fit' as a benchmark for entry and progression in PR sets up clear potential disadvantages for BAME practitioners, whose bodies unavoidably signify them as 'other' in a white profession, and who must overcome racist stereotypes before their right to belong can be established.

Reclaiming history: speaking back to 'post-race racism'

The seriousness of discrimination notwithstanding, interviews with BAME practitioners show that they draw on alternative histories and identity narratives to address the challenges that client-related discourses present to their ambitions in the field, and adopt a range of practical strategies to overcome them. Their resistance begins with a rejection of the normative superiority of Whiteness, explicitly recognising its arbitrary nature and dependence on historical privilege. As one practitioner put it:

> [B]eing from a minority background we don't have well established like a long kind of family lineage in this country (…) So we might have really close family ties but in terms of moving anywhere professionally, I think families of an ethnic minority, it's going to take several generations before we're on a par with… like, the established English families here.
>
> *(Angela)*

Monica's experience as a trainee intern revealed to her not only a set of skills she required, but also the importance of Whiteness as the benchmark for 'fit' that automatically excludes 'others.'

> I think [PR] started with the whites and they, they said that's the standard,
> that you have to be polished, that you have to come from this background
> (…) [At the] internship, it was about, you know, even how to talk, just the
> mannerism, how to talk, how to conduct ourselves in meetings and that,
> that's when it becomes a reality how different you are and you're told that
> if you have to fit you have to start consciously getting to that mannerism to
> get there and feel comfortable and fit in, otherwise you will always feel like
> an outsider.
>
> *(Monica, focus group 1)*

These insights are made possible by BAME practitioners' liminal position in the
occupation, a position that facilitates the development of 'double-consciousness,'
or knowledge of different institutions and ideologies associated with both dominant and dominated locations in social hierarchies. Double-consciousness allows
practitioners to know themselves as Whiteness knows them (Fanon 2008[1952]),
but also to draw on resources associated with their personal identities and histories, and their knowledge of how Whiteness operates as a dominant professional
ideology, to negotiate their occupational position (Acker 2006; Atewologun and
Singh 2010; Holvino 2008; King 1988). By transforming exclusion into 'successful
marginality' (Hurtado 1996:376), practitioners manage their occupational identity in ways that can overcome the barriers presented by the racial structures that
underpin the field.

Practitioners used their liminal knowledge to challenge Whiteness by
rejecting its implicit superiority, rejecting their assumed inferiority and
adopting practical strategies to work around the barriers it presented. Rejecting
Whiteness involved revealing its fictional character and poking fun at the dis-
comfort generated by their presence as the 'other.' For example, stereotypes
were reinterpreted as necessary fictions that accommodated their colleagues'
ignorance of 'other' lives. Practitioners recognised the colonial lens of inferiority through which they were often perceived, but reversed the position when
their colleagues' ignorance was betrayed by their palpable surprise to stereotypes being overturned: 'They're like "oh you *did* go to university" and "oh
you're *not* the tea boy," that kind of thing' (Andy, focus group 3). Stereotypes
were also challenged when practitioners provided unequivocal evidence of
unjustified stigmatisation, as Shoma did: 'The interesting thing is I am the head
of a department, I've got a team, I've got a budget and, you know, the president
and his wife sometimes introduce me, "Meet Shoma, [whispers] she's our press
officer"' (Shoma, focus group 5).

The power that participants drew on through their liminal knowledge extended
even to understanding the kinds of internalised fears and uncertainties that their
presence prompted as colleagues who might not 'fit,' because colonial histories continue to deny them an assumed right to belong in professional space. In a vivid illustration of this power, Cordelia 'voices' the thoughts that emerge when the 'other'
comes too close.

> [T]here is just that, 'We're not used to dealing with those sorts of people,' or 'Those sorts of people are only fit for certain situations.' So, 'I only meet those people when I'm on the tube, or when one of them's trying to steal my bag,' or, you know, so 'to have them sitting round a board table on equal terms, I just… it's outside of my reality and I don't know how to treat them, I don't know how to behave.' (…) [They] assume that I won't have had any of the experiences or the background that they've had. And then they think, 'Well, you know, she won't have gone skiing over Easter, or she won't have popped down to Prada to buy a new… so what are we going to talk about? She won't have been to the theatre, you know, and maybe we're going to have to talk about the MOBOs or we're going to have to talk about jerk chicken…'
>
> *(Cordelia)*

These kinds of strategies helped practitioners to reassert their identities in the face of the visible and invisible stigmatisation to which they were subjected. Alongside them, practical strategies of resistance included directly addressing their 'deficient' attributes (as defined by the racial structures underpinning occupational norms). For example, Amy recognised that her accent was a form of embodiment that repeatedly highlighted her difference, and so for her, 'skills' related not to the practical skills of the job, but to refining her accent in ways that would mitigate this aspect of her physical presence.

> [W]e have a training budget and they were asking what kind of training would I like to have, and, well, writing press releases? Not really, because I've been doing this for like for how many years and I've written more press releases than some people here (…) Anyway I said that one of the things I might want to do is having pronunciation classes or something. So actually my training budget didn't go to PR but to language classes.
>
> *(Amy)*

Other practitioners took opportunities to demonstrate their professional skill, or go beyond the call of duty, as a way of redirecting the gaze of their colleagues towards their skills and abilities, which did illustrate their 'fit,' rather than their embodiment. As Sharon put it, 'you have to juggle, you have to show something that will let them maybe not look at [ethnicity] so much.' Such strategies could lead to positive outcomes. As Thomas noted: 'when they have such low expectations and then they see me and maybe they see my output they go, 'Wow this is really good. This report is really good. This proposal is really good.' Sometimes, difference was reframed as an occupational advantage – for example, when ethnic minority groups were being targeted: 'I think it's been quite beneficial to be a part of a team that's not necessarily got that many ethnic minorities within it, because it brings in a different perspective and it can help' (Aaron). Working extra hard was also a common strategy, although it came at a price, both in terms of the potential for personal burn-out: 'I've always just worked extra, extra hard. Which isn't always the answer actually. It's very unfair because you just end up physically done in' (Cordelia). Working hard also carried with it the risk of becoming hyper-visible, which could lead to more scrutiny and a danger of sacrificing creativity for a more cautious, process-oriented approach.

The practitioners' experience of the professional environment was grounded in an understanding of how the legacy of social, political and economic histories shaped the position of the 'other' in the UK public relations industry. Their resistance to discrimination and stigmatisation, on the other hand, drew on an understanding of the fictional superiority of Whiteness, born of the liminal reality that these practitioners, and other members of their family and community, had experienced throughout their lives. While they could not combat racial structures directly (one of the disheartening realities of 'post-race' public relations is that practitioners repeatedly encountered discrimination and stigmatisation across different situations and over time), their actions ensured that their identities were never completely fixed, and their persistent, insistent presence always had the potential to prompt a reframing and re-evaluation of occupational hierarchies.

Conclusion

Understanding the effect of histories of racism and racialisation in UK public relations requires taking the perspective of the 'other' so that the daily experience of subjugation and resistance is made visible. BAME practitioners negotiate narratives of themselves as 'other' on a daily basis. These narratives are both visible and predictable because they reflect the structures of racism that mark other areas of their lives. At the same time, their histories of resistance, migration and settlement, which also accompany them into the workplace, tell stories of cultural hybridity, creativity and political agency (Hall 2000), which they can use to both challenge the idea that public relations is 'post-race,' and contest their professional marginalisation.

The moniker 'post-race' denies the continued influence of racial structures on the lives of marginalised groups and therefore presents a significant danger to anti-racist struggles in professional fields. Engaging critically with the social, professional and individual histories that make up the context for the contemporary occupational field can reveal the ways in which such structures underpin norms that appear neutral, but in practice favour Whiteness over the 'other.' Equally, the rich cultural, social and political heritages of BAME communities provide resources and forms of knowledge that allow them to reveal the superiority of Whiteness as a convenient professional fiction. The influence of history on contemporary manifestations of racism in the profession will continue to evolve as the relationship between dominant racial norms and alternative histories is continually recast. While racism remains persistent even in post-race professions, this ongoing change means that there is a faint possibility that, at some point in the future, alternative histories of the strength rather than the subjugation of the 'other' (Yosso 2005) will have a transformative effect and create an occupational field where race is no longer a difference that 'matters' (Werbner 2013).

Notes

1 I use scare quotes here to indicate the socially constructed nature of 'race.' This principle underpins the use of the word in the rest of the chapter.
2 I follow Owen (2007) in arguing that Whiteness is best understood as part of the racial structures that underpin the social world. It normalises the social location of those racialised as White as a position of advantage, is invisible to 'Whites' but highly visible to non-Whites, and is embodied in ways that go beyond skin colour to encompass a particular way of being in the world.
3 For information on other professions, see, for example, Sommerlad (2015), Duff (2011), Edgley, Sharma and Anderson-Gough (2016).
4 These quotes are taken from a small interview-based study carried out in the UK in 2015. Seventeen interviews were conducted with in-house human resource managers (10) and consultant recruiters (7) to the PR industry, focusing on how the recruitment process unfolds and what approach they took to diversity in that context. Participants responded to an email invitation to participate in the study, circulated via two professional HR/recruitment associations, and they were mainly based in London. Each interview lasted between 45 and 90 minutes.

References

Acker, J. 2006, Inequality Regimes: Gender, Class and Race in Organizations, *Gender & Society*, 20(4), pp. 441–464.

Ahmed, S. 2007, The Language of Diversity, *Ethnic and Racial Studies*, 30(2), pp. 235–256.

Aitken, I. 1990, *Film and Reform: John Grierson and the Documentary Film Movement*, London: Routledge.

Anderson-Gough, F., Grey, C. and Robson, K. 2000, In the Name of the Client: The Service Ethic in Two Professional Services Firms, *Human Relations*, 53(9), pp. 1151–1174.

Anthony, S. 2012, *Public Relations and the Making of Modern Britain: Stephen Tallents and the Birth of a Progressive Media Profession*, Manchester: Manchester University Press.

Atewologun, D. and Singh, V. 2010, Challenging Ethnic and Gender Identities: An Exploration of UK Black Professionals' Identity Construction, *Equality, Diversity and Inclusion: An International Journal*, 29(4), pp. 332–347.

Baptist, E. 2014, *The Half Has Never Been Told: Slavery and the Making of American Capitalism*, New York: Basic Books.

BBC 2018, Windrush Generation: Who are They and Why are They Facing Problems? *bbc.co.uk*. Available online www.bbc.com/news/uk-43782241.

Bonilla-Silva, E. 2015, The Structure of Racism in Colour-Blind, Post-Racial America, *American Behavioral Scientist*, 59(11), pp. 1358–1376.

Brewis, J. and Grey, C. 1994, Re-Eroticizing the Organization: An Exegesis and Critique, *Gender, Work and Organization*, 1(2), pp. 67–82.

Carbado, D. and Gulati, M. 2003, The Law and Economics of Critical Race Theory, *The Yale Law Journal*, 112, pp. 1757–1828.

Chartered Institute of Public Relations 2018, *State of the Profession 2018*. Available online www.cipr.co.uk/stateofpr.

Coates, R. 2008, Covert Racism in the USA and Globally, *Sociology Compass*, 2, pp. 208–231.

Couldry, N. 2010, *Why Voice Matters: Culture and Politics after Neoliberalism*, London: Sage.

Davis, A. 2018, *Reckless Opportunists: Elites at the End of the Establishment*, Manchester: Manchester University Press.

Du Gay, P. and Salaman, G. 1992, The Cult[ure] of the Customer, *Journal of Management Studies*, 29(5), pp. 615–633.

Duff, A. 2011, Big Four Accounting Firms' Annual Reviews: A Photo Analysis of Gender and Race Portrayals, *Critical Perspectives on Accounting*, 22(1), 20–38.

Edgley, C., Sharma, N. and Anderson-Gough, F. 2016, Diversity and Professionalism in the Big Four Firms: Expectation, Celebration and Weapon in the Battle for Talent, *Critical Perspectives on Accounting*, 35, pp. 13–34.

Edwards, L. 2008, PR Practitioners' Cultural Capital: An Initial Study and Implications for Research and Practice, *Public Relations Review*, 34, pp. 367–372.

Edwards, L. 2014, *Power, Diversity and Public Relations*, London: Routledge.

Evetts, J. 2013, Professionalism: Value and Ideology, *Current Sociology*, 61(5–6), pp. 778–796.

Fanon, F. 2008[1952], *Black Skin, White Masks*, London: Pluto Press.

Fishburn Hedges 2010, About us. Available online www.fishburn-hedges.com/aboutus.

Ford, R. and Brown, C. 2016, *State of the PR Industry: Defining & Delivering on the Promise of Diversity*. Available online http://nbprs.org/wp-content/uploads/2017/11/NBPRS-State-of-the-PR-Industry-White-Paper-FINAL.pdf.

Fournier, V. 1999, The Appeal to 'Professionalism' as a Disciplinary Mechanism, *The Sociological Review*, 47, pp. 280–307.

Freud Communications 2010, Our people. Available online www.freud.com [accessed 4 January 2010].

Gilroy, P. 1987, *There Ain't No Black in the Union Jack: The Cultural Politics of Race and Nation*, 2nd edn. London: Routledge.

Gilroy, P. 1993, *The Black Atlantic: Modernity and Double-Consciousness*, Boston, MA: Harvard University Press.

Goldberg, D.T. 2015, *Are We All Postracial Yet? Debating Race*, Cambridge: Polity Press.

Hall, S. 1996, Who Needs 'Identity'? In Hall, S. and DuGay, P. (eds), *Questions of Cultural Identity*, London: Sage, pp. 1–17.

Hall, S. 1997, The Spectacle of the 'Other'. In Hall, S. (ed.), *Representation: Cultural Representations and Signifying Practices*, London: Sage/Open University Press, pp. 223–290.

Hall, S. 2000, Conclusion: The Multi-Cultural Question. In Hesse, B. (ed.), *Un/settled Multiculturalisms*, London: Zed Books, pp. 209–241.

Hall, S., Critcher, C., Jefferson, T., Clarke, J. and Roberts, B. 2013, *Policing the Crisis: Mugging, the State and Law and Order*, 2nd edn. Basingstoke: Palgrave Macmillan.

Hanlon, G. 1999, Professionalism as Enterprise – Service Class Politics and the Redefinition of Professionalism, *Sociology*, 32(1), pp. 43–63.

Harris, C. 1993, Whiteness as Property. *Harvard Law Review*, 106(8), pp. 1707–1791.

Hesmondhalgh, D. and Baker, S. 2011, *Creative labour: Media Work in Three Cultural Industries*, Abingdon, Oxon: Routledge.

Hesse, B. 2000, Introduction: Un/settled Multiculturalisms. In Hesse, B. (ed.), *Un/settled Multiculturalisms: Diasporas, Entanglements, Transruptions*, London: Zed Books, pp. 1–30.

Hochschild, A. 1983, *The Managed Heart: The Commercialization of Human Feeling*, Berkeley, CA: University of California Press.

hooks, b., 1994, *Outlaw Culture: Resisting Representations*, London: Routledge.

Holvino, E. 2008, Intersections: The Simultaneity of Race, Gender and Class in Organization Studies, *Gender, Work and Organization*, 17(3), pp. 248–277.

Hughes, S. 2018, Declare an Annual Day to Mark Partition of India, MPs Told, *Guardian*. Available online www.theguardian.com/world/2018/jul/15/uk-annual-day-commemorate-partition-india-my-family-partition-and-me.

Hurtado, A. 1996, Strategic Suspensions: Feminists of Color Theorize the Production of Knowledge. In Goldberger, N., Tarule, J., Clinchy, B. and Belenky, M. (eds), *Knowledge,*

Difference and Power: Essays Kinspired by Women's Ways of Knowing, New York: Basic Books, pp. 372–388.

Imoagene, O. 2018, The Nigerian Second Generation at Work in Britain: Ethnoracial Exclusion and Adaptive Strategies, *Sociology*, online first. doi:10.1177/0038038518 776866.

King, D. 1988, Multiple Jeopardy, Multiple Consciousness: The Context of a Black Feminist Ideology, *Signs*, 14(1), pp. 42–72.

Korczynski, M. 2003, Communities of Coping: Collective Emotional Labour in Service Work, *Organization*, 10(1), pp. 55–79.

L'Etang, J. 2004, *Public Relations in Britain: A History of Professional Practice in the 20th Century*, Mahwah, NJ: Lawrence Erlbaum Associates.

Ladson-Billings, G. 2009, 'Who You Callin' Nappy-Headed?' A Critical Race Theory Look at the Construction of Black Women, *Race, Ethnicity and Education*, 12(1), pp. 87–99.

Lamont, M., Silva, G.M., Welburn, J., Guetzkow, J., Mizrachi, N., Herzog, H. and Reis, E. 2016, *Getting Respect: Responding to Stigma and Discrimination in the United States, Brazil and Israel*, Princeton, NJ: Princeton University Press.

Lawrence, E. 1982, Just Plain Common Sense: The Roots of Racism. In C. f. C. C. Studies (ed.), *The Empire Strikes Back*, London: Hutchinson/Routledge, pp. 47–94.

Leveson, B. 2012, *An Inquiry into the Culture, Practices and Ethics of the Press: Report*. Available online www.gov.uk/government/publications/leveson-inquiry-report-into-the-culture-practices-and-ethics-of-the-press.

McClintock, A. 1995, *Imperial Leather: Race, Gender and Sexuality in the Colonial Conquest*, New York: Routledge.

McIntosh, P. 1997, White Privilege and Male Privilege: A Personal Account of Coming to Correspondences through Work in Women's Studies. In Delgado, R. and Stefancic, J. (eds), *Critical White Studies: Looking Behind the Mirror*, Philadelphia, PA: Temple University Press, pp. 291–299.

Owen, D. 2007, Towards a Critical Theory of Whiteness, *Philosophy and Social Criticism*, 33(2), pp. 203–222.

Public Relations and Communications Association 2016, *PR Census 2016*. Available online www.prca.org.uk/assets/files/PR%20Census%202016.pdf.

Puwar, N. 2004, *Space Invaders: Race, Gender and Bodies Out of Place*, Oxford: Berg.

Ramamurthy, A. 2012, Absences and Silences: The Representation of the Tea Picker in Colonial and Fair Trade Advertising, *Visual Culture in Britain*, 13(3), pp. 367–381.

Ramdin, R. 1999, *Reimaging Britain: 500 Years of Black and Asian History*, London: Pluto Press.

Saha, A. 2016, The Rationalizing/Racializing Logic of Capital in Cultural Production, *Media Industries*, 3(1). doi:10.3998/mij.15031809.0003.101.

Said, E. 1995, *Orientalism*, 2nd edn. Harmondsworth: Penguin.

Skeggs, B. 1994, Refusing to be Civilised: 'Race', Sexuality and Power. In Afshar, H. & Maynard, M. (eds), *The Dynamics of Race and Gender* (Vol. 106–127). London: Taylor and Francis.

Solomos, J. 2003, *Race and Racism in Britain*. Houndmills, Hants: Palgrave Macmillan.

Solomos, J. and Back, L. 1995, *Race, Politics and Social Change*. London: Routledge.

Sommerlad, H. 2015, *The 'Social Magic' of Merit: Diversity, Equity, and Inclusion in the English and Welsh Legal Profession*. Available online http://epapers.bham.ac.uk/1962/5/cepler_working_paper_2_2015(2).pdf.

Syedain, H. 1993, 1 April, Major Minority Interest. *Marketing*, pp. 37–39.

Tallents, S. 1932, *The Projection of England*, London: Olen Press.

The Cabinet Office 2018, *Race Disparity Audit*, London: Crown Copyright. Available online https://assets.publishing.service.gov.uk/government/uploads/system/uploads/attachment_data/file/686071/Revised_RDA_report_March_2018.pdf.

Waymer, D. and Street, J. 2015, HBCUs as Relics or Reminders Race Remains Relevant in a 'Post-Racial' Society? Exploring and Expanding the role of Memory in Public Relations, *Public Relations Inquiry*, 4(2), pp. 145–162.

Werbner, P. 2013, Everyday Multiculturalism: Theorising the Difference between 'Intersectionality' and 'Multiple Identities', *Ethnicities*, 13(4), pp. 401–419.

Yosso, T.J. 2005, Whose Culture Has Capital? A Critical Race Theory Discussion of Community Cultural Wealth, *Race, Ethnicity and Education*, 8(1), pp. 69–91.

Yuval-Davis, N., Anthias, F. and Kofman, E. 2005, Secure Borders and Safe Haven and the Gendered Politics of Belonging: Beyond Social Cohesion, *Ethnic and Racial Studies*, 28(3), pp. 513–535.

6

INTERSECTIONAL ACTIVISM, HISTORY AND PUBLIC RELATIONS

New understandings of women's communicative roles in anti-racist and anti-sexist work

Jennifer Vardeman, Amanda Kennedy and Brittany Little

Introduction

In this chapter, we review two illustrations to articulate historic and contemporary intersections between race and gender: women of color in the US civil rights movement of the 1950s and 1960s, and the Women's March on Washington of 2017. We situate these illustrations and interdisciplinary theories of identity, power, and social change to interrogate dominant understandings of who and what 'counts' as 'doing' PR. First, we consider different approaches of the writing of PR history, namely the 'traditional' versus the 'reappraisal' approach, which reframes PR actors' goals in history in more culturally situated ways. Next we look at gendered and raced subjects as PR practitioner-activists operating in complex systems of social oppression through a lens of intersectionality (Crenshaw 1991). Then, we engage theories of agency/activism via resistance and performance – including (in)visibility, infrapolitics (Scott 1990), and politics of respectability (Higginbotham 1992; Scott 1990) – by oppressed, intersectional subjects in historical and contemporary contexts of emancipatory activist PR.

Reappraising the gendered history of public relations

Jacquie L'Etang's work on public relations history has been instrumental in highlighting the problems with traditional readings and bringing forth approaches and methods for uncovering additional, revisionist readings. This is particularly important when considering the status of gender and race in the field, and how political identities like these have contributed to the character of PR historically versus today. One salient context by which to examine race and gender is through activism and social movements.

Traditional vs revisionist histories of PR. The history of public relations is a contested subject. One major critique has been that 'traditional' readings of PR history rely on the centering of the 'Four Models' in the Excellence project (L'Etang 2008) and on US readings of PR history (L'Etang 2016) in which PR evolved from pure publicity to moral relationship-building. This traditional, descriptive history emerged according to a temporal succession of 'great men' (e.g., P.T. Barnum, Ivy Lee, Edward Bernays) who brought innovative approaches to how organizations can motivate publics to comply with organizational messages.

The purpose of taking this broader historical approach is to understand depths and ranges of PR's reach than previously considered. L'Etang (2016) argued that we learn more about PR history as well as cultural/national histories if we contextualize PR history within social movements' histories: 'use of social theory, may offer new ways of understanding public relations in macro-historical processes, so that public relations history is not solely the history of public relations activities (the occupational development), but rather is positioned more fundamentally within social development' (31). This analysis attempts to pair PR history with the critical social concept, intersectionality, to identify stories that may have been left out of traditional PR history, a main one being that of gender.

Gender in the history of PR. Other major critiques on PR history have been on the emphasis on men's 'contributions' to the success and growth of PR (Creedon 1989) as well as on the development of a feminist theory *for* public relations rather than a feminist theory *of* public relations (Rakow and Nastasia 2009). Revisionist history of PR should examine individuals, organizations, and societies rather than the typical textbook and biographical approach of promoting the singular successes of 'fathers' of PR (L'Etang 2008). Creedon brought forth the first critique of two major themes in PR history writing: (1) women were either absent or were 'add-ons' at the end of a list of male practitioners who forged the field; and (2) the 'contribution' approach to PR history privileges one type of PR activity (e.g., succeeding or winning a campaign) versus a 'reappraisal' approach, which values examining both why certain people succeeded at PR when others failed (e.g., privilege of being male, white, etc.) as well as embracing a collection of practitioners' failures. A reappraisal of public relations history, 'would account for diverse racial, gender, and class perspectives on the development of the field (…) rather than victory, independence, and autonomy, public relations values are more along the lines of compromise, cooperation, and communication' (Creedon 1989:29).

Another revisionist lens of history would build theory through seeing women as affected by public relations:

> [A feminist theory of public relations] enables us to see that concerns expressed to date about women and public relations have been concerns about the lives of women in public relations rather than concerns about public relations in the lives of women.
>
> *(Rakow 2001:3)*

Both revisions of public relations history provide fundamentally new ways from which to build and learn and conduct public relations, around an understanding that women formed the field equally to and uniquely from the men we've traditionally understood to have powered the industry. Repositioning public relations around a gender lens also behoves scholars and educators to relearn how a racial lens is equally important to the foundations of public relations.

Applications of intersectionality theory in public relations' history

To fully understand the role of race *and* gender in PR history, scholars, educators, and activists need to engage history in conjunction with other social theories. Intersectionality provides that engagement. As a way to rationalize how multiple identities of race and gender play a role in the communicative practices of people performing PR roles historically, we incorporated intersectionality as one of our theoretical frameworks to examine the illustrations. Intersectional analyses of the field – pedagogical, applied, and scholarly – provide context for why our field continues to have diversity problems, which are problematic for the future of public relations practitioners' and educators' ability to reach increasingly diverse, global publics, as suggested by Pompper (2005): 'Shortages of female African American public relations practitioners further delay incorporation of multicultural diversity in the workplace' (298).

Intersectionality explains how Black women were oppressed twofold in systems of domination (e.g., the US legal system) that worked against both their gender and race by favoring maleness and Whiteness as normative identities (Crenshaw 1989). While it was coined 'intersectionality' in 1989, the concept was theorized in Black feminism and critical race theory well before then, and it has since gained prominence not only in Black feminist thought (Collins 2009), but it has also gained popularity in wider milieu.

PR scholars are increasingly adopting an intersectional approach in research with publics as well as in examining how race and gender affect practitioners' experiences in the field today (e.g., Edwards 2010; Pompper 2007). However, intersectionality has not yet been used as a lens through which to learn about practitioners' experiences in the past. We hope to add research to the body of knowledge about how PR has been performed by activists pushing for anti-sexist and anti-racist solutions, particularly in the histories of PR practices by women practitioner-activists in important social movements.

In/visible politics and resistance as activism

In James C. Scott's (1990) *Domination and the Arts of Resistance: Hidden Transcripts*, Scott theorized what might be called invisible and subversive activism: strategic performances of resistance by subordinate groups against hegemonic discourses and ideologies that work in the interest of dominant classes. Scott used the metaphor of a stage to introduce and illustrate concepts such as hidden and public transcripts, infrapolitics, and performing respect by oppressed subjects with much to lose from visible and public dissidence.

Public and hidden transcripts. Scott (1990) analyzed how dominant and subordinate classes have strategically engaged what he termed public and hidden transcripts to reinforce and/or resist dominant discourses across history and society. Scott described the public transcript as discourses enacted by both dominant and subordinate groups (e.g., masters/slaves, lords/serfs, etc.,) when visible to each other, or 'on stage' (2). The public transcript is largely determined by the powerful for the powerful and includes displays or rituals of domination and subservience in ways that are flattering to the dominant class, reinforce existing power relations, and legitimize subservience by subjugated groups.

On the flip side, 'If subordinate discourse in the presence of the dominant is a public transcript, I shall use the term hidden transcript to characterize discourse that takes place "offstage," beyond direct observation by powerholders' (Scott 1990:4). In this 'offstage' space where subordinate interactions remain invisible to those in power, subjugated and disenfranchised groups are afforded more freedom to be candid, strategize and organize, practice religious and cultural rituals, share violent fantasies of retaliation and revenge against the dominant class, and openly express hatred, frustration, despair, pain, rage, and other feelings that would otherwise disrupt the public transcript – even to the extent of endangering (subordinate) lives (39).

One example of an offstage space where hidden transcripts emerged in the civil rights movement was weekly meetings held in cities across the South where Blacks (and some White allies) would come together to share stories of racial and sexual violence and discrimination away from the menacing gaze of White segregationists and opponents of racial justice (McGuire 2010). These gatherings were sites of organization, mobilization, commiseration, and catharsis fed by testimony of mostly Black women. McGuire described one of these scenes in which a Black woman recalled being asked to give up her seat on a public bus for a white man to sit instead:

> 'I am filled up to my bones, in this, it's way down in my bones and when there ain't no protest,' she said, offering a profound defense of her humanity, 'I'm still gonna have it. I'm still gonna have my protest.' After her moving testimony, the congregation sang the Negro spiritual 'Nobody Knows the Trouble I've Seen,' translating the troubles they had all seen into 'Glory, Hallelujah'.
>
> *(95)*

Somewhere in the middle, Scott (1990) theorized a 'subordinate group politics that lies strategically between the first two (…) a politics of disguise and anonymity that takes place in public view but is designed to have double meaning or to shield the identity of actors' (19). Scott coined these public/hidden practices by subordinate group infrapolitics.

Infrapolitics. Infrapolitics is defined by Scott (1990) as 'a wide variety of low-profile forms of resistance that dare not speak in their own name' (19). Scott offered helpful analogies to explain the 'infra' of infrapolitics. First, Scott likened the invisibility of infrapolitics to infrared light: 'the circumspect struggle waged daily by subordinate groups is, like infrared rays, beyond the visible end of the spectrum' (183); further, 'That [infrapolitics] should be invisible (…) is in large part by design – a tactical choice born of a prudent awareness of the balance of power' (183). An example of infrapolitics prominent in shaping recent US history is a politics of respectability strategically deployed by African Americans in pursuit of civil rights and racial justice.

Performing respect/politics of respectability. One strategic infrapolitical move by subordinate groups involves 'a continuous stream of performances of deference, respect, reverence, admiration, esteem, and even adoration' (Scott 1990:93) that, on the surface, serve to validate existing power relations and modes of domination for the dominant class. At the same time, those performances of respect – subjugated groups' visible displays of reverence for official public transcripts and rules of the dominant class – also work to ingratiate subordinates to those in power even while actively – and invisibly – resisting that very power and domination. As Scott explained, 'The dominant never control the stage absolutely, but their wishes normally prevail,' and, 'it is in the best interest of the subordinate to produce a more or less credible performance, speaking the lines and making the gestures he knows are expected of him' (4).

Other theorists have situated the 'politics of respectability' more specifically in Black history in the US, from slavery to Reconstruction, the civil rights era, and beyond (Higginbotham 1992; McGuire 2010). According to McGuire (2010), 'political respectability required middle-class decorum' (93) and was deployed strategically by Black men and women since Reconstruction to combat racist, anti-Black stigmas that persisted among middle- and upper-class White Americans (i.e., the dominant class). Similarly, Higginbotham's (1992) depiction of respect/respectable/respectability might be described as the oppressive counterpart to Scott's more strategic, subversive, and emancipatory version of respectable performances: 'The politics of "respectability" disavowed, in often repressive ways, much of the expressive culture of the "folk," for example, sexual behavior, dress style, leisure activity, music, speech patterns, and religious worship patterns' (Higginbotham 1992:272).

An example of the politics of respectability is reflected in the strategic positioning of Rosa Parks as a face of the movement instead of any number of Black women of lower-class statuses and more stigmatized subject positions (e.g., sharecroppers, pregnant unwed teenagers) whose experiences with racial and sexual violence were often more extreme than that faced by Parks. Deliberately publicizing Parks as a 'respectable' (read unthreatening, sympathetic) African American woman and victim of racial injustice became even more critical in the historical-political context of White backlash and paranoia post-*Brown v. Board of Education*:

E. D. Nixon undoubtedly sensed this hysteria when he refused to raise a pregnant teenager up as the symbol of the integration struggle. In mid-1950s Alabama, he had to find someone whose class background, moral reputation, and public record could withstand withering white scrutiny and inspire African-American.

(McGuire 2010:98)

Connections to public relations. As public relations is an anthropologic activity (L'Etang 2010), and as messages, information subsidies, events, and other public relations products carry scripts of meaning about valuable identities, it is relevant to explore how the communicators of resistance movements have utilized public relations activities for infrapolitical purposes. Some scholarship in public relations outside of the traditional, dominant research trajectories has clear parallels to in/visibility, infrapolitics, and resistance as activism as covered in this section. For example, Holtzhausen (2012) theorized about PR practitioners as organizational activists who engage resistance strategies, work within dominant organizational structures and discourses to challenge existing power structures and what might be described as official public transcripts to promote justice and emancipatory ends. Similarly, Dutta-Bergman (2006) and Dutta and Pal (2010), among others, have favored critical-cultural and subaltern approaches to public relations research to interrogate power relations and privilege often-silenced, even invisible, subjects and discourses for social change and justice. These are but a few examples of the growing but still scattered body of literature grounded in critical and historical theories and methods to challenge traditionally dominant 'paradigms' in public relations.

The chapter examines women's use of PR to enact social change in their communities that are mired in racist systems. The first illustration is of Rosa Parks, as depicted in Danielle L. McGuire's *At the Dark End of the Street* (2010), as Parks seemingly performed the PR function for the civil rights movement. Parks was a well-known figure of the civil rights movement for her role in starting the Montgomery Bus Boycott. She was also secretary of the National Association for the Advancement of Colored People (NAACP), and did influential work for them during the civil rights movement (McGuire 2010). The second case is of the Women's March on Washington, as its leaders employed social media and PR messaging with intersectional purposes and rhetoric in unprecedented ways. Both illustrations temper previous notions of how women practitioner-activists have been viewed in the field by answering the guiding question, *what practices characterize PR work performed by women doing intersectional activist work over the past 75 years?*

Illustration 1: Rosa Parks, Black women and the civil rights movement

The civil rights movement was inherently a public relations campaign against racism and inequality (Hon 1997). It turned everyday people into activists, who regularly practiced the art of public relations. As activists, women had to fight for equality within and outside their communities. We illustrate that women activists like Parks played PR practitioner roles in historical social movements, which is characterized by in/visibility and the presence of public and hidden transcripts, infrapolitics of the civil rights movement within existing structures, and nuances of the politics of respectability.

In history books and general social discourse, Parks' involvement in the civil rights movement was diminished. She is remembered as an aging woman, who indirectly started the Montgomery Bus Boycott only because she refused to stand and give her seat to a White man on the bus, because she had worked a hard day and was too tired to move. However, Parks was an activist well before her involvement with the Montgomery Bus Boycott, and she was not a meek, old woman. She was a secretary for the NAACP, and readily worked to bring rape cases to the attention of the media to force police to take some form of legal action. For example, Parks was instrumental in bringing the injustice done in Abbeville, Alabama, in 1944, when six White men raped Recy Taylor, a Black woman. Parks, along with allies, formed a group called the Alabama Committee for Equal Justice, which utilized the Black media to nationally spread the injustice done in Abbeville. Parks' efforts gained national attention, support and money for Taylor's defense, and forced the Abbeville police department to file charges (although the men were never indicted). Despite the outcome, the garnering of resources and formal charges were abnormal occurrences in rape cases involving White men and a Black woman (McGuire 2010). Thus, this campaign changed how US justice departments reacted to these cases and set the stage for a large-scale campaign against White supremacy.

Additionally, Parks was raised in a culture of civil rights activism, as her grandfather openly spoke and acted against racism, despite the danger. Her husband was also a member of the NAACP and because of his involvement, Parks was able to procure the release of nine Black men who were wrongly convicted of rape with no evidence (McGuire 2010:13). Parks and her husband did other types of activist work, as well. They held voters' league meetings to encourage Black citizens to register to vote by describing the registration process and preparing them for the test (which was designed to make Black citizens fail). Parks spoke at NAACP conventions and strategically allowed herself to be arrested to spur the Montgomery Bus Boycott into action (McGuire 2010). It is important to understand that Parks was a civil rights activist decades before she refused to give up her seat on the bus.

In/visibility: public and hidden transcripts of the civil rights movement

The story of the civil rights movement features many men, but glosses and sometimes ignores the complex and diverse stories of women in the movement. Jo Ann Robinson was one of these women whose story is not commonly shared.

Robinson, a member of the Women's Political Council (WPC), was adamant on the need to desegregate buses to take back the dignity of women who were constantly abused physically and verbally by the driver and riders of the buses (McGuire 2010).

Members of the WPC set up a registration school to help members of the community prepare to register and to accompany them to register, in addition to confronting bus drivers who mistreated women with true political action (McGuire 2010). The main goal of this organization was to fight institutionalized racism in Montgomery, Alabama, while providing opportunities for women to hold leadership positions (Crocker 2017). After hearing of Parks' arrest, Robinson and the other members of the WPC drafted plans for what would become the Montgomery Bus Boycott. They drafted flyers and promoted the boycott over the next few days, successfully garnering significant support and participation (Robinson 2007).

However, their role in the Montgomery Bus Boycott is rarely if ever mentioned; instead, the movement is credited to Martin Luther King, Jr. and his team. Although the men took over leadership of the Montgomery Improvement Association (MIA), the group that took charge of the boycott, Robinson made sure the women of the WPC joined the MIA and handled the day-to-day operations, ensuring that the women managed the communication except for the speeches at 'the podium,' where men took the spotlight (McGuire 2010:110). Robinson and other members of the WPC may have taken on a more invisible role in the fight for civil rights, but they were still doing just as much if not more than their male counterparts, despite receiving little to no recognition.

Women didn't remain invisible or silent in their fight against the systematic rape of Black women. It wasn't uncommon for Black women to endure abuse by White men in the time between 1940 and 1980, but it was uncommon for Black women to take action to receive justice from them. Recy Taylor, Rosa Lee Cherry, Rosa Lee Coates and many other women raped by White men began telling their stories despite the threat of retribution and the backlash from the trials, where lawyers would try to demean their characters. Their willingness to not only share their stories but the attempt to seek justice all within the public eye contributed to the fight against the idea that 'a Black women's body was never hers alone' (Lee 2000). They did not fight alone; other people, especially women, like Parks and Daisy Bates (the owner of State Press) would fight with them however they could (McGuire 2010).

The intersectional identities of – and intersecting systems of oppression encountered by – Black women in the civil rights movement help illuminate their systematic erasure from popular histories of the movement and era. For example, while their racial status compelled Black women to be part of the struggle for civil rights almost by default (whether they liked it or not), gender largely subjugated them to their male counterparts in the movement – Black women activists' roles in the movement were often limited to supporting the Black men who emerged, both at the time and still in popular memory, as brave leaders and social justice visionaries (McGuire 2010). Further, social class added another layer of intersectionality that routinely dictated Black women's experiences and roles in the civil rights movement; while Black women from lower class backgrounds encountered racial and sexual violence at disproportionately higher rates than middle- and upper-class Black women, lower class status for many Black women also led them to be silenced and rendered absent across many of the more publicly visible platforms of the civil rights movement (McGuire 2010).

Infrapolitics of the civil rights movement within existing structures

Infrapolitics refers to how historically marginalized, silenced, or subordinated groups and individuals strategically operate within and appropriate existing structures and dominant discourses to achieve social change and emancipatory ends, typically in conflict with dominant values and interests (Scott 1990). Parks and other activist women deployed infrapolitics to navigate and take advantage of the visible dominant systems, and used communication tactics and strategies familiar to those in power (but unexpected coming from subordinate groups), which allowed for strategic uses of both invisibility and visibility – 'official' public and hidden transcripts and discourses – by disenfranchised subjects and publics (Scott 1990).

Many influential moments in infrapolitics of Black women activists during the civil rights movement played out in courthouses, schools, voting booths, buses, and other public (as in both visible and civic) and 'legitimate' structures and systems as resistance to racist and sexist domination. For example, organizers of the Montgomery Bus Boycott took advantage of highly visible spaces of public transportation to wage and eventually win a legal battle in court with material policy implications (McGuire 2010). To ensure victory, Black organizers strategically chose Black women who would be sympathetic victims of racist White male bus drivers to testify in court, while Black men – mostly Christian ministers, most notably Martin Luther King, Jr. – were positioned as chaste and courageous leaders of the boycott (McGuire 2010). Arguably, the outcome may have been different had center stage been ceded to the scores of Black women who, in reality, constituted a much stronger driving force behind the boycott than the select group of Black ministers (men) who received almost all public credit for it nationally (McGuire 2010).

Another example of infrapolitics, the Black Press, was a long line of Black-owned newspapers dating back to the early 1800s with a major role in giving voice and visibility to an otherwise disenfranchised Black communities, played an essential part in the civil rights movement. Parks and other Black leaders in the movement and from the Black Press strategically published shocking and graphic representations of violence against Black men and women, including rapes and lynchings (McGuire 2010). The Black Press not only served Black audiences, it also worked as a pipeline to dominant (White) media and audiences, delivering news and testimony from Black communities to more mainstream outlets and to the living rooms of middle- to upper-class White America. Sensational images and graphic stories covering violence against Blacks worked to both garner sympathy for Black victims of racial and sexual violence, leading to growing national support for civil rights causes, as well as creating global embarrassment for the US when such shocking stories of social and racial violence and injustice reached international audiences (Scott 2010).

The politics of respectability and the civil rights movement

Long before Parks refused to give up her seat on the bus to a White man, she was fighting for the rights and dignity of African Americans. As a member of numerous civil rights organizations and the NAACP, Parks participated in numerous campaigns about Black women who were rape victims. Parks and other activists performed a sort of media relations role by spreading women's stories to Black Press papers through the USA in efforts to force states to arrest and prosecute White men accused of rape and other violent crimes against Blacks (McGuire 2010) (see Figure 6.1):

> For example on July 17, 1942, the State Press published photographs of two white Little Rock police officers who raped Rosa Lee Cherry (...) Daisy Bates even printed a transcript of Cherry's grand jury testimony. This helped secure public support for an indictment (...) Bates's vigilance on the Cherry case and others like it made it impossible for white authorities to ignore crimes against African-American women. Her outspoken attacks on rape and other forms of sexualized violence helped secure trials and, in some instances, even rare convictions of white assailants who attacked Black women in Arkansas during the early 1940s and early 1950s.
>
> *(McGuire 2010:139)*

$600 To Rape Wife? Ala. Whites Make Offer To Recy Taylor Mate!

By FRED ATWATER
(Defender Staff Correspondent)

MONTGOMERY, Ala. — "Nigger—ain't $600 enough for raping your wife?"

Stocky Willie Lee Taylor considered it.

He talked to white Marvin White, who wanted him to forget prosecuting the six white men who raped and ruptured Recy, his 24-year-old wife.

White spoke for his clients, all youths from prominent Abbeville families who had been identified by Recy. They were Hugo Wilson, Penute Hastings, Sam Skippy, Billie Hilder, Dillard York and Luther Lee.

They were willing to pay $100 each if Recy Taylor would forget it, White said.

By then the rape of Recy, mother of a two-year-old daughter, had become known in every town in Alabama and every Negro community in the nation. The Grand Jury was to meet within a week to act upon one of the few cases ever to be brought to court of white youths raping a Negro woman.

White repeated his offer of $100 for each man as a "settlement."

Willie blurted out "No." But that didn't end it. White came back and again after more pressure and threats had been leveled at the Taylors and Willie said, "Come back later and I'll tell you." He came back later and Willie answered "Yes."

Defendants Dismissed

Willie may as well have stuck to his first no. For the Grand Jury called on October 3, 1944, dismissed all the defendants. For a white

VICTIM OF WHITE ALABAMA RAPISTS

First published photo of Mrs. Recy Taylor, victim of six white rapists in Alabama, and her little family is this picture received from their refuge in an Alabama city some distance from their hometown of Abbeville, where the crime occurred. With the young mother is her daughter, little Jayce Lee Taylor and her husband, Willie Guy Taylor.

FIGURE 6.1 Newspaper headline in October 1944 from the *Chicago Defender*, which was read primarily by African Americans, about Recy Taylor's rape.

Most of Parks' activist past is forgotten because in December 1955 she became the public face of the Montgomery Bus Boycott (McGuire 2010). Her willingness to fight publicly against the buses' mistreatment of African Americans, women in particular, made it crucial for her to adhere to the politics of respectability. A respectable woman in 1955 was not a disruptive woman, but she was a middle-class woman of principle and chastity. Other Black women boycotted the buses, but the movement leaders did not promote them as the 'face' of the boycott (McGuire 2010:85). Rather, Parks fit the bill, but her activist past did not, so it wasn't mentioned to reporters, judges or anyone because Parks has to be seen as the 'perfect' women to gain support for the boycott and ultimately win her case against the mistreatment of African Americans on buses. Parks was seen as a 'sainted' woman and 'celebrated for her quiet dignity, prim demeanor, and middle-class propriety' (McGuire 2010:107); her radical and activist past was strategically hidden. Her respectability gave her the ability to withstand the common negative stereotypes lawyers would try to place on women of color and afforded legitimacy to the boycott.

The standard of respectability made it important for activists to frame themselves and their messages carefully to ensure their goal of justice and equality. Parks and other activists who led the charge against racially motivated rape found the concept of respectability to be a major factor in the campaign of a case. The first tactic by officers and lawyers hinged on painting the accusers as a jezebel to dehumanize women to the jury, but also to the media (McGuire 2010). The rhetoric used by the lawyers and supporters of the accused were careful to paint the women as 'productive' members of the community, as mothers and as respectable women, to garner effective positive media and actual results (even unfavorable results).

Illustration 2: Women's March on Washington and intersectional messaging

The Women's March on Washington (WMW), held in January 21, 2017, immediately followed the inauguration of Donald J. Trump as President of the United States, to advocate for policies that protect marginalized groups of people and the environment, which WMW and other groups argued were significantly threatened by the imminent Trump administration. Via social media tactics, the singular event of the march morphed quickly into a global movement that lauds 673 individual marches to date on all seven continents, 4.95+ million marchers (Women's March n.d.), and the 'largest coordinated protest in U.S. history and one of the largest in world history' (Women's March n.d.). The Women's March, now an official non-profit organization, supports multiple coordinated programs supporting youth empowerment, voter registration, and women's rights and health globally.

The march and the organization have stated their messaging and mission work are grounded in intersectionality as a guiding approach; as such, this chapter and related work is one of the first to document intersectionality work as part of PR practice. To demonstrate the stream of intersectional public relations activism through time, this section will analyze the WMW's work in the similar context as that of Rosa Parks' civil rights movement activism, by showing how the WMW similarly employed *in/visible politics*, *public/hidden transcripts*, and *politics of respectability*. This case study will also demonstrate how these *infrapolitical* actions are different today than in the 1950s/1960s USA: women can and are at the forefront of sociopolitical and economic movements now. However, this case suggests the undertones of Whiteness are the *infrapolitical* system undermining this.

Reappraising history, accepting invisibility and transforming transcripts

To this point, as historical context is a backdrop for the distinctions of power is one of the tenets of intersectionality theory (Crenshaw 1991), and the WMW leaders explicitly looked backward in time to situate the current march, this chapter aims to highlight the history in the WMW, despite the fact that it is relatively recent. In order to erase the *invisibility* of women of color's historic efforts and demonstrate the current movement's commitment to intersectionality, the WMW took a *reappraisal approach* (Creedon 1989) in their spotlighting civil rights acts, specifically by demonstrating the problems of previous movements. They do this by highlighting past failures, showing corrections, grounding in Constitutional edicts, and recalling icons from the past civil rights efforts.

For example, conflict arose quickly in the campaign among women from different groups (Stockman 2017). Specifically, one of the largest critiques to the WMW was that women of color had been fighting 'this' fight for decades before but had been ignored by White activists. The leadership addressed these critiques in a number of ways (Vardeman-Winter 2017) to negotiate tensions of political identities in and for this campaign. The WMW co-chairs used explicit messaging to communicate their belief that the current march had to be more inclusive of women of color and other historically marginalized groups in order to overcome the past movements' White-centric efforts: 'We cannot talk about the history of women's liberation in the US w/o talking about the racism w/in the movement for women's suffrage' (@womensmarch 2017, January 10). The systemic errors of historic movements of making women of color's work and experiences invisible are the *hidden transcripts* of the past women's movements as well in the White origins of the WMW.

As a marked difference from 75 years prior, the political and mediated environment of today made *public transcripts* of identity transparency salient. Specifically, the WMW producers dedicated a significant amount of media space and time to demonstrating the origin and concerted intention of the WMW being an intersectional campaign. The campaign messages consistently noted that privileged individuals/groups must accept *invisibility* in order to correct an historic wrong.

Specifically, this meant that White women needed to retreat from claiming authority and defining campaign goals and needs and instead support the direction women of color determined for WMW efforts. The campaign regularly vocalized that although all women's lives matter, pivoting identities place some women's needs at higher priority of political and economic action today than others:

> For too long, the march organizers said, the women's rights movement focused on issues that were important to well-off white women, such as the ability to work outside the home and attain the same high-powered positions that men do. But minority women, they said, have had different priorities. Black women who have worked their whole lives as maids might care more about the minimum wage or police brutality than about seeing a woman in the White House. Undocumented immigrant women might care about abortion rights, they said, but not nearly as much as they worry about being deported.
>
> *(Stockman 2017)*

Building consensus through politics of respectability

Furthermore, the WMW producers reappraised the failures of the past but also conjured up iconic leaders, messages, and events to build consensus. Past leaders' words served as a common *public transcript* for the campaign, almost as a form of apology to the wrongful direction of past movements' leadership as well as in gestures of deference for timeless wisdom about the nature of civil rights work. For example, WMW tweeted well-respected author-activists' quotes to encourage unity: "'I am not free while any woman is unfree, even when her shackles are very different from my own." –Audre Lorde #WhyIMarch #WomensMarch' (@womensmarch 2016, December 12). They also embedded historic feminist and anti-racist movements and iconic leaders into the strategic structuring and messaging for the organization. In their 'Guiding Vision' document, they quoted Martin Luther King, Jr.: 'As Dr. King said, "*We cannot walk alone. And as we walk, we must make the pledge that we shall always march ahead. We cannot turn back.*"' (@womensmarch 2017, January 12). The document also *performed respect* to myriad historically marginalized groups by showing that the WMW organization is composed of and directed by past and current activists:

> leaders of organizations and communities that have been building the foundation for social progress for generations. We welcome vibrant collaboration and honor the legacy of the movements before us – the suffragists and abolitionists, the civil rights Movement, the feminist movement, the American Indian Movement, Occupy Wall Street, Marriage Equality, Black Lives Matter, and more (…) We are empowered by the legions of revolutionary leaders who paved the way for us to march, and acknowledge those around the globe who fight for our freedoms (…) They are #WHYWEMARCH.
>
> (@womensmarch 2017, January 12)

Discussion

This chapter examined these illustrations from the standpoint of Jacquie L'Etang's critical, anthropologic-based historical work. In particular, L'Etang (2016) likened activist movements and PR: 'it is possible to understand social movements as long-term campaigns; activism as specific historical event and conflicting agents; and public relations as organizational strategic communication' (32). By examining commonalities of social movements and PR over time, we can see how the implementation of intersectionality as a mission and rhetoric was both a hindrance and a bridge for women practitioner-activists over the past 75 years.

Because of the significant dearth of histories of and including women practitioners (Creedon 1989), scholars have to unearth untold stories. We've attempted this in analyzing Parks' acting as a PR agent in the civil rights movement (McGuire 2010), as Parks performed the 'backroom' work to promote Martin Luther King, Jr. to the 'forefront,' particularly in the traditional PR activity of the time, podium speeches, a form of *public transcript*, as well as by employing the Black Press to spread the news of the events because otherwise, these violent acts would not get any coverage. These cultural acts by Black women suggest an historic, particular, *infrapolitical* scope of women in the field of public relations in the 1950s and 1960s USA, as well as other Western countries (see L'Etang's analysis of women in postwar Britain 2015).

The women leaders of the WMW performed similar PR strategies as did the Black women practitioner-activists of the civil rights movement, but three main differences emerged between their performances/flow in PR versus those of Parks and her cohort in the 1950s/1960s: (1) social media allowed for more open, conducive outlets for women's strategic management of the campaign; (2) intentional intersectionality emerged as a prominent mission, strategy, and message prominent in the campaign and as the primary *public transcript* of all women in the WMW effort; and (3) women of color emerged necessarily at the *visible* forefront of the WMW campaign. The illustrations contrast one another but provide a revisionist history of gender, activism, and PR, and demonstrate the importance of considering the politics surrounding PR practices, which dominant PR paradigms do not.

Many of the 'old' hidden transcripts that operated 'behind the scenes' around the civil rights movement have moved into public transcripts unfurling surrounding race and gender (and identity politics in general) in the USA. Relatively 'radical' (i.e., challenging heteronormative White male privilege) rhetorics of contemporary social movements like Black Lives Matter and #MeToo are examples of conversations that used to happen among subordinated groups in private but are now taking center stage in public transcripts.

However, while seeing this kind of progress in national and wider conversations about race, gender, power and privilege is heartening on one hand, making once-hidden transcripts public also presents new dangers and challenges. For one, increased vulnerability accompanies heightened visibility of marginalized individuals and groups who are now empowered to speak out against those in power who historically benefited from public transcripts (e.g., women who speak out against male sexual harassers may become targets of retaliation and public shaming). Also, theories and analytical tools originally intended for rendering visible and critiquing social injustice and systems of power and oppression – like intersectionality – stand the risk of being misappropriated and depoliticized in dominant and popular discourses for less-than-emancipatory ends.

Furthermore, regarding what 'new' hidden transcripts are being (re)produced by subordinate groups now (like those operating behind the scenes of the Women's March, for example), we argue that's difficult if not impossible for us (authors) to 'see' from our positions of relative privilege. We can learn and 'know' about the hidden transcripts we talk about in this chapter thanks to the benefits of hindsight and social progress made since the civil rights and women's movements of the twentieth century and beyond; but that's only because the hidden transcripts circulated among oppressed groups behind those social movements at the time stayed hidden long enough to enable infrapolitics and resistance as activism necessary to drive real social change. Hidden transcripts are meant to stay hidden to avoid cooptation by dominant classes and, as such, we would argue they wouldn't be hidden transcripts anymore if we (the authors) knew and wrote about them in this chapter.

However, even though we can't know hidden transcripts of subordinate groups today, just knowing of them and acknowledging how hidden transcripts are strategically communicated and function behind closed doors to enable oppressed subjects to organize, mobilize, and resist domination by powerful elites prompts us to recognize another flow of public relations that has otherwise remained largely invisible to us, and to recognize agency in subaltern subjects and publics often invisible in dominant histories of PR and social movements and change more broadly. We want to expand/re-envision/reappraise traditional conceptualizations and dominant histories of PR to include subaltern and subversive communication strategies and tactics such as engagement with hidden transcripts, infrapolitics, and resistance as activism that may not even be visible to us now (or possibly ever).

Concluding thoughts on future work

A preliminary conclusion for this analysis – one that should be explored in future research – suggests that the undermining of women in PR history is cultural and infrapolitical, is tied to the contemporary secondary status of women in the field today, and is determined almost completely by the angle and purpose with which we employ historicity in our field.

Furthermore, this analysis and case studies are relevant for international readers because the US civil rights movement was conducted on an international stage, as key members of the movement utilized US international power struggles to legitimize the movement. Furthermore, much of the USA' involvement internationally hinged on the situation of African Americans in the military, educational, and industrial systems in the USA (Gaines 2007). Finally, the civil rights movement paved the way for many future social movements, domestically and globally, as its strategies and tactics (e.g., sit-ins, nonviolent direct action) were born in bridging racial, class, gender, and other cultural boundaries to establish new policies and structures in social, legal, educational, workplace, and financial settings. The many connections, historically and presently, between civil rights domestically and internationally suggest a future generation that can more ably understand class and race issues on a global scale: 'Studying the black freedom movement within a global perspective can better prepare students to understand contemporary global affairs, helping them draw connections between postwar U.S. history and the histories of Africa, Asia and the Middle East' (Gaines 2007:58).

References

Collins, P.H. 2009, *Black Feminist Thought*, New York: Routledge Classics.

Creedon, P.J. 1989, Public Relations History Misses 'Her Story', *Journalism Educator*, 44(3), pp. 26–30.

Crenshaw, K.W. 1989, Demarginalizing the Intersection of Race and Sex: A Black Feminist Critique of Antidiscrimination Doctrine, Feminist Theory, and Antiracist Politics, *University of Chicago Legal Forum*, 1989(1), pp. 139–167.

Crenshaw, K.W. 1991, Mapping the Margins: Intersectionality, Identity Politics, and Violence Against Women of Color, *Stanford Law Review*, 43, pp. 1241–1299.

Crocker, J. 2017, September 5, Women's Political Council. Available online www.britannica. com/topic/Womens-Political-Council [accessed 26 November 2018].

Dutta, M.J. and Pal, M. 2010, Dialog Theory in Marginalized Settings: A Subaltern Studies Approach, *Communication Theory*, 20(4), pp. 363–386.

Dutta-Bergman, M.J. 2006, U.S. Public Diplomacy in the Middle East: A Critical Cultural Approach, *Journal of Communication Inquiry*, 30(2), pp. 102–124.

Edwards, L. 2010, 'Race' in Public Relations. In Heath, R.L. (ed.), *The Sage Handbook of Public Relations*, 2nd edn. Thousand Oaks, CA: Sage, pp. 205–221.

Gaines, K. 2007. The Civil Rights Movement in World Perspective, *OAH Magazine of History*, 21(1), pp. 57–64.

Higginbotham, E.B. 1992, African-American Women's History and the Metalanguage of Race, *Signs*, 17(2), pp. 251–274.

Holtzhausen, D.R. 2012, *Public Relations as Activism: Postmodern Approaches to Theory & Practice*, New York: Routledge.

Hon, L.C. 1997, 'To Redeem the Soul of America': Public Relations and The Civil Rights Movement, *Journal of Public Relations Research*, 9(3), pp. 163–212.

L'Etang, J. 2008, Writing PR History: Issues, Methods and Politics, *Journal of Communication Management*, 12(3), pp. 319–335.

L'Etang, J. 2010, 'Making it Real': Anthropological Reflections on Public Relations, Diplomacy, and Rhetoric. In Heath, R.L. (ed.), *The Sage Handbook of Public Relations*, 2nd edn. Thousand Oaks, CA: Sage, pp.145–162.

L'Etang, J. 2015, 'It's Always Been a Sexless Trade'; 'It's Clean Work'; 'There's Very Little Velvet Curtain': Gender and Public Relations in Post-Second World War Britain, *Journal of Communication Management*, 19(4), pp. 354–370.

L'Etang, J. 2016, History as a Source of Critique: Historicity and Knowledge, Societal Change, Activism and Movements. In L'Etang, J., McKie, D., Snow, N. and Xifra, J. (eds), *The Routledge Handbook of Critical Public Relations*, New York: Routledge, pp. 28–40.

Lee, C.K. 2000, *For Freedom's Sake: The life of Fannie Lou Hamer*, Champaign, IL: University of Illinois Press.

McGuire, D.L. 2010, *At the Dark End of the Street: Black Women, Rape, and Resistance – A New History of the Civil Rights Movement from Rosa Parks to the Rise of Black Power*, New York: Vintage Books.

Pompper, D. 2005, Multiculturalism in the Public Relations Curriculum: Female African-American Practitioners' Perceptions of Effects, *Howard Journal of Communications*, 16, pp. 295–316.

Pompper, D. 2007, The Gender-Ethnicity Construct in Public Relations Organizations: Using Feminist Standpoint Theory to Discover Latinas' Realities, *Howard Journal of Communications*, 18, pp. 291–311.

Rakow, L. and Nastasia, D. 2009, On Feminist Theory of Public Relations: An Example from Dorothy E. Smith. In Ihlen, Ø. and Fredriksson, M. (eds), *Public Relations and Social Theory: Key Figures and Concepts*, New York: Routledge, pp. 252–277.

Robinson, J.A. 2007, *The Montgomery Bus Boycott and the Women Who Started it: The Memoir of Jo Ann Gibson Robinson*, 9th edn. Knoxville, TN: University of Tennessee Press.

Scott, J.C. 1990, *Domination and the Arts of Resistance: Hidden Transcripts*. New Haven, CT: Yale University Press.

Stockman, F. 2017, January 9, Women's March on Washington Opens Contentious Dialogues About Race, *NYTimes.com*. Available online www.nytimes.com/2017/01/09/us/womens-march-on-washington-opens-contentious-dialogues-about-race.html [accessed 19 October 2017].

Vardeman-Winter, J. 2017, 'We Are Being Intentional about Being Inclusive.' The Inclusivity of Identity in Public Relations: Reflecting on the Relationship between Intersectionality and Public Relations Management in the 2017 Women's March. In: *Organisational and Strategic Communication Section of the European Communication and Research & Education Association*, Edinburgh, November 13–14.

Women's March n.d., The March. Available online www.womensmarch.com/ [accessed 1 July 2018].

7

PUBLIC RELATIONS IN THE MASTER'S HOUSE

Camille Reyes

Paul,[1] a self-described 'freelance revolutionary,' was the founding member of the Occupy Wall Street (OWS) Press Relations Working Group (PRG) in New York City from September to November of 2011. A young, educated man, Paul – who had been unemployed at the time – joined a movement in OWS that Chomsky (2012) described as the first mass, popular response to some 30 years of class warfare in the United States. In the wake of the Arab Spring, OWS rode an international wave of dissatisfaction with the neoliberal status quo and dared to hold those responsible to account (at least rhetorically) for the financial crisis of 2008. The NYC encampment – the first of hundreds throughout the country and the world – became the headquarters of a movement committed to direct action and consensus-based decision-making. In New York, the protestors were forcibly removed by the NYPD on November 15, 2011, a blow from which the movement never recovered. The role of public relations within the movement was fraught – with some finding the practices of public relations (e.g., creating talking points for the mainstream media) to be antithetical to movement goals that shunned all actors in a capitalist system, including most journalists (Reyes 2018). Yet, as the OWS PRG attempted to demonstrate, practices of public relations could be useful to promote movement ideals.

As the 'activist-turn' in public relations research continues to gather steam, scholars and practitioners alike have opportunities to push boundaries, in some cases moving scholarship toward a shared critical project of casting light on global conditions of marginalization by demonstrating that public relations tools are not inherently oppressive; in fact, they are also used by the oppressed. Using new examples from a qualitative study of OWS, as well as previous lessons from movements past, this chapter explores whether it might be possible to dismantle the 'master's house' using the 'master's tools' (to borrow from the self-described black, lesbian, feminist, warrior, poet Audre Lorde). In other words, this work examines the relative efficacy of using practices of public relations, so rooted in the public imagination as weapons of corporate power, to advance non-corporatist aims of social justice.

It is not the aim of this chapter to answer yes or no to Audre Lorde's formulation; besides, as a child I looked up to a poster of Lorde, arms spread wide to the sun, on the wall of my mother's bedroom. One might say I was born to agree with Lorde. No, this work will not argue in favor of the master's tools – of dishonesty, misdirection, and obfuscation – the hallmarks of many unethical uses of public relations today. The extension of Lorde's metaphor here is meant to take the strategic ambiguity of her historic speech and apply it to a contemporary moment of public relations activism, a moment reminiscent of similar struggles for unity within the women's movement. Excerpts from Lorde's interviews accentuate this process, as do selections from another feminist icon, Nancy Fraser.

Although best known for her critique of the Habermasian public sphere, Fraser's recent work tackled the shifts in feminist movements through neoliberalism today. (This work is also more fitting since public sphere theory is inherently tied to the state and OWS had no interest in statist politics – see comparisons with the contemporaneous rise of the Tea Party for contrast.) Through the angles of capitalist critique, framing, and difference, the chapter considers the connections between neoliberalism, public relations, and feminism, leading to two interrelated points: (1) a celebration of the dialectic of difference identified by Lorde is vital to effective practices of public relations in social movement contexts; (2) through difference, public relations may help facilitate coalition-building to challenge neoliberal power. Before the thought experiment with the metaphor, the chapter is situated within public relations histories and critical feminist work, followed by theoretical framing, method, and the voices of OWS PRG related to the theme of gender.

Public relations histories that eschew progressive arcs (with their focus on influential white male power brokers) offer explanations of complicated patterns of dominance and resistance. Unlike the chronologies of the powerful, such studies analyze marginalized groups (see Miller 1995; Hon 1997; Murphree 2006; Demetrious 2013). Such maneuvers are important in the context of social movements in particular because without them '[a]ctivists become marginalized actors in the discussion of U.S. public relations history rather than driving forces' (Coombs and Holladay 2012:351).

This invigorates L'Etang's (2013) assertion that '[h]istorians need to see public relations as part of the political, economic and socio-cultural fabric rather than ideologically neutral management technocracy, a notion that is implicit in the longstanding campaign for the public relations of public relations' (803). Activists in particular present a thorny challenge to this neutral, technocratic image of public relations practice and open space for further understanding of the sociopolitical implications of public relations. Such foci answer a call by Fitch, James, and Motion (2016): 'For public relations, the challenge is to open up multiple agentic possibilities for women in popular culture and, more generally, our professional and everyday lives' (283). This chapter with its consideration of gender within the OWS

PRG seeks to contribute to the resurgent awareness of activists as public relations practitioners (Curtin 2016; Ciszek 2017; Hon 2016).

In addition to an historical perspective, this chapter also explores activist public relations through a critical feminist lens. Much of the feminist scholarship in public relations has focused on women practitioners in professional organizations. Although the publication of *Gender and Public Relations* (eds. Daymon and Demetrious) in 2014 supported a robust variety of contexts from migrant work to breastfeeding, all viewed from a critical cultural perspective. This chapter shares the definition of public relations offered in that volume: 'a communicative activity used by organizations to intervene socially in and between competing discourses in order to facilitate a favourable position within a globalized context' (Daymon and Demetrious, 2014:3).

This chapter engages with second-wave feminism. The second wave is typically defined as the period of the feminist movements approximately between 1960 and 1990 that was concerned with women's equality (especially economically) with men, although it is correctly criticized for having racist and homophobic strains. It was far from monolithic, as evidenced by a number of black feminist and lesbian separatist organizations (Springer 2005). Lorde (1984) was a staunch critic of the dominant white feminist movement. Despite her dissatisfaction with the mostly white and heteronormative leadership of the movement, Lorde (1984) fought for change from within. In her landmark speech dubbed 'The Master's Tools,' she challenged white feminists at the second sex conference in 1979. The 'master' of her metaphor was twined – a reference both to slavery and the patriarchy, the latter usage deriving from Simone de Beauvoir's work. In this chapter, neoliberalism is the oppressive power.

Framing the house

Harvey (2005) defined neoliberalism in practice as primarily a '*political* project to re-establish the conditions for capital accumulation and to restore the power of economic elites' (19). Fraser (2013) among others mined the connections between neoliberalism and second-wave feminism to powerful effect. Although some feminist scholars, such as Hewitt (2010), have argued that separating feminisms into waves is arbitrarily limiting and potentially oppressive, an historian's role 'as *bricoleur*' (L'Etang 2008:323) repositions the writing of history as a polysemic enterprise. Fraser (2013) has called second-wave feminism 'among the most visionary' of the social movements emerging since the 1960s (3).

The second wave, according to Fraser (2013), centered 'redistribution' as the political push for women, i.e., the inclusion and elevation of 'women's work' in political economy and the concomitant redistribution of wealth. Subsequent waves shifted the focus to the politics of recognition or identity when the 'deep gender structures of the capitalist economy' proved difficult to change under neoliberalism (Fraser 2013:4). 'Instead of arriving at a broader, richer paradigm that could encompass both redistribution and recognition, feminists effectively traded one truncated paradigm for another – a truncated economism for a truncated culturalism' (Fraser 2013:5). In 2011, OWS missed an opportunity to speak truth to neoliberal power by failing to combine the cultural with their more articulated economism. However, many of the activists had no intention of speaking to *anyone* in power, embracing instead an anarchist bent that, like movements past, wished to be the change they wanted to see.

The social movement literature explicated this idea – prefigurative politics – in a variety of contexts from movements of the 1960s (Brienes 1989; Polleta 2002) to contemporary direct-action movements (Gerbaudo 2012; Wolfson 2014) such as OWS (Brown 2011; Graeber 2013; Calhoun 2013). The encampments were meant to be embodiments of the desired change – through consensus-based governance and a non-hierarchical approach to living where the activists serving food were meant to be on equal footing with the activists setting up an Internet connection or working at the press table or in the library. Although there were reports of violence and discord (Writers for the 99% 2012), the energy of living anti-capitalist ideals was palpable (Gitlin 2012). This rejection of the hierarchical and plutocratic outside world rubbed uncomfortably for the PRG members who, to paraphrase their words, wanted to change the national conversation about economic justice – a move they felt required a compromise, namely interaction with the corporate-controlled media system (Reyes 2018).

This chapter analyzes the emergent theme of gender from 16 semi-structured interviews the author conducted with former members of the OWS New York PRG. The snowball sample represented 64 percent of the approximately 25 active members. Their recollections of the most active period of the movement were triangulated with work product (e.g., press releases) and 450 emails from the group's listserv, which were delimited to 102 with the participation of the informants (Reyes 2018). The author selected the 'Occupy Gender' story at hand due to its representativeness of multiple stories of gendered oppression told by many in the group.

The OWS PRG consisted solely of volunteers, many of whom were current or former institutional practitioners of public relations (Reyes 2018). The group focused on media relations, despite the opinion of many movement participants that engagement with the mainstream media was tantamount to sleeping with the enemy. They were inundated with more than 10,000 press queries via email and numerous in-person requests at the press table in Zucotti Park.

Managing the incoming press requests was challenging. Nathan, a 27-year-old web designer during OWS, explained,

> A lot of it was logistics. We had, by the end of the first month, our contact list for press was thousands and thousands of various outlets from around the world, from like local radio stations in Australia to BBC and everybody in between[.]

Since the PRG eschewed formal leadership roles in keeping with the movement ethos, this flow of press requests was difficult to control.

PRG members regretted the opportunity cost of stories that went untold. Eric, a 48-year-old film producer, said,

> Every working group wanted you to go cover them and you would see things every day in the park and think, "Oh my God, someone's got to tell that story. Someone's got to tell that story," and then there was only a limited number of people.

Those stories that were uplifted to the press were typically in reaction to a press query rather than part of a strategic plan (although there were frequent PRG meetings to write press releases and other collateral). Sam, a 31-year-old former publicist, thought they did not have (or want) the infrastructure to execute such a plan. He explained, 'In the beginning I was suggesting we should be doing that [proactive story pitching] and I think on the one hand that was (…) we didn't have the ability to do that. (…) We didn't have very much infrastructure.'

Despite the largely reactive quality of their press engagements, the PRG did manage to influence a discursive shift in the American press at least toward a focus on income inequality (Reyes 2018). For example, Politico's Ben Smith (2011) found the use of the phrase 'income inequality' had quintupled across media outlets from pre-OWS to the second month of the movement (Reyes 2018). The OWS PRG contributed to these media placements. The critique that follows is in no way meant to diminish their impressive work ethic or success.

Occupying gender

In terms of message content, the practitioners promoted the idea of economic justice. This is to say that they agreed that the middle and working classes – the 99 per-cent –should usurp neoliberal power, represented by the 1 percent of American plutocrats. Despite this unity, many group members identified tensions concerning the messaging. Gender, in particular, became problematic as the majority-male group struggled to incorporate more inclusive perspectives. This problem was not structural, per se, because they decided to form a sub-group devoted to an expan-sive, gender non-conformist idea open to everyone except cisgendered men, i.e., the already dominant majority of the larger group. This subgroup would create content that explored economic justice through the lens of marginalized, fem-inist perspectives. Skylar, a 24-year-old graduate student in 2011, was a part of this process.

The trouble, according to Skylar, began when content was shared with the larger group for the purposes of producing materials for the press (press releases, talking points, etc.). The hope was that if, for example, there was '(…) a list of five things that are wrong with the economy, one of those five things needs to be the wage gap or the expense of child care for working women.' In practice, Skylar (as well as others) felt that the larger, male-dominated group dismissed women's issues. When asked to speculate about the larger group's reticence on women's issues, Skylar said,

> You know, I think it would just come down to like 'oh we only have space
> for the really important stuff' and then so often things would dissolve
> into: 'If you want to have your own gender movement and go like Occupy
> the gender, you can go do that.' You can't have a human conversation about
> intersectionality with a bunch of 19-year-olds. You can't do it.
>
> *(Skylar)*

For Skylar, the immaturity of the other members was tied to the lack of sensitivity
to the plight of people struggling with multiple kinds of overlapping, systemic
inequalities, or what is known as intersectionality (Crenshaw 1989; see Vardeman-
Winter and Tindall 2010 for usage in public relations). She added, 'So I felt like
I ended up trying to convince people that didn't respect me and that I didn't
respect that I was there to talk about the economy and that talking about women is
talking about the economy.' Of the members interviewed for this study, the average
age of the group was 32.5, considerably older than she was at 24. Perhaps the
meetings she attended skewed younger on those days, and/or perhaps the younger
men of the PRG had more influence when it came to high-profile decisions such
as public talking points.

For example, one member with a reportedly outsized influence was founder
Paul. Paul knowingly created strategies that played upon gendered stereotypes. In
an interview about his public relations practices, Paul explained, 'One, I termed the
sitcom strategy, which was a fat, dopey-looking dude and a really hot girl, which
worked – which is definitely like riding on some patriarchal coattails, but… [trails
off].' Paul would use this pairing in his role as casting director-cum-fixer. He would
find spokespeople that fit these physical descriptions and match them with television outlets in order to gain favor from journalists by providing 'good tv' and to
deliver movement messages in a sympathetic light. Paul's 'sitcom strategy' intention-
ally violated inclusive norms of social justice movements by relying on American
media stereotypes, where the fat guy gets the girl, in order to receive favorable press
coverage for OWS. Paul was so in touch with this patriarchal double standard (the
fat girl seldom gets the guy, much less the starring role) that he recognized the trope
as being popular on television (e.g., *King of Queens*), hence the name he gives to
his strategy. He added, 'Yeah, I knew it would be used. It creates a common touch.'

Other members shared that the erasure (rather than the manipulation above) of
women's voices – particularly women of color – also happened in relation to who
was put forward to the press as spokespeople for interviews. According to multiple
members, these women were often passed over for white men for the high-profile
interviews. However, this was not by design. The PRG's media training facilitators
especially sought out women to counteract what one participant said was 'being
perceived [by the press] as a white kids, spoiled white kids demonstration.' Another
member added,

> I mean there would be white men often that were doing good work and were
> the bright people to talk to about a particular action, but if there was a very

> strong female presence to an action (…), we would (…) privilege that over
> the white dude who we knew would get contacted anyway. We weren't too
> worried that he would be marginalized. It would be different if it meant that
> white men would be written out of history if we didn't supply their names.
>
> *(Rachel)*

Thus, despite the organized *intention* to include women's voices through interviews, message creation, and other practices of public relations, the public-facing, frequent erasure of women's perspectives was a subject of consternation. They were using public relations tools to further social justice aims within the larger anti-capitalist frame; however, these tools were being subsumed in many cases by the decisions of the white male majority. Victor, a Latino, thought that on the occasions when diverse voices did go public, it was a token, condescending recognition by the majority. Victor said, '[the PRG] kind of acquiesced, capitulated, but they did it [included diverse voices] with the reservation that they don't want "the others" to dilute the message, as if they were not as informed.' The token inclusion Victor spoke about took a toll on group morale. Skylar summarized it this way:

> I think that the experience of being in the park became this kind of smack
> down of being reminded like oh, well you're a girl. Get out. You don't matter.
> It doesn't matter to us that you feel comfortable here.

Here the voices of Victor and Skylar represent the majority of the members interviewed. In fact, 14 of the 16 interview subjects (88 percent) shared the opinion that, in practice, white men dominated the engagements with the press despite a unanimous desire to include the voices of women of color. As discussed, the white male majority reportedly struck down messages concerning women and the economy. In addition, other participants told the story of two OWS Twitter accounts controlled by a white male who blocked a PRG member and woman of color from using them. Still more members explained that white men in the PRG would routinely take press interviews for themselves. Clearly neoliberal, patriarchal power dynamics that exist in larger society were reified within the PRG to the detriment of the movement. Public relations produced power for some, but not all. Importantly, if the PRG (re)produced oppression within their ranks, it is difficult to imagine how a movement ostensibly designed to confront such oppression could be sustained. On the other hand, what social movement has not had division from within? The women's movements certainly experienced such division despite the unity of gender power.

Background of the metaphor

Lorde (1984[1979]) had been asked to comment on papers about difference (to be explored in this chapter) at the second sex conference. Instead, she spoke truth to white power – angered by the dearth of work by/or about women of color and lesbians. Much has been written about the speech. It notably sparked debate between Lorde expert Lester Olson (2000) and Jessica Benjamin, feminist scholar and one of the organizers of the conference in 1979. Benjamin (2000) wrote, 'To accept her [Lorde's] view that the event was organized with no effort to include women of color by oblivious, racist white women is surely not what happened' (286). Beyond the 'she said, she said,' if we reconfigure Lorde's formulation, how might public relations relate to her metaphor and open ways of understanding and addressing the kinds of internal divisions that impede the progress of social change?

Extending the metaphor

Rather than slavery and/or the patriarchy, neoliberalism is a suitable update for the 'master's house' in 2018, although the patriarchy is thriving within neoliberalism and the ghosts of slavery are still very present in the current struggles for racial justice. However under neoliberalism, feminism has been 'taken into account' (McRobbie 2007:28). In other words, feminism has been re-branded as post-feminism resulting in 'an uncritical relation to the dominant, commercially reproduced, sexual representations' (McRobbie 2007:34). Paul in OWS was certainly aware of this co-optation within the culture – so much so that he tried to 'weaponize' it. Contemporary women do not need feminism, so the neoliberal thinking goes; they can have the corner office, a bikini-ready body, and choose the fat guy if they want to because individual 'empowerment' of this sort is a matter of will power and the right protein powder. The neoliberal house is not furnished with collective power.

The 'master's tools' in this scenario are practices of public relations, some more ethical than others. The 'sitcom strategy' was questionable. The subgroup formed to create feminist messaging was progressive; however, the larger group effectively erased this work as demonstrated. The PRG engaged in at least 13 different practices of public relations from fixing interviews, to monitoring media, to utilizing social media (Reyes 2018). Many of the PRG's reported instances of practice were unproblematic. On the other hand, there were frequent examples of gendered erasure and/or manipulation within these practices – a fact better understood by working through the metaphor.

Is it possible to destroy (or at least dent) neoliberalism using public relations? This question is not to suggest that public relations practices are inherently evil anymore than the practitioners are. On the contrary, the public imagination concerning public relations is fueled by caricatures in popular culture and the occasional, though not representative, ethical shambles (e.g., Bell Pottinger or Kellyanne Conway). Rather, the question opens space to consider the efficacy of social change through public relations placed on a continuum between more or less socially just.

When Skylar was told to go 'Occupy gender,' her male peer failed to recognize that he was narrowing the field of economic justice by consigning so-called women's issues to the closet just as many white feminist activists had done with racism and homophobia in part of the second-wave feminist movement. This reification of a classic divide-and-conquer maneuver builds upon neoliberalism by suggesting that the women could pull themselves up by their own gendered bootstraps in a separate movement, leaving the white men in power in the context of a movement ostensibly against the very same power. Furthermore, the 'Occupy gender' comment is a matter of misrepresentation.

Fraser (2013) identified two levels of misrepresentation: 'ordinary-political misrepresentation' where 'political decision rules wrongly deny some of the included the chance to participate fully, as peers' (196) and 'misframing' (197). The first level is an issue of 'intraframe representation,' which according to Fraser (2013) includes political science debates about proper electoral systems, or systems that strive to be gender blind and might inadvertently work against parity for women (196). The second level of misrepresentation is even more serious, and characterized the gender strife within the OWS PRG.

Fraser (2013) wrote,

> The deeper character of misframing is a function of the crucial importance of framing to every question of social justice. (…) Constituting both members and nonmembers in a single stroke, this decision effectively excludes the latter from the universe of those entitled to consideration within the community (…).
>
> *(197)*

Women were often excluded from the final public relations work product of the OWS PRG, despite egalitarian gestures to process. One could argue, as many did, that the erasure of women's issues in economic justice was a practical choice – 'if we include women, then we'll need to include LGBTQ, race, <marginalized group> ad infinitum.' This internal debate reflected tensions in movements past, but particularly larger, contemporary debates about identity politics versus class-centric approaches to social movements, or recognition versus redistribution.

Questions of misframing, despite their paramount value to social justice, are often pushed to the margins (Fraser 2013). This is often done subconsciously due to a lack of recognition of there being anyone outside of a political community – a common-sense approach (Fraser 2013). Fraser (2013) said,

> globalization has put the question of the frame squarely on the political agenda. (…) Among those shielded from the reach of justice are more powerful predator states and transnational private powers, including foreign investors and creditors, international currency speculators, and transnational corporations.
>
> *(198)*

In other words, this global rogue's gallery constituted what was meant by Wall Street – the subject of the occupation and the movement. While the majority of the PRG thought it possible to exclude women's concerns from the battle against Wall Street, the misrepresentation compromised morale and mobilization. This is to say that the erasure of gender from the public relations efforts of the OWS PRG unintentionally served to strengthen the house of neoliberalism and was at the very least a missed opportunity for good PR. 'The political dimension is implicit in, indeed required by, the grammar of the concept of justice. Thus, no redistribution or recognition without representation' (Fraser 2013:199) From a public relations perspective, this meant that the PRG constructed messaging framed by a limited sense of economic justice – one that prioritized redistribution at the expense of women's voices. Again, this was not for lack of trying.

PR as the master's tools

Although sometimes manipulative (e.g., Paul's 'sitcom strategy'), the activist practitioners were earnest in their work. In other words, they did not rely upon the worst tools of the PR toolbox – deception, misdirection, obfuscation, to name but three. Instead, they met a flurry of interest from the press with an organized, albeit reactive, approach to media relations in particular. Although they had little time for proactive story pitching, they organized a spreadsheet indicating spokes-people with particular expertise and language skills and they staffed a popular table for the press at the encampment among other activities (Reyes 2018). They were arguably instrumental in pushing the narrative of economic justice, which was then filtered by the press into stories about income inequality and what the press largely interpreted as an inchoate movement. This relatively effective use (after all, the issue of income inequality is still on the map) of activist public relations advances social justice, thus damaging the house. On the other hand, the exclusions of women and people of color within the PRG and the larger movement buttress the master's house through public relations.

A demolition using PR: powered by difference

As revealed, the OWS PRG missed opportunities to use public relations as a way to express power through difference. Again, this omission is an old tale from social movements past. During an interview in 1986, Lorde said,

> (…) when people of a group share an oppression, there are certain strengths that they build together. But there are also certain vulnerabilities. For instance, talking about racism to the women's movement results in "Huh, don't bother us with that. Look, we're all sisters, please don't rock the boat".
>
> *(Wylie Hall 2004:86)*

The connection with OWS here is clear: go Occupy gender. Get in line.

A celebration of difference is one way to dismantle the master's house. Far from a problem of identity politics, the promotion of difference creates opportunities for connection and through connection, social change. What some contemporary critics on the Left fail to imagine is the power of 'both and,' the very same power hoped for by Skylar and some of her peers. This echoes Fraser's (2013) ideal combining of economist and cultural paradigms. And following Lorde (1984), who wanted racism to take center stage of the women's movement, a focus on women's issues in the OWS PRG might have served to disturb further the foundations of the neoliberal house.

Although she was speaking in the context of the study of literature, Lorde constructed difference in a way that resonates with critical cultural public relations:

> We should see difference as a dialogue, the same way we deal with symbol and image, in literary study. 'Imaging' is the process of developing a dialectic, a tension between opposites that illuminates the differences and similarities between things in apparent opposition. It is the same way with people. We need to use these differences in constructive ways, creative ways, rather than in ways to justify our destroying each other.
>
> *(Wylie Hall 2004:86)*

It is this Hegelian dialectic that explains this tension as the acorn to the tree – the same, but different. Feminism and economic justice in the OWS example are clearly in dialectical relation to the women of the sub-working group, but the dominant men in power take that 'don't-rock-the-boat' approach. In so doing, they miss the seed of their growth as a movement, convinced that gender is separate from class – part of another movement.

How fitting for the scholar of public relations that Lorde uses symbol, image, and dialogue – all tools of public relations – to construct difference as a creative, productive dialectic. To the extent that the public relations activist is able to use these tools and to recognize that any destructive 'ism shares a 'root in the same inability to accept difference in a structure that depends for its survival upon profit' (Lorde quoted in Wylie Hall 2004[1987]:167), she will succeed in creating powerful connections. Far from a nice-to-have, Lorde framed the importance of celebrating difference, of resisting the divide-and-conquer strategy of the status quo, as one of survival, not just of black women, but all women (Wylie Hall 2004). In social movement terms, the resulting connections of the dialectic of difference forge coalitions. 'Of course, I'm dedicated to believing that it's through coalitions that we'll win out. There are no more single issues' (Lorde quoted in Wylie Hall 2004[1982]:88).

Rebuilding the house

In an interview with Marion Kraft in 1986, Lorde and Kraft had the following exchange:

MK: In 'The Master's Tools Will Never Dismantle the Master's House,' (…) you made it clear that all women need these different tools (…) if we want to bring about change.

> AL: It means different tools in language, different tools in the exchange of information, it means different tools in learning. It means that we use the tools of rationality, but we do not elevate it to the point that it is no longer connected to our lives.
>
> *(Wylie Hall 2004:151–152)*

Lorde's point seems especially important to the storytelling aspect of public relations. The dominant members of the OWS PRG arguably elevated class to the point that it was not recognizable to the most marginalized of their audience; the erasure of women and people of color effectively made that happen. Connection was lost in the shadow of economic rationality.

What might this 'new power' or new house look like? Clearly, difference is the power necessary to dislodge entrenched structures of oppression. 'Both racism and homophobia are institutionalized into the structure that we live in. So, as part of those structures, we cannot help but reflect those feelings unless we take an *active* position against them' (Lorde quoted in Wylie Hall 2004[1982]:103). One could say that in this moment of late capitalism, free-market individualism, like racism and homophobia, is mixed into the concrete. It will take connected, collective power to remove them. As Lorde said, 'Coalition building is not romantic; it's very annoying, it is constant, it is very slow' (Wylie Hall 2004:104).

To be fair, the OWS PRG did undertake coalition-building, or what would be considered stakeholder outreach in public relations terms. However, this work was hampered by time and by the type of internal divisions previously described. For example, Mike, an anarchist grad student who wrote a book about the movement, said, 'I think it [OWS] could be more useful if we had already done the hard work over a number of years of building alliances between groups.' Plus, for every win, there were individuals within the PRG actively working against coalition-building strategies. Paul, the group founder, wanted nothing to do with unions. He said, 'I want a revolution and these people wanted healthcare.'

Public relations has an important role to play in coalition-building to the extent that the activist practitioner is able to privilege difference in the context of social justice. Of course, this is easier said than done in large part because the structures of neoliberal power run deep, controlling all institutions, including ones vital to success in public relations, such as the press. If the mainstream press pigeonholes movements, as it has long done (Gitlin 2003), then how is the public relations practitioner supposed to break free? The Black Lives Matter movement, for example, offers an interesting nexus for future research as its own messaging is inclusive of difference in a way that the dominant white second-wave feminist movement was not (Matthews and Noor 2013). However, it is doubtful that their progressive messaging maintains curb appeal to the public at large. Perhaps it is a matter of mobilization – one need not persuade everyone at first, but rather undertake that slow build toward coalitions and something resembling social justice – a new home for our better, future selves.

Note

1 All names of participants have been changed.

References

Benjamin, J. 2000, Letter to Lester Olson, *Philosophy & Rhetoric*, 33(3), pp. 286–290.

Brienes, W. 1989, *Community and Organization in the New Left, 1962–1968: The Great Refusal*, New Brunswick, NJ: Rutgers University Press.

Brown, W. 2011, Occupy Wall Street: Return of a Repressed *Res-Publica*, *Theory & Event*, 14(4). DOI: 10.1353/tae.2011.0064.

Calhoun, C. 2013, Occupy Wall Street in Perspective, *British Journal of Sociology*, 64, pp. 26–38.

Chomsky, N. 2012, *Occupy*, Brooklyn, NY: Zuccotti Park Press.

Ciszek, E. 2017, Activist Strategic Communication for Social Change: A Transnational Case Study of Lesbian, Gay, Bisexual, and Transgender Activism, *Journal of Communication*, 67(5), pp. 1–17.

Coombs, W.T. and Holladay, S.J. 2012, Privileging an Activist vs. a Corporate View of Public Relations History in the U.S., *Public Relations Review*, 38, pp. 347–353.

Crenshaw, K. 1989, Demarginalizing the Intersection of Race and Sex: A Black Feminist Critique of Antidiscrimination Doctrine, Feminist Theory and Antiracist Politics, *University of Chicago Legal Forum*, p. 139.

Curtin, P.A. 2016, Exploring Articulation in Internal Activism and Public Relations Theory: A Case Study, *Journal of Public Relations Research*, 28(1), pp. 19–34.

Daymon, C. and Demetrious, K. (eds) 2014, *Gender and Public Relations: Critical Perspectives on Voice, Image and Identity*. New York: Routledge.

Demetrious, K. 2013, *Public Relations, Activism, and Social Change: Speaking Up*, New York: Routledge.

Fitch, K., James M. and Motion, J. 2016, Talking Back: Reflecting on Feminism, Public Relations and Research, *Public Relations Review*, 42, pp. 279–287.

Fraser, N. 2013, *Fortunes of Feminism from State-Managed Capitalism to Neoliberal Crisis: Reframing Justice in a Globalizing World*, New York: Verso Books.

Gerbaudo, P. 2012, Tweets and the Streets, London: Pluto Press.

Gitlin, T. 2003, *The Whole World is Watching: Mass Media in the Making and Unmaking of the New Left*, Oakland, CA: University of California Press.

Gitlin, T. 2012, *Occupy Nation: The Roots, the Spirit, and the Promise of Occupy Wall Street*, New York: HarperCollins.

Graeber, D. 2013, *The Democracy Project: A History, a Crisis, a Movement*, New York: Spiegel & Grau.

Harvey, D. 2005, *A Brief History of Neoliberalism*, New York: Oxford.

Hewitt, N. 2010, *No Permanent Waves*, New Brunswick, NJ: Rutgers University Press.

Hon, L.C. 1997, 'To Redeem the Soul of America': Public Relations and the Civil Rights Movement, *Journal OF Public Relations Research*, 9(3), pp. 163–212.

Hon, L.C. 2016, Social Media Framing within the Million Hoodies Movement for Justice, *Public Relations Review*, 42, pp. 9–19.

L'Etang, J. 2008, Writing PR History: Issues, Methods, and Politics, *Journal of Communication Management*, 12(4), pp. 319–335.

L'Etang, J. 2013, Public Relations: A Discipline in Transformation, Sociology Compass, 7(10), pp. 799–817.

Lorde, A. 1984, *Sister Outsider*, Freedom, CA: Crossing Press.

Matthews, S. and Noor, M. 2013, *Celebrating Black Lives Matter*, Black Lives Matter.

McRobbie, A. 2007, Postfeminism and Popular Culture: Bridget Jones and the New Gender Regime, in Tasker, Y. and Negra, D. (eds), *Interrogating Post-Feminism*, Durham, NC: Duke University Press, pp. 27–39.

Miller, K.S. 1995, National and Local Public Relations Campaigns during the 1946 Steel Strike, *Public Relations Review*, 21 (December), pp. 305–323.

Murphree, V. 2006, *The Selling of Civil Rights: The Student Nonviolent Coordinating Committee and the Use of Public Relations*, New York: Routledge.

Olson, L.C. 2000, The Personal, the Political, and Others: Audre Lorde Denouncing 'The Second Sex Conference', *Philosophy & Rhetoric*, 33(3), pp. 259–285.

Polletta, F. 2002, *Freedom is an Endless Meeting: Democracy in American Social Movements*, Chicago, IL: University of Chicago Press.

Reyes, C. 2018, Spokesperson is a Four-Letter Word: Public Relations and Power in Occupy New York, *Public Relations Inquiry*, 7(3), pp. 243–259.

Smith, B. 2011, Occupy Wall Street is Winning, *Politico*. Available online www.politico.com/blogs/bensmith/1111/Occupy_Wall_Street_is_winning.html.

Springer, K. 2005, *Living for the Revolution: Black Feminist Organizations, 1968–1980*, Durham, NC: Duke University Press.

Vardeman-Winter, J. and Tindall, N.T.J. 2010, Toward an Intersectionality Theory of Public Relations, *The Sage Handbook of Public Relations*, Thousand Oaks, CA: Sage, pp. 223–235.

Wolfson, T. 2014, *Digital Rebellion: The Birth of the Cyber Left*, Urbana, IL: University of Illinois Press.

Writers for the 99% 2012, *Occupying Wall Street: The Inside Story of an Action that Changed America*, Chicago, IL: Haymarket Books.

Wylie Hall, J. (ed.) 2004, *Conversations with Audre Lorde*, Jackson, MI: University of Mississippi Press.

8

COMMUNICATING IDENTITY HISTORIES IN ETHNIC MUSEUM PUBLIC RELATIONS

Melissa A. Johnson

Preoccupied with juggling their daily organizational responsibilities, most public relations practitioners rarely consider the roles they play in society. One such function is to communicate the histories of organizations, peoples, regions, or nations. After all, histories are promulgated by those who control the communication platforms, whether they are scribes composing in Mayan hieroglyphics or twenty-first-century communicators in charge of organizations' digital channels. This is true for ethnic museum public relations experts.

The purpose of this chapter is to unpack how public relations practitioners describe the identity histories of the cultures associated with the ethnic museums where they work and convey how professionals communicate about evolving ethnic identities. Ultimately, museum communication practitioners amplify identity and collective memory, transcending museum walls via digital and mobile platforms, along with traditional communication tools.

Ethnic museums are found worldwide, ranging from Norway's Sami National Museum to Melbourne's Chinese Museum. In the United States, institutions were formed to serve immigrant diasporas beginning in the 1800s, and continued to open through the present. These museums not only educate visitors who partake of exhibits and events. They also reach citizens outside the organizations via the museums' communication.

Following a literature review and a brief methodology overview, the chapter will present the results of interviews with ethnic museum professionals. The first section defines identity concepts, summarizes the literature about public relations history and ethnic museum history, and reviews a few studies concerning the public relations field's contributions to society.

Race, ethnicity and identity

The terms *ethnicity* and *culture* are used interchangeably throughout to signify identification with a specific heritage, such as a national or regional origin. Sometimes they are applied as expressions embracing racial groups, recognizing that race is just one component of a socially constructed identity (e.g., Orbe and Allen 2008). The phrase *pan-ethnic* refers to a shared identity perceived as having cultural, geographic, and/or language commonalities. This may be placed upon a group by others or embraced by a collective of cultures. For example, Dávila argued that Latino and Hispanic were used to package a homogeneous depoliticized market segment for corporate advertisers (2001). *Hybrid* cultures are blended cultures, where a group combines elements from various ancestries (e.g., Japanese Peruvians).

Some communication scholars have approached race and ethnicity with a post-positivist lens, focusing on the ability of individuals to function in majority-White environments (Kim 2001). A concern in capitalist societies has been the transformation of immigrants into consumers. For instance, Veresiu and Giesler said that in Canada, 'a colonizing consumer culture may transform the ethnic "other" (…) into an exoticized subject that helps reproduce entrenched divides' (2018:568). Critical race theory (CRT) diverges from the consumer-oriented or post-positivist approaches, identifies Whiteness as the undifferentiated standard, and is oriented toward societal change (Pompper 2005). Pompper included race, ethnicity, and culture in her essay on incorporating CRT into public relations research. However, Latina/o scholars rebel against the binary approach of some of the work underpinned by CRT, and note that it omits issues such as language or immigration ethnicity (Anguiano and Castañeda 2014:113). Still others fear that communication highlighting diversity leads to societal fragmentation and the lack of consensus needed for functioning democracies, a negative outcome of celebrating differences.

Most important, experts have emphasized that cultural identities are fluid, not static, a limitation of all labels (e.g., Kim 2006). Concerned about the use of identities in 'intergroup collisions' rather than as collective confidence-builders for all groups, Kim argued that identity can be adaptive and transformative (2006:284). She conceptualized interethnic identities as bridges in multicultural societies. Her optimism guides this study.

Public relations histories

By centering on non-profits, this research addresses one of the criticisms of public relations histories – most have focused on large public relations agencies and/or corporations (e.g., Combs and Holliday 2012; Lamme and Russell 2010). Another negative appraisal of public relations histories has been their masculine nature. For instance, Cutlip's text traced the 'great men' responsible for the discipline's foundations, although Leone Baxter, Doris Fleischman, and the despicable Elizabeth Tyler were briefly mentioned (1994).

A third critique of public relations histories was that they tended to be linear narratives. This was especially true of US histories that leaned on Grunig's models of public relations – from press agentry, to Lee's public information, to Bernays' two-way asymmetric, to present-day two-way symmetric (L'Etang 2008). Although the main periods of ethnic museum formation are delineated, in this chapter specific public relations practices are not connected to those epochs.

A fourth criticism of public relations histories was that many focused on the United States and the aforementioned models as if they could be exported into any culture (Rodríguez-Salcedo 2008). L'Etang described the importance of studying public relations practice in different cultures, as she showed in her history of British public relations (2004). Other recent studies have added to this trajectory. For instance, Larsson (2006) demonstrated that public relations' origins in Sweden started in state-owned institutions, with agencies not arriving on scene until the 1980s. Likewise, Rodríguez-Salcedo (2015) noted the late start in Spanish consultancies, saying the first Spanish public relations firm began in 1960. As in Sweden and Britain, early Canadian public relations was not dominated by corporations but was government-centric, focusing on issues such as agriculture or immigration (Thurlow 2017). In addition, Fitch found mid-twentieth-century Australian public relations in government, business, and community organizations, before 'the arrival of MacArthur' (2016:15) – relinquishing the impression that US influence was paramount.

Differences in public relations development occurred even among juxtaposed nations like England and Ireland, according to Hora (2017). He also asserted that Ireland became one of the world's most stable democracies in part because of the communication of its identity as Catholic and Celtic (2017), highlighting the centrality of cultures in public relations history and the role of communication that 'benefited both state and citizens' (2017:202). Like culture, politics also affected public relations development. A study comparing public relations in Southern and Eastern Europe found that the discipline advanced in multiple political systems, not just among democracies (Rodríguez-Salcedo and Watson 2017). Initially, as described when outlining public relations during the Franco dictatorship, Spain differed from nearby European post-World War II democracies (Rodríguez-Salcedo 2008, 2015; Rosendorf 2014).

Further, as Rosendorf noted, 'Even unpleasant regimes and repellent leaders have it within their grasp to formulate effective reputation-enhancing programs' (Rosendorf 2014:12). Somerville and Purcell extended this idea through their examination of the public relations actions of a terrorist organization, the Irish Republican Army (IRA), and its political wing, Sinn Fein (2011). They found that that although the IRA engaged in political violence, Sinn Fein also effectively used public relations tactics to forge the peace process that remains today.

A fifth observation is that public relations histories lack global range. The subfield of international public relations research highlighted contemporary topics rather than historic data, and cross-border histories were rare. For instance, history topics comprised 7 percent of international public relations journal articles in a

1990–2005 meta-analysis (Molleda and Jaskin 2005), and another meta-analysis mentioned no histories in 2006–2011 (Jain, DeMoya and Molleda 2014). As historical resources are difficult to acquire, it is easy to understand why there have been few public relations histories involving multiple countries. In fact, even an ambitious text entitled 'North American Perspectives' investigated Canada and the United States but overlooked Mexico, North America's third component (Watson 2017).

Perhaps due to its focus on businesses, public relations history has not yet documented its start in museums, at least in English-language journals and books. Lee's non-profit public relations history (1900–1956) described universities, religions, social service agencies, public health organizations, professional associations, and civic organizations, but no museums or culture organizations (2011). However, a museum public relations text noted that in a 1980 American Association of Museums survey, 25.2 percent of the 317 respondent institutions reported public relations enterprises (Adams 1983), an indication of the profession's role in the sector. The next section delves into the specialty field of ethnic museums, the organizational context for this chapter's discussion of public relations.

Ethnic museums

An *ethnic museum* is a 'permanent institution open to the public that acquires, conserves, researches, exhibits and communicates material artifacts related to a particular racial, ethnic, or cultural group' (Johnson and Sink 2013:358). Among English-language publications about ethnic museums, most research has concerned US institutions, despite their growth elsewhere (Horn 2006). Ethnic museum studies have focused on institutional missions (Loukaitou-Sideris and Grodach 2004); roles in their cities (Davis 2013; Jennings-Rentenaar and Kraus 2012; Sze 2010); and functions in societies (Atwater and Herndon 2003; Davalos 2001; Ransaw 2015). Use of digital media has also received attention (Johnson and Carneiro 2014; Johnson and Pettiway 2017). Whatever the focus,

> ethnic and minority groups have responded to their perceived and often real exclusion and the growing interest in their own culture and heritage by creating distinct institutions to document, interpret, and exhibit the art, culture and history of their communities and cultures.
>
> *(Loukaitou-Sidaris and Grodach 2004:51)*

These institutions' beginnings differed from traditional museums, which typically engaged in nation-building efforts and reinforced societal hierarchies (Hooper-Greenhill 1997).

Some ethnic museums were formed during the 1800s to serve as community resources, corresponding to migration periods of European immigrants to the United States. An example is the Vesterheim Norwegian-American museum, founded in 1877. Later cohorts of early twentieth-century immigrants inspired more museum launches – again, mostly obliging European diasporas.

Regarding African American museums, the Hampton University Museum in Virginia was the first African American museum, established in 1868 (Burns 2013; Ransaw 2015). Initial African American museums unaffiliated with universities included the DuSable Museum of African American History (Chicago, 1961) and the Charles H. Wright Museum of African American History (Detroit, 1964), still among the genre leaders. Although some museums and centers related to various Asian and Latina/o cultures started in the late nineteenth or early twentieth century, many rose during the 1960s and 1970s, reflecting not only immigration trends but ethnic consciousness promulgated by activism such as the Chicano Movement. Examples include El Museo del Barrio (New York, 1969) and the Chinese Culture Center of San Francisco (1965). These reflected the second wave of ethnic museums founded during the civil rights era.

Finally, the liberalization of US banking laws helped enable the urban gentrification that assisted museum formations like the 1980 New York opening of the Museum of Chinese in America (Sze 2010). Financial deregulation in the 1970s and 1980s allowed larger US banks and transnational lenders to penetrate areas such as New York's Chinatown, where previously local thrifts and Chinese-owned banks had more modest operations. Public policies on land use, taxation, and the like also contributed to such urban changes, such as the turn toward mixed-use development in downtown Los Angeles starting in the 1990s. This third period highlighted museums' contributions to cities, in addition to their importance in cultural tourism.

Societal role of public relations

Whereas public relations histories contested the accuracy and precedents of public relations' impacts (Miller 1999), the literature about museums emphasized their contributions – past and present – to local communities or to society more broadly. The role of ethnic museums, according to Loukaitou-Sidaris and Grodach, was to promote a culture, to interpret the culture, to maintain its traditions, and to be a 'zone of contact between the ethnic culture and the culture of others' (2004:59).

Thus, the ethnic museum literature aligned with public relations scholarship that highlighted public relations' influences in society. These include decreased prejudice (Blythe 1947) and increased intercultural understanding. As L'Etang noted, 'The connection between public relations work and culture is fundamental, as public relations is involved in *border crossings*, continually crossing cultures within and between organizations and communities' (2012:167). Further, 'public relations historical work is the process of thinking and writing about the history of meaning generation' (L'Etang 2014:659). In line with these directives, the present study explores how practitioners communicate the meanings of cultural identification.

In short, public relations histories are understudied, and museum public relations is an under-researched organizational segment. Criticisms of public relations histories include a narrow range of countries studied, tendencies toward linearity, privileging corporate and agency practices, and negligible inclusion of women professionals. Scholars have also worked to overcome concerns about US model dominance. Given the history literature and public relations' role in society, along with backgrounds on ethnic museums and museum public relations, the following research questions were set forth.

RQ1: How do public relations practitioners at ethnic museums and cultural centers communicate the identity histories of the cultures associated with the museums? What are the challenges?
RQ2: How do public relations practitioners at ethnic museums and cultural centers communicate about contemporary and evolving ethnic identities? What are the challenges?

Methodology

Communicators from ethnic museums in the US's four largest immigration gateway cities (Chicago, New York, Los Angeles, San Francisco) participated in the research.[1] The locales varied widely in demographics. Digital audio devices recorded the interviews, which were conducted in person and ranged from 45 to 75 minutes. All 22 interviews were transcribed, generating 328 pages of transcripts. Constant comparison analysis was employed to reduce the interview data. Member checks were conducted to ensure accuracy of direct quotes or other information. Five interviewees were men and 17 of the 22 interviewees were women (77 percent), providing female voices in observations about identity communication.

Some of the practitioners had job titles that clearly identified their sphere of work as public relations, communication, and/or marketing. However, depending on the size of the museum or staff vacancies at the time of interviews, other chief communication officers served multiple roles, including two who were museum directors.

Results

According to Somerville (2019), 'the present is always historical, and the past and present can power imagined futures.' The following discusses patterns in how communicators conveyed histories of museums' stakeholders in present-day communication. Practitioners differentiated identities by immigration cohorts (which enveloped histories of originating countries), by US history periods where minorities were associated with national markers, and by local community histories. Organizational histories – why the museums were started and for whom – also affected practitioners' identity expressions. In addition, the professionals grappled with forms of identities, including specific, pan-ethnic, and hybrid identities. This section reviews professionals' categorizations by historic period and concludes with a look at the types of identities that museum communicators pinpointed as pertinent.

Immigration cohorts

Museum professionals were well-versed in the histories of their key publics. These histories drove the way practitioners conceptualized their contemporary audiences. Several organization representatives observed that tourists from originating nations, such as China, did not necessarily want to come to the United States and view an exhibit that they could see at home. However, as one museum professional noted, recent immigrants living in the United States had high interest: 'The amount of cultural families is growing, and they especially want to reconnect to their heritage and want to teach their children about their heritage, so that's one of the key drivers.' In other words, current immigrants wanted to extend past heritages into the future through their children, illustrating Somerville's point about imagined futures (2019).

However, talking about the past could be slippery. One museum official discussed the various forms of Chinese that a museum might select for its communication materials, observing that Chinese residents who moved to the United States after 1947 might be bilingual, but were more comfortable speaking or reading Chinese. Groups that debarked from Taiwan may have had original roots in Mainland China or be native Taiwanese speakers. Knowing stakeholder origins was paramount for effective communication.

Immigrants from Ukraine also had a complicated history. According to a museum specialist:

> People who came in 1950; they really wanted to maintain everything, maintain their heritage. But those that came in 1991, they were more concerned with catching up with what they missed in Ukraine. They didn't have money, they didn't have jobs, they didn't have clothes; [when they] came here they wanted to buy those fancy cars and build big homes. The people who come now – they are again different – because they were born after Ukraine was free. And I would say that they are a little more interested in maintaining [the culture]; they're coming to the museum.

Such intricate histories were also observed among Polish Americans, and museum public relations practitioners were sensitive to nuances. A communicator noted that some Poles came during the Polish partitions, 'so there was no Poland when they came over. A lot of them went back to Poland when Poland was recreated after World War I, and then were forced to return after World War II.'

However, she related that because many Polish residents had previously lived in the city beforehand and had businesses that had thrived, 'it was easy for them to come in as refugees.' Consequently, among museum constituents, some Polish Americans wanted to hold onto culture and language, and others preferred to distance themselves from Polish identity. In other words, not all embraced their histories as an element of their present-day identities.

Although many of the discussions centered on 'push factors' of immigration such as political upheavals or wars, economic rationales for migration also affected conceptualization of publics. For example, the Mission Cultural Center for Latino Arts was founded by former Central Americans in San Francisco involved in political activism but has expanded to include Latina/o culture more broadly. As an expert at the Center said, 'People have migrated for political reasons, now it is shifting. Now we are migrating for economic reasons.'

Community histories and cultural history heritage seekers

One professional noted that local ethnic museums not only tell the histories of the ethnic groups in the United States, but that by 'telling their stories, it's also telling a story of a city.' For example, an expert at the Italian American Museum of Los Angeles observed that 'this story of Italians in Southern California has really never been told, and it's such a valuable part of understanding this region as a whole.' She said that in Los Angeles, residents from the suburbs are 'returning to our historic core' and thus the downtown ethnic museums can provide a history of the urban community, including the contributions of the racial and ethnic groups.

Similarly, an expert at the California African American Museum stated his commitment to featuring African American art, but also, 'the California journey, the California unique story because African Americans in the West had a very different experience than if you were in Mississippi.'

He added, 'A lot of people that came here are from the South but (…) it wasn't a majority African American city. They did amazing things, like Tom Bradley for example, or Willie Brown.' (Tom Bradley was the first African American mayor of Los Angeles, serving from 1973 through 1993. Willie L. Brown, Jr. was a longtime legislator in the California Assembly, speaker of the California Assembly, and mayor of San Francisco.)

Conversely, African Americans in Chicago are a sizeable, long-standing population, comprising 33 percent of the population compared to 10 percent in Los Angeles. But a specialist on African American marketing and media remarked that because Chicago is one of the top three US tourism and convention cities, the DuSable Museum of African American History attracted 'tourists primarily of African American descent or any tourists that come to Chicago and want to learn about the integral and fundamental history of those who built this city, those who continue to influence its culture, its politics, etc.'

Locals are heritage seekers, too. For instance, a professional at the Museo Italo Americano in San Francisco said the institution caters to Italians and Italian Americans who have been members for 30 years, but it also reminds younger generations with Italian ancestry that the museum is trying to 'preserve and protect the Italian heritage and culture for their sakes.' Despite the hardships experienced by earlier-twentieth-century groups of Italians, now in the Bay Area, she articulated that 'the Italian community and the Italian heritage is much appreciated.'

Organizational histories

Although national and local histories were integral, organizational histories also played a role in conceptualizing publics. Some ethnic museums were founded by cultural group members and others were started by wealthy patrons. For instance, prominent New Yorkers started the Japan Society in 1907 and, post-World War II, John D. Rockefeller helped to revitalize it. Similarly, Rockefeller founded the Asia Society in 1956. Art collectors in California, on the other hand, were the impetus behind the Mexican Museum (San Francisco) and the Museum of Latin American Art (Long Beach). These differed from the origins of neighborhood-based museums or cultural centers founded by activists.

However, many museums' missions have evolved since the time of their origins. As one practitioner declared, 'We are still representing a living community that is a living *changing* community. And because of our name, people hold us responsible for that, and we feel like we have responsibility.'

Fluctuating identities were not just a pre-occupation in how to transmit one-way communication 'at' the primary publics. Sociocultural change made museums reconsider their missions, and how – or when – they needed to alter their missions to remain relevant. This demonstrated responsiveness to their communities.

This phenomenon was apparent at Scandinavian museums because the largest groups of immigrants arrived more than 100 years ago. Thus, one Swedish American museum changed its mission from concentrating on the Swedish immigration story to talking about immigration more broadly. 'The whole concept of emigrating (…) leaving your family behind somewhere else, for a child that concept is so different than for an adult,' said an expert.

She continued, 'And I do believe that we have a little advantage because having a Swedish background is not very controversial.' In other words, longtime societal integration – aided by Sweden's global reputation – allowed this museum to discuss various immigration topics without the burden of being from a US group that currently is stigmatized.

Additional museum professionals also discussed how the immigration experience or identification as a minority were relevant to various contemporary events. They pointed out that even if museum visitors did not share a cultural heritage with a museum, a history of prior discrimination or simply a look at the challenges of moving to a different country could educate or create empathy.

For instance, one public relations manager said about the history of experiences in World War II internment camps in the United States:

> The other thing we share, sadly, is that the only Japanese Americans still alive today who experienced the camps themselves were children when that happened, and they're now in their 70s and 80s and they're passing. And the exact same thing is true of Holocaust survivors. So, one of the things that I think those two types of ethnic museums really share right now is this turning point in our history where very soon there will not be first-person

> stories anymore. We will not have docents who can say to a group of 8-year-olds visiting, 'when I was your age this is what happened to me.'

Luckily, oral history projects at such museums are capturing these narratives before they are lost.

Specific, pan-ethnic, and hybrid identities

As noted, museum professionals also wrestled with specific, pan-ethnic, and hybrid identities, which were affected by the histories just described. Local histories and organizational histories tended to govern museums' use of specific or pan-ethnic identities. An example was described by a cultural promotion expert associated with the Mexican Museum (San Francisco): 'First off, it is the Mexican museum. It was founded by a Mexican American and at first it was just all Mexicano. It's evolved to be more inclusive of other Latino art.' Regarding the founder, she said:

> It's the realization of his vision to present the aesthetic expression of Mexican and Mexican American people. Today the museum's vision has expanded to include the full scope of the Mexican, Chicano, and Latino experience, including the arts, history and heritage of their respective cultures.

A savvy public relations director at the Museum of Latin American Art in Long Beach described the shifting demographics in Southern California that affected communication at her museum and others:

> I know that people imagine that everybody here who is Latino is from Mexico or they have roots in Mexico. But it's not true. There are plenty of Central Americans here and lots of other representatives from countries in South America.

However, sometimes audience confusion about pan-ethnic identities created a challenge for pan-ethnic museums in promoting an exhibit or event. For instance, according to a practitioner publicizing an Asian museum, 'People who are Persian may not consider themselves Asian American; they think they're Persian American.' Thus, she said, the museum had 'to spend time cultivating these communities when we do a show that's of interest to them,' because the Persian American group, for instance, might not be interested in other exhibits such as Chinese landscapes or artifacts from the Philippines.

In addition to specific or pan-ethnic identities, museum practitioners sometimes created programming around hybrid identities. In fact, museum practitioners were savvy about applying this notion in their communication. As a communication professional at the Museum of the African Diaspora (MOAB) said, 'We are embracing all cultures because of how far the diaspora is spread throughout the globe. There's Afro-Cuban, Afro-Brazilian, even Afro-Asian, and Afro-European.'

In summary, the histories of the organizations and their current missions helped govern whether public relations employed specific, pan-ethnic, or hybrid identities. Also, programs or exhibits helped direct the choices. Because of these multi-layered identities and complicated communication transactions, this resulted in situational ethnic identity communication in organizations, just as in interpersonal communication (Kim 2006). Thus, the data provide additional evidence about intercultural identity dynamism and the part public relations plays in bolstering it.

Discussion

The main limitation of the research is that interviews were in four US cities. Two study participants who were the chief communication officers were also museum directors. Thus, the viewpoints were the experiences of those managing communication for museums, but the data were not limited to those with public relations educations. However, occupational role specialization is limited among many small organizations, not just museums, and consequently reflects non-profit communication realities.

Despite these shortfalls, the study addresses some of the weaknesses of prior public relations history research. The chapter's attention to minorities, its inclusion of women's voices, and its spotlight on non-profits rather than businesses are key contributions. Although this study's interviews are US-based, its discussion of diaspora groups engenders global connections that the public relations history literature has bemoaned are missing. Another asset is its scrutiny of public relations' societal role, rather than a narrower examination of organizational factors. Although the interviews were in the United States, the themes in the findings can be applied to ethnic museums worldwide. Readers in the public relations discipline will benefit from the explorations of concepts, as these are common to various types of organizations – not just museums.

Lee noted that even ethnic minority PR practitioners are unable to 'challenge oversimplified understandings of different ethnic communities' (2013:247). However, in the niche settings of ethnic museums, practitioners were able to do so. For instance, many organizations rely on pan-ethnic demographic data to describe their target publics, such as the percentage of Latina/os or Asians in a market. As scholars have described, this can lead to treating cultural group members as homogenized consumer subjects (Dávila 2001; Veresiu and Giesler 2018). However, the ethnic museum professionals in this study showed that identities are more nuanced than the traditional methods of categorizing audiences. This helped the organizations reach their institutional goals of cultural education and promotion, but also meant that the practitioners' cultural work benefited society.

In fact, ethnic museum public relations up-ended some received immigrant histories because of the specificity of their segmentation and messaging, which contradicted beliefs in homogeneous encounters. For example, public relations professionals recognized that not all Chinese Americans spoke the same language, and that African Americans' histories on the US West Coast differed from those in the South. This specificity of histories also enabled communicators to refrain from some stereotypes, especially when ethnic or racial histories were embedded into local histories. Another realization of practitioners was that they could not separate organizational histories from the histories of their regions. As their communities evolved, the organizations adapted. This supported L'Etang's assertions about the 'border crossings' that occur between organizations and communities (2012).

Public relations' communication of imagined futures

One museum communicator said the ethnic group associated with the museum's mission was a 'living, changing community.' Injecting the history of a group into the community's history altered the traditional history of the area, which tended to focus on White accomplishments. By inserting the cultural group into the historic stream, ethnic museum communication also enabled it to flow forward into the future. This could lead to Kim's dream of truly interethnic citizens (2006).

Public relations messages were a 'production of difference' (L'Etang 2014), but they also symbolically linked disparate groups by asserting their shared narratives. One of the most important message strategies used by communicators associated present-day immigrants with nineteenth- and twentieth-century immigrants. Comparing histories of ethnic groups now looked upon favorably (such as formerly marginalized Italians or Swedes) with the experiences of stigmatized newer immigrants is one method practitioners used to power a successful future for twenty-first-century cultural groups. They showed, as a California museum demonstrated, that one can survive even internment camps and achieve the 'American Dream.'

Nevertheless, ethnic museums associated with European immigrants also were protective of groups that were amalgamated into White identity. This required a fine balance between communicating distinct cultural heritages and cultural integration. Pan-ethnic approaches allowed museums to be inclusive, but this also risked creating 'merchandised' identities or confusion, rather than authentic identities.

These findings further public relations scholars' calls to 'cross cultures' and decrease prejudice (Blythe 1947; L'Etang 2012). They also address intercultural communication researchers' appeals to increase intercultural understanding in order to create truly multicultural democracies (Anguiano and Castañeda 2014; Kim 2006). Future research regarding how museum public relations (ethnic or mainstream) generates meaning about identities (e.g., L'Etang 2014) could include delineating how identities are presented in various tools of museum communication (e.g., news releases or brochures) over time. Documenting how political and social trends intersected would also be of interest.

Acknowledgments

Funding for travel and transcription was provided by the Association of Educators in Journalism & Mass Communication Senior Scholar Award, NC State University's

College of Humanities and Social Sciences Professional Development Grant, and NC State University's Department of Communication Faculty Research Fund.

Note

1   Communicators from indigenous museums were not included in this interviewee set. For more on this topic, see Curtin (2011), Cuillier and Ross (2007), or Leuthold (1998).

References

Adams, D.G. 1983, *Museum Public Relations*, Nashville, TN: American Association for State and Local History.

Anguiano, C. and Castañeda, M. 2014, Forging a Path: Past and Present Scope of Critical Race Theory and Latina/o Critical Race Theory in Communication Studies, *The Review of Communication*, 14(2), pp. 107–124.

Atwater, D.F. and Herndon, S.L. 2003, Cultural Space and Race: The National Civil Rights Museum and MuseumAfrica, *The Howard Journal of Communications*, 14, pp. 15–28.

Blythe, J. 1947, Can Public Relations Help Reduce Prejudice? *The Public Opinion Quarterly*, 11(3), pp. 342–360.

Burns, A.A. 2013, *From Storefront to Monument: Tracing the Public History of the Black Museum Movement*, Amherst, MA: University of Massachusetts.

Coombs, W.T. and Holladay, S.J. 2012, Privileging an Activist vs. a Corporate View of Public Relations History in the U.S., *Public Relations Review*, 38, pp. 347–353.

Cuillier, D. and Dente Ross, S. 2007, Gambling with Identity: Self-Representation of American Indians on Official Tribal Websites, *Howard Journal of Communications*, 18, pp. 197–219.

Curtin, P. 2011, Discourses of American Indian Racial Identity in the Public Relations Materials of the Fred Harvey Company, 1902–1936, *Journal of Public Relations Research*, 23(4), pp. 368–396.

Cutlip, S.M. 1994, *The Unseen Power: Public Relations, A History*, Hillsdale, NJ: Lawrence Erlbaum.

Davalos, K.M. 2001, *Exhibiting Mestizaje: Mexican (American) Museums in the Diaspora*, Albuquerque, NM: University of New Mexico.

Dávila, A. 2001, *Latinos, Inc.: The Marketing and Making of a People*, Berkeley, CA: University of California.

Davis, P. 2013, Memoryscapes in Transition: Black History Museums, New South Narratives, and Urban Regeneration, *Southern Communication Journal*, 78(2), pp. 107–127.

Fitch, K. 2016, Rethinking Australian Public Relations History in the Mid-20th Century, *Media International Australia*, 160(1), pp. 9–19.

Hooper-Greenhill, E. 1997, *Cultural Diversity: Developing Museum Audiences in Britain*, London: Leicester University Press.

Hora, K. 2017, *Propaganda and Nation Building: Selling the Irish Free State*, New York: Routledge.

Horn, B. 2006, Barriers and Drivers: Building Audience at the Immigration Museum, Melbourne, Australia, *Museum International*, 58(3), pp. 78–84.

Jain, R., DeMoya, M. and Molleda, J.-C., 2014, State of International Public Relations Research: Narrowing the Knowledge Gap about the Practice across Borders, *Public Relations Review*, 40, pp. 595–597.

Jennings-Rentenaar, T. and Kraus, A. 2012, The Cleveland Ukrainian Museum-Archives: Its Role as a Cultural Ambassador, *The International Journal of the Inclusive Museum*, 4(3), pp. 1–9.

Johnson, M.A. and Carneiro, L. 2014, Communicating Visual Identities on Ethnic Museum Websites, *Visual Communication*, 13(3), pp. 357–372.

Johnson, M.A. and Pettiway, K. 2017, Visual Expressions of Black Identity: African American and African Museum Websites, *Journal of Communication*, 67, pp. 350–377.

Johnson, M.A. and Sink, W. 2013, Ethnic Museum Public Relations: Cultural Diplomacy and Cultural Intermediaries in the Digital Age, *Public Relations Inquiry*, 2(3), pp. 355–376.

Kim, Y.Y. 2001, *Becoming Intercultural: An Integrative Theory of Communication and Cross-Cultural Adaptation*, Thousand Oaks, CA: Sage.

Kim, Y.Y. 2006, From Ethnic to Interethnic: The Case for Identity Adaptation and Transformation, *Journal of Language and Social Psychology*, 25(3), pp. 283–300.

Lamme, M.O. and Russell, K.M. 2010, Removing the Spin: Towards a New Theory of Public Relations History, *Journalism & Communication Monographs*, 11(4), pp. 281–362.

Larsson, L. 2006, Public Relations and Democracy: A Swedish Perspective, In L'Etang, J. and Pieczka, M. (eds), *Public Relations: Critical Debates and Contemporary Practice*, Mahwah, NJ: Lawrence Erlbaum, pp. 123–141.

Lee, M. 2011, Historical Milestones in the Emergence of Nonprofit Public Relations in the United States, 1900–1956, *Nonprofit and Voluntary Sector Quarterly*, 40(2), pp. 318–335.

L'Etang, J. 2004, *Public Relations in Britain: A History of Professional Practice in the Twentieth Century*, Mahwah, NJ: Lawrence Erlbaum.

L'Etang, J. 2008, Writing PR History: Issues, Methods and Politics, *Journal of Communication Management*, 12(4), pp. 319–335.

L'Etang, J. 2012, Public Relations, Culture, and Anthropology – Towards an Ethnographic Research Agenda, *Journal of Public Relations Research*, 24(2), pp. 165–183.

L'Etang, J. 2014, Public Relations and Historical Sociology: Historiography as Reflexive Critique, *Public Relations Review*, 40(4), pp. 654–660.

Leuthold, S. 1998, *Indigenous Aesthetics*, Austin, TX: University of Texas.

Loukaitou-Sideris, A. and Grodach, C. 2004, Displaying and Celebrating the 'Other': A Study of the Mission, Scope, and Roles of Ethnic Museums in Los Angeles, *The Public Historian*, 26(4), pp. 49–71.

Miller, K.S. 1999, *The Voice of Business: Hill & Knowlton and Postwar Public Relations*. Chapel Hill, NC: University of North Carolina.

Molleda, J-C. and Jaskin, A.V. 2005, *Global, International, Comparative, and Regional Public Relations Knowledge from 1990 to 2005: A Quantitative Content Analysis of Academic and Trade Publications*, Gainesville, FL: Institute for Public Relations.

Orbe, M.P. and Allen, B.J. 2008, 'Race Matters' in the *Journal of Applied Communication Research*, *The Howard Journal of Communications*, 19, pp. 201–220.

Pompper, D. 2005, 'Difference' in Public Relations Research: A Case for Introducing Critical Race Theory, *Journal of Public Relations Research*, 17(2), pp. 139–169.

Ransaw, L.A. 2015, The Challenges Facing African American Museums along the Eastern Corridor, *International Review of African American Art*, 25(4), pp. 41–49.

Rodríguez-Salcedo, N. 2008, Public Relations before 'Public Relations' in Spain: An Early History (1881–1960), *Journal of Communication Management*, 12(4), pp. 279–293.

Rodríguez-Salcedo, N. 2015, Contributions to the History of Public Relations in the Midst of a Dictatorship: First Steps in the Professionalization of Public Relations in Spain (1960–1975), *Journal of Public Relations Research*, 27, pp. 212–228.

Rodríguez-Salcedo, N. and Watson, T. 2017, The Development of Public Relations in Dictatorships – Southern and Eastern European Perspectives from 1945 to 1990, *Public Relations Review*, 43, pp. 375–381.

Rosendorf, N.M. 2014, *Franco Sells Spain to America: Hollywood, Tourism, and Public Relations as Postwar Spanish Soft Power*, New York: Palgrave Macmillan.

Somerville, I., Edwards, L., and Ihlen, O. 2019, 'Introduction', *Public Relations, Society and the Generative Power of History*, London: Routledge, pp. 1–25.

Somerville, I. and Purcell, A. 2011, A History of Republican Public Relations in Northern Ireland from 'Bloody Sunday' to the 'Good Friday Agreement', *Journal of Communication Management*, 15(3), pp. 192–209.

Sze, L. 2010, Chinatown Then and Neoliberal Now: Gentrification Consciousness and the Ethnic-Specific Museum, *Identities*, 17(5), pp. 510–529.

Thurlow, A. 2017, Canada – Development and Expansion of Public Relations, in Watson, T. (ed.), *North American Perspectives on the Development of Public Relations: Other Voices*, London: Palgrave Macmillan, pp. 113–126.

Veresiu, E. and Giesler, M. 2018, Beyond Acculturation: Multiculturalism and the Institutional Shaping of an Ethnic Consumer Subject, *Journal of Consumer Research*, 45, pp. 553–570.

Watson, T. (ed.) 2017, *North American Perspectives on the Development of Public Relations: Other Voices*, London: Palgrave Macmillan.

PART III

Histories of public relations in the political sphere

9

SELLING MUNICIPAL SOCIALISM

Local government, the Left and the transformation of political public relations in Britain

Dominic Wring

Introduction

It has been customary to link many of the innovations associated with the professionalisation of political communication with developments during the closing stages of the twentieth century. It has been widely perceived that politicians' embrace of advertising and public relations concepts, personnel and techniques has been a relatively new phenomenon. This assumption has, however, been challenged by a new generation of work inspired by various historically minded scholars who have collectively demonstrated that there are some significant continuities as well as changes in practices and processes. Foremost among these studies has been Jacquie L'Etang's comprehensive and groundbreaking study into the origins and development of *Public Relations in Britain* (L'Etang 2004).

The merits of the approach taken by L'Etang are varied. Foremost among these is her longitudinal focus on excavating and explaining how the embryonic public relations business came to be in a major country other than a United States traditionally seen as the main crucible for the industry's development. This is important because it offers a parallel historical account that demonstrates how innovation and creativity in this domain were not solely an American-driven phenomenon and neither were they necessarily a product of private enterprise-related activities. Rather, as L'Etang illustrates, significant changes came about through the agency of the (British) state. Furthermore she shows how these public-sector practices were not the exclusive preserve of the most senior or centrally located civil servants in Whitehall; rather, a more complex picture emerges whereby officials in local government were in the vanguard of some of the important changes made in terms of public information dissemination (L'Etang 2004:21–28).

If Jacquie L'Etang's pioneering historical contribution demonstrates the importance of looking beyond the US and private sector for the source of change she also highlights the significant role played by primarily non-profit-making actors. Unlike commentators who situated the origins of political public relations in the post-1945 era of growth, L'Etang recognised crucial links had already been forged between the industry and politicians during the interwar years. While the British Conservatives sought to understand and capitalise upon the latest professional communications methods during this period, some associated with the progressive Left were also proactive in this respect. Significantly it was staff working in municipal authorities and associated with their National Association of Local Government Officers trade union who played a major role in establishing the network that eventually coalesced into what became the UK's Institute of Public Relations launched in 1948 (L'Etang 2004:62–67).

Conscious of different aspects in L'Etang's influential study, this chapter analyses the development of political public relations within the unlikely context of 'municipal socialism.' Far from being a late and reluctant adopter, it will be demonstrated how a key division of the Labour Party embraced strategic communication techniques at local-government level to successfully outflank the then seemingly hegemonic Conservative central administrations. Intriguingly this happened on two occasions 50 years apart. The cases are the 1937 campaign to re-elect the first ever Labour-controlled London County Council and the ultimately ill-fated but nonetheless groundbreaking attempt to Save the Greater London Council during the mid-1980s. Both were planned and executed from the same location of County Hall, then the seat of the capital's government. Respectively these campaigns were led by Herbert Morrison and Ken Livingstone, two of the best-known local British politicians of the twentieth century.

It is no coincidence that it was London-based politicians Morrison and Livingstone who would oversee major campaigns that incorporated significant strategic input from advertising and public relations experts. During both periods in question the capital played host to a vibrant part of a marketing industry whose influence extended out to the rest of the UK, Europe and further afield. The relatively youthful creatives who worked in the field included several who identified with progressive political causes and, as will be explored, were prepared and able to work with Labour politicians in producing two memorable campaigns. Both partnerships also anticipated the more obvious presentational changes that followed at the national level during the leaderships of Harold Wilson, Neil Kinnock and ultimately Tony Blair. Intriguingly it would be none other than Morrison's own grandson Peter Mandelson who managed the overhaul of party campaigning during the Kinnock and Blair eras.

By the time Tony Blair entered Downing Street in 1997, Peter Mandelson had spent over a decade working for the party. In 2002 a panel of industry experts underlined the so-called spin doctor's then mythic reputation when they agreed that the *PR Week* award for 'the best PR campaign of all time' should go to 'New' Labour. An admittedly Anglo-centric list featuring Richard Branson in second place, the citation explicitly mentioned the work done by Peter Mandelson in creating the brand from the mid-1990s onwards. It was another prime example of

New Labour's ability to generate publicity and was somewhat generous to a self-styled 'project' that achieved its aims due to a highly fortuitous set of circumstances rather than just its own strategic acumen. Furthermore, as will be explored here from a historical vantage point, the attribution of success to any such campaign is questionable. A purpose of this chapter is to place more recent events in broader context by revisiting how two teams of Labour politicians presided over promotional innovations that both marked significant departures from past practices.

To educate and emancipate?

Labour's development was comparatively swift following its foundation at the beginning of the twentieth century. The party formed its first minority government after it polled well in the 1923 general election. Within a couple of decades of its creation, the party had supplanted the Liberals as the major Centre-Left opposition to the Conservatives. Labour's organisation differed to its established rivals, grounded as it was in a grassroots' approach to campaigning that emphasised the importance of education and conversion in addition to the more short-termist goal of gaining votes. This fostered an evangelical style socialist movement antithetical to capitalism and then developing industries associated with corporate business such as advertising and public relations (Barker 1972; Hollins 1981). Aside from ideological objections, early Labour campaigners raised practical objections to using commercial techniques seen as an expensive waste of scare resources. These pioneering 'educationalists' believed their mission to emancipate society would be realised through 'making' socialism rather than merely 'selling' it (Wring 2005:15–19). This worldview was of course in keeping with the challenging times that helped encourage the party's progression during the first half of the twentieth century.

The educationalist philosophy was embodied in iconic early Labour posters such as 'Landless,' 'Workless' and 'Forward! The Day is Breaking' produced for the 1910 General Election by Gerald Spenser Pryse (Burgess and Wring 2017:346–347). Pryse himself was a sympathetic artist rather than an advertising agent. His and other forms of communication enabled Labour to directly reach an audience rather than have to rely on co-operation from a growing print media then dominated by pro-Conservative newspapers owned by largely hostile proprietors. By 1917 the party had, however, created a publicity section led by former journalist Herbert Tracey partly devoted to liaising with the press. The following two decades saw this department expand as well as considerable debate involving Tracey's successor W.W. Henderson and others over how Labour could best communicate its case (Beers 2010). Foremost among those urging re-evaluation of the party's approach to campaigning was Herbert Morrison during his emergence as one of the most influential figures in Labour history.

Herbert Morrison's formative career afforded him a greater understanding of the then burgeoning news media industry than most politicians. In 1912 he had started working for the circulation department of the party-supported *Daily Citizen* journal in a job that provided Morrison with insights into newspaper layout, advertising and the wider role of the press: 'With his experience which, though small, had been intensive he saw the value of what later came to be known as public relations but which was then known quite bluntly as propaganda' (Edelman 1948:30). Unlike many of his contemporaries on the Left, he was more favourably disposed to journalists, seeing them and their work as an opportunity to promote the Labour case rather than an irredeemably hostile force. Writing an essay on how to campaign in a municipal election, the now-Councillor Morrison urged colleagues to cultivate rather than shun members of the press:

> Discretion is always desirable, but generally speaking it is best to assume that newspapermen are your friends, and to send Party publications to the Press, treating all papers equally. Newspapermen often write things we do not like and capitalism is as bad for journalism as it is for other occupations, but it is no more a reason for treating journalists with personal discourtesy than the need for housing would justify a housing reformer abusing a building trades operative engaged in the erection of a cinema.
>
> *(Morrison 1920:202)*

Throughout his time in politics Herbert Morrison demonstrated an awareness of how to craft and promote a complex message; 70 years before John Major popularised the term, he wrote *The Citizen's Charter* in 1921 to advocate for councils to be able to intervene if businesses were monopolising markets in their community (Morrison 1921). Although the related parliamentary bill was unsuccessful, Morrison later had the prime opportunity to forge an activist local state in 1934 when, for the first time ever, Labour took power in London. Under his leadership the Council embarked on an ambitious programme of public works and welfare provision (Weightman and Humphries 2007:218–219). In partisan terms this project was vital for Labour because it happened during a hugely adverse political environment dominated by the more laissez-faire Conservative led-National Coalition government formed in 1931 and re-elected by a landslide in 1935. Mindful of the need to communicate his party's vision for London, not to mention as an example to wider opinion, Morrison expanded and upgraded the functions of the Publicity Department at the LCC's County Hall headquarters. The leader pointedly took an active interest in the section's work to the extent that: 'Presentation sometimes became more important than content, and he would judge an official's memorandum by its usefulness for reporters' (Donoughue and Jones 1973:207–208).

The London Labour leader had already shown himself adept at giving discreet briefings to favoured journalists while Mayor of Hackney during the 1920s (Donoughue and Jones 1973:55.). He transferred this practice to the LCC, where he promoted stories through press correspondents such as Preston Benson of the *Star*, who became known as 'Herbert's anchor' (*ibid.*:208). Aside from his behind-the-scenes activities, Morrison also played a prominent role in front of the cameras. His talent for self-publicity was demonstrated when he climbed down a ladder onto a fire engine parked beneath his office at County Hall to launch an event promoting volunteering for London's Auxiliary Fire Service (*ibid*.:208). The stunt, an early example of the 'photo-opportunity' that would come to dominate politics, was co-ordinated by one of the various communication specialists hired to help promote Labour's radical vision for the capital.

Some of the marketing and public relations personnel advising Herbert Morrison at County Hall would later serve with him in central government after World War II. They included Clem Leslie, who guided various projects associated with the by-then-Deputy Prime Minister, and Robert Fraser, who Morrison appointed to head the Central Office of Information created in 1946 (Moore 2006:31). The pair had originally met during the previous decade while working together at London Press Exchange, at the time a leading British advertising agency that boasted a public relations division (Foster 1985). Fraser subsequently recommended Leslie to Morrison for a role in the team convened to manage the Labour campaign for the 1937 London elections (Moore 2006:35). What transpired would demonstrate the extent to which the latest professional political communication techniques were no longer the preserve of the Conservatives. In doing so the campaign posed the most important challenge to Labour's previously dominant educationalist approach and its valorisation of frugal, interpersonal and labour-intense methods.

'Let Labour finish the job'

The 1937 re-election campaign benefitted from a comparatively large budget of £8,000 (the equivalent of over half-a-million now) in donations from the party's trades union affiliates and sympathisers, including John Maynard Keynes (Jones 1967). Keynes had recently published his *General Theory*, and his support for the Labour-led LCC reflected a shared belief in an interventionist economic programme of the kind now being implemented across the capital (Keynes 1936; Morrison and Daines 1935). While Morrison clearly hoped such policies would mobilise the core vote he had also long been conscious of the need for the party to reach out to those not regarded as natural Labour supporters, including the self-employed and middle-class 'brainworkers' (Morrison 1923; Morrison 1927). Consequently with the funding and expertise available, the campaign explicitly targeted what one of their adverts called 'fair-minded' Conservatives. This copy, featuring a dialogue between an imaginary pair, appeared in the high-circulation national *Daily Express* on polling day (Daily Express 1937a).

Campaign adverts encouraging readers to vote appeared in daily morning and evening newspapers on polling day. Pointedly in an election-related radio broadcast, Morrison called out two newspapers, the *Daily Mail* and *Evening News*, for refusing to publish Labour copy (Morrison 1937). Despite being costly the adverts were an effective way of reaching a significant number of Londoners, particularly in response to an attempt by the *Evening Standard* to identify Labour with the Communist Party and 'red ruin' (Robson 1937). This controversial line of attack emulated the Conservative-backed Municipal Reform candidate leaflets' stark claim that 'Socialism means Slaughter.' Morrison retorted by using his BBC capital-wide broadcast to disavow the alleged links between his party and the Communists (Morrison 1937). Interventions such as this reinforced the leader's dominant prominence in fronting the Labour campaign with the *Daily Express* going as far as to describe him as the 'Prime Minister of London' (Daily Express 1937b).

Clem Leslie chaired the London Labour re-election campaign team and was greatly impressed by his principal client:

> We were responsible for the strategy of the publicity, the writing, the layout and some of the ideas. Herbert was a good client. He didn't interfere. He told us the message and I could see that housing offered a good theme.
>
> *(Donoughue and Jones 1973:209)*

The latter policy featured in another key advertisement with the strapline 'Labour Gets Things Done,' in which Morrison appeared with two children against a backdrop of flats constructed by his administration. This and other campaign imagery was created by the renowned artist Tom Purvis, the illustrator responsible for iconic posters, including those for the rail operator LNER.

Another Purvis-designed advert featured five policies chosen to best convey Labour's appeal: 'Better Homes, Good Schools, Health Care, Play Fields, Lidos.' The latter commitment, a reference to the provision of outdoor swimming pools, might have seemed bizarre given the often inclement British weather. But its inclusion was designed to help promote and represent the party's public health strategy. The deployment of a few choice symbolic policies to promote a manifesto would become a familiar practice during elections and was adopted by those responsible for Labour's hugely successful 1997 general election campaign. Fittingly, the team responsible for co-ordinating those efforts also promoted five policy 'pledges' and was managed by Morrison's own grandson, Peter Mandelson. Mandelson himself would help oversee other campaigns with slogans that resembled those used in 1937, such as 1986's 'Putting People First' ('Labour Puts Human Happiness First') and Tony Blair's 1994 mantra 'New Labour, New Britain' ('Let Labour Build the New London').

'New Britain' was a phrase originally popularised by Harold Wilson, another Labour leader who succeeded in becoming prime minister. As with Blair, there is an uncanny similarity between Wilson's 1963–1964 campaign slogan 'Let's Go with Labour and We'll Get Things Done,' and the 'Labour Gets Things Done' strapline that appeared on many of the posters devised in 1937. However, it wasn't just the messaging that was similar, it was also the rationale behind them. Like future generations of party strategists, notably Blair's chief adviser Philip Gould, the advisory group working for Morrison set about popularising and simplifying the party's message with pithy slogans of the kinds already mentioned. They did so because they believed many of the voters they needed to reach and persuade would lack the opportunity or inclination to read the Labour or indeed any other manifesto.

London Labour's reliance on commercial-style marketing techniques went against the educationalist ethos that had previously informed and dominated the party's campaigning. Those involved were able to experiment because they had the practical resources and personal support of Morrison, himself an obvious beneficiary of their efforts. The significant amount of advertising copy devised for the 1937 campaign leant itself to being recycled in public discourse, be it through interpersonal campaign methods or the news media. The decision to promote key policies through use of slogans and phrases was integral to this strategy. Some of these were usefully reproduced in the press coverage of the election, forming a very welcome byproduct of the drive to simplify the party's message (see, for instance, *Daily Express* 1937b). More sympathetic newspapers such as the *Daily Herald* and *News Chronicle* also helpfully reprinted images of the Labour posters alongside statements by Morrison in which he emphasised key campaign themes (*Daily Herald* 1937; *News Chronicle* 1937).

Labour was convincingly re-elected, having doubled the party's majority at County Hall on an improved vote share of 51 per cent following what Morrison's biographers described as 'the most professional (campaign) ever fought in Britain' (Donoughue and Jones 1973:209). Contemporary observers were also effusive, with Ralph Casey, an American scholar who had collaborated with Harold Lasswell, claiming the strategy had 'set a new standard for electioneering publicity' and that it had been 'successful because of the exclusive focus (…) upon the plain man and his relationship to local government' (Casey 1944). Significantly, Dean McHenry, another visiting academic from the United States, concurred with his fellow countryman. McHeny, an activist who had supported radical Democrat Upton Sinclair's 1934 bid for the Governorship of California, applauded the 1937 campaign, suggesting it: 'perhaps surpasses in effectiveness the most highly perfected American political machines sustained by spoils' (McHenry 1938:303). Casey agreed, concluding the London party's use of 'young liberal-minded advertising men and public relations specialists (…) [that] marked a departure from the usual labour-movement tradition of relying on a staff of journalists for propaganda services' (Casey 1944).

The scale of the 1937 victory may have vindicated Morrison's approach but the campaign was not without its critics. Some in the London party executive committee were disquieted by the lack of transparency in the way the strategy had been planned and then implemented. One of them, Joan Bourne, voiced her objections to the use of personnel drawn from a marketing industry she associated with capitalist exploitation. Bourne's views were emblematic of the still-strong educationalist ethos within the party, which particularly objected to the way the leader's team of advisers' 'unanimous recommendation [had been] to personalise it [the campaign] in Morrison' (Jones 1973). Critics suggested this approach to politics had uncomfortable echoes of the 'Fuhrer' principle then in the ascendancy across continental Europe (Donoughue and Jones 1973:209).

Writing in the aftermath of the London triumph, 'a prominent advertising expert' explored 'the psychology of attention and interest' in a piece for the party's capital-wide newspaper that suggested the overwhelming majority of the electorate were 'fairly indifferent to politics.' The author concluded what works best 'avoids detail and concentrates on very broad simple human issues, which mean something at a glance to everybody, including the harassed preoccupied housewife and mother; uses colour, both literally and metaphorically; and uses pictures' (*London News* 1937). Later that year, the pro-Labour think tank the Fabian Society sponsored a conference, Selling Socialism, featuring discussion of the latest developments in political communication at home as well as abroad (Fabian Society 1937). The event fielded contributions from Richard Crossman, Hugh Gaitskell and members of the London re-election team in a wide-ranging discussion exploring the impact of the media on democracy. In perhaps the ultimate tribute to the 1937 campaign, the Conservative leadership established an inquiry into how their party might re-organise to win back control of London County Council in future elections (*Daily Telegraph* 1938).

Save the GLC

Aside from being the first Labour figure to occupy the role, Herbert Morrison was one of the most high-profile leaders in the history of London County Council. Another was Ken Livingstone, the last politician to lead Greater London Council, the LCC's direct successor. Like Morrison, Livingstone would be involved in a memorable bid to sustain the party's rule at County Hall. However, in the later case the campaign would be about winning over public support in defence of the GLC's right to continue existing. This was because Margaret Thatcher's government, re-energised from their second general election victory in 1983, was ready to implement an ambitious Conservative manifesto that included a commitment to abolish the Metropolitan County Councils, a tier of local government serving the most heavily populated conurbations. All Labour-controlled, these authorities included the Greater London Council.

The GLC had been the focus of great controversy following the succession of Ken Livingstone to its leadership after a 'palace coup' had removed his more mainstream predecessor soon after Labour's victory in the 1981 elections. Livingstone and his deputy John McDonnell began to implement more radical measures, including the implementation of policies to boost public transport use, multiculturalism and the arts among other things. The leadership team also clashed with the Thatcher government over the GLC's promotion of homosexual equality, engagement with the Irish republican movement and their public display of unemployment statistics on the front of County Hall overlooking the Houses of Parliament. Initially derided as a 'loony' left-wing extremist by vocal opponents in the media and government, Livingstone would nevertheless establish himself as an effective politician and able communicator (Carvel 1987). His belief in an activist local state inevitably made him an opponent of the free-marketeer Thatcher. However, that Livingstone emerged as an enduring critic of this most determined of prime ministers in the highly adverse political climate of the mid-1980s was a not inconsiderable feat, particularly given the bleak fate of others on the Left involved in other high-profile struggles against the government at that time.

The new GLC leadership around Livingstone recognised the existential threat posed to their authority. A strategy group was convened to consider how a campaign might be launched to try and thwart the plan to abolish the Metropolitan County Councils being drawn up by the Department of Environment, the ministry overseeing local authorities. Initial research commissioned by Tony Wilson, the Council's Head of Public Relations, indicated there was only limited knowledge about the work done by the GLC (Carvel 1987:221). This did not, however, deter strategists from planning an anti-abolition campaign that would run between October 1983 and March 1985 at a cost of an estimated £14 million, a huge budget for this kind of initiative. What ensued contributed to changing the terms of debate, if not necessarily public attitudes that were already sceptical about the proposed government plans not to mention their legitimacy (Curran et al. 2005:58). The GLC campaign also had an important political legacy in that they helped transform attitudes on the Left towards more professionalised forms of campaigning involving marketers (Myers 1986; Carvel 1987:219).

In devising their strategy, the GLC campaign team hired the services of Boase Massimi Pollitt (BMP), one of the most innovative advertising agencies in London. Chris Powell, the managing director of BMP, had previously advised Labour and his firm had worked for trade union and other progressive clients (Powell 2000). Preliminary opinion research work undertaken by the agency helped identify several salient themes in order to provide a clearer definition of campaign objectives. Denis Robb, the executive who helped manage the GLC account, recognised focus groups were a valuable means of testing copy for this kind of initiative. Potential advertisements were devised, each highlighting one of several different scenarios associated with the now-threatened Council. These were shown to selected groups of Londoners to gauge and understand reactions. The mocked-up adverts failed to inspire much of a response, with one important exception. When respondents were shown copy detailing government plans for the so-called 'paving bill,' they were disquieted to learn this would mean the cancellation of GLC elections scheduled for 1985. Many participants believed this to be a profoundly undemocratic act and a denial of their basic rights as citizens to express themselves at the ballot box (Clark 1986:443).

Results from the BMP focus groups provided the inspiration for the subsequent GLC campaign. Agency copywriters designed a series of visually arresting adverts based around the core strapline of 'Say No to No Say.' A seemingly omnipotent but complacent central government had assumed its parliamentary bill was a largely administrative measure involving the cancellation of elections and thereby 'paving' the way for abolition. But the GLC's campaign would make this a defining issue and one that would embarrass and undermine ministers in ways few of Thatcher's opponents had previously managed. One prominent 'No Say' advert featured a picture of Livingstone alongside the slogan 'If you want me out, you should have the right to vote me out.' Like Morrison before him, the London Labour leader became the personification of the campaign and his presentation skills would be integral to its success (Myers 1986:116). Variations on the No Say theme were advertised throughout the capital.

The anti-abolition campaign budget allowed for some imaginative message placement, with posters even appearing on hoardings at the Romanian national team's stadium during an international football match involving the visiting England squad (Carvel 1987:233). GLC press officer Nita Clarke believed a major benefit of such a heavy spend on paid media content was the subsequent journalistic interest and public sympathy it helped to generate (Myers 1986:115). Clarke followed this up by tailoring stories to newspapers so that those about democracy went to the *Guardian*, items concerned with efficiency were passed to the *Telegraph*, and stunts were designed to attract the attention of the more popular papers. The PR team at County Hall also successfully targeted and forged relationships with radio and television broadcasters, generating coverage that if not necessarily favourable was questioning of the central government's plans for abolition (Curran et al. 2005:59–60). Aside from these attempts to influence the news coverage, the GLC also heavily invested in other forms of awareness-raising activities through sponsorship of a range of community events (*ibid.*:66–67).

The legacy of 'No Say'

James Curran and his colleagues have suggested the impact of the GLC publicity efforts is difficult to evaluate in isolation from the policies and other activities implemented by the Council over the preceding years (Curran et al. 2005:57). That said the 'No Say' strategy was a success if judged by its ability to raise awareness of the issue. This was reflected in survey research findings. Polling taken in January 1984, prior to the start of the anti-paving bill campaign, suggested 45 per cent of Londoners were unaware that their Council was facing abolition. By June this figure had halved to just 21 per cent, recognition as to the general impact of the 'No Say' message on levels of popular consciousness (Channon 1989). This trend was further reflected in a subsequent MORI poll of Londoners, in which 71 per cent said they believed the advertisements had helped shift public sentiment in favour of the GLC. Similarly, by the summer of 1984, 74 per cent of those questioned were expressing their opposition to abolition, an increase of 20 per cent on the previous year (Forrester et al. 1985:80). Growing public disquiet combined with vocal opposition expressed through both the media and in parliament culminated with a dramatic vote by the House of Lords against the proposals for abolition. Although this proved to be a temporary setback, delaying the plan for only a year, it was a humbling experience for what had largely been seen as an unassailable government. It was for reasons like this that leading industry expert Winston Fletcher applauded No Say as 'the finest political campaign of the decade, perhaps ever' (Fletcher 1988).

The success of the GLC campaign has been questioned because it ultimately failed in realising its objective: self-preservation (Waller 1988). Although the

Council was eventually abolished together with the Metropolitan County bodies, it is worth noting that this was of little surprise given the government's huge majority in the House of Commons at that time. Even then, several Conservative MPs led by former prime minister Ted Heath had joined the opposition in a highly publicised rebellion during the passage of the legislation through the House of Commons (Carvel 1987:237). But beyond this the campaign demonstrated how Ken Livingstone, a former hate figure once demonised by the then-agenda-setting right-wing press, was able to humiliate the most formidable of premiers at the height of her powers. Whereas the best-selling *Sun* had attacked the GLC leader as 'the most odious man in Britain,' he ended his time at County Hall rehabilitated and something of a 'Robin Hood' figure (Curran 1987). This reputation would later prove vital when Livingstone ran to be the first ever Mayor of London after the Labour government reinstated a capital-wide authority in 2000. Having fallen out with the Blair government, he stood against his former party and was elected as an independent in what was one of the most profound comebacks in British political history (D'Arcy and MacLean 2000).

The 'No Say' campaign had other effects beyond its immediate impact on the government's paving and abolition bills. In a survey of Conservative MPs when the issue was still live, 43 per cent of those questioned expressed a belief that the changes involved were a potential vote-loser (Curran 1987). Further to this the GLC campaign helped undermine confidence in Patrick Jenkin, the then Secretary of State for the Environment, charged with bringing in the paving bill and implementing abolition of the Metropolitan County Councils. It has been argued his subsequent departure from the Cabinet in 1985 was partly a result of his failure to effectively respond to the No Say message (Channon 1989). Jenkin's successor Kenneth Baker took steps to ensure there would be no further GLC-style campaign by sponsoring a parliamentary bill outlawing so-called 'propaganda on the rates' (Myers 1986:117). If this reflected a belief in the potency of marketing, so did the same government's decision to spend millions on promoting the value of buying shares in the public utilities that they were privatising at that time (Scammell 1995:225–230).

The 'Say No to No Say' initiative greatly challenged attitudes within the Labour movement towards the value and nature of marketing and public relations, as Peter Herd, a BMP executive who worked on the account, argued: 'It is hard to overestimate the importance of the GLC campaign; it made advertising politically acceptable to the left' (Wring 2005:83). It greatly helped those seeking to transform the wider party's approach to campaigning that Ken Livingstone himself was an avowed radical because, as the leadership supporting Labour Co-ordinating Committee pamphlet put it: 'Who dares accuse the GLC of socialist betrayal?' Professional communication, it was argued, could greatly benefit the party's cause. The then-relatively new Labour MP Gordon Brown came to this conclusion when he argued: 'The GLC showed that it was possible to employ glossy public relations without diluting the basic socialist message and it is encouraging' (Wring 2005:83).

Conclusions

The piece has drawn inspiration from Jacquie L'Etang's groundbreaking work on a topic – public relations – that is routinely conceived of as a largely contemporary phenomenon associated with the later half of the twentieth century. Following L'Etang's example, this study underlines the necessity of taking a longitudinal approach to the subject through exploration of relevant developments over a more considerable period of time. The chapter has necessarily focused for reasons of brevity on one arena, politics, that featured throughout *Public Relations in Britain*. The resulting comparative analysis has explored and highlighted the similarities and differences between two historically significant campaigns relating to the UK capital's Labour Party.

Half-a-century apart, the London County Council and Greater London Council campaigns have obvious differences in that they did not share the same core political objective (election versus survival), nor were they operating in a similar media environment (before and after the introduction of mass television). They did, however, command significantly more attention than they might, given both operated out of a County Hall base literally facing the seat of power, directly across the Thames at the Palace of Westminster. It was thus comparatively much easier for even a Labour-led London authority to generate publicity compared with their peers running similarly sized local councils beyond the capital.

Although they differed in their core objective, the campaigns Herbert Morrison and Ken Livingstone presided over are comparable to one another, as well as important, for various reasons. Foremost here was their ability to attract and manage news interest, including from a notoriously hostile right-wing press. Both combined what was at the time state-of-the-art advertising with public relations techniques to help generate paid and free media content, and in doing so were able to draw on professional expertise backed by relatively high levels of funding. The campaigns were thereby important in that they demonstrated how progressive leftist politicians might harness marketing communication for their own ends. So, more considered use of sloganeering, the simplification of messaging and the personification of the cause in the guise of the individual leader's own image became integral features of Labour campaigns; perhaps more then anything, both efforts demonstrated how Centre-Left politicians could use strategic promotion to successfully influence political agendas then hitherto largely determined by two of the most seemingly hegemonic Conservative governments.

Beyond their immediate impact the LCC and GLC innovations anticipated strategic changes that would be later taken further prior to the Labour victories of 1964 and 1997. The London campaigns also demonstrated that innovation in strategic political communication was not necessarily the preserve of the Conservatives. Herein there are marked parallels between Morrison's approach and the similarly controversial career and work of his 'spin-doctoring' grandson Peter Mandelson. Mandelson used the kind of 'symbolic policies' and even similar slogans to promote the party in the mid-1980s that the team working for his illustrious forefather had deployed during the 1937 LCC campaign (Mandelson 1988). Likewise, during the former period, it was Save the GLC's similar ability to communicate that helped boost the stature and profile of Ken Livingstone. It gave the GLC leader a valuable platform from which he was later able to mount his ultimately successful attempt to resume the leadership of the capital's authority as Mayor of London when city-wide local government was restored in 2000. Ironically, in doing so Livingstone would become embroiled in a protracted battle of 'spin' with Mandelson, by now an influential member of the Labour government.

References

Barker, B. 1972, The Politics of Propaganda: A Study in the Theory of Educational Socialism and its Role in the Development of a National Labour Party. Unpublished M.Phil thesis, York University.

Beers, L. 2010, *Your Britain: Media and the Making of the Labour Party*, Cambridge, MA: Harvard University Press.

Burgess, C. and Wring, D. 2017, Electoral Posters in Britain. In Holtz-Bacha, C. and Johansson, B. (eds), *Political Campaigning in the Public Space Election Posters around the Globe*, New York: Springer.

Carvel, J. 1987, *Citizen Ken*, London: Hogarth.

Casey, R. 1944, British Politics: Some Lessons in Campaign Propaganda, *Public Opinion Quarterly*, Spring, pp. 72–83.

Channon, C. 1989, The GLC's Anti-Paving Bill: Advancing the Science of Political Issue Advertising. In Channon, C. (ed.), *Twenty Advertising Case Histories*, London: Cassell.

Clark, E. 1986, *The Want Makers*, Sevenoaks: Coronet.

Curran, J. 1987, The Boomerang Effect: The Press and the Battle for London 1981–86. In Curran, J. et al. (eds), *Impacts and Influences*, London: Methuen.

Curran, J., Gaber, I. and Petley, J. 2005, *Culture Wars: The Media & the British Left*, Edinburgh: Edinburgh University Press.

Daily Express 1937a, Why Morrison Gets Our Vote: By Two Fair-Minded Conservatives, *Daily Express*, 4 March, p. 2.

Daily Express 1937b, Two Men Who Would Rule London Seek Your Vote Today, *Daily Express*, 4 March, p. 9.

Daily Herald 1937, Mr Morrison Calling London, *Daily Herald*, 25 February, p. 4.

Daily Telegraph 1938, Conservative Party Reform, *Daily Telegraph*, 13 June, n.p.

D'Arcy, M. and MacLean, R. 2000, *Nightmare! The Race to Become London's Mayor*, London: Politico's Publishing.

Donoughue, B. and Jones, G.W. 1973, *Herbert Morrison: Portrait of a Politician*, London: Weidenfeld and Nicolson.

Edelman, M. 1948, *Herbert Morrison*, London: Lincolns Prager.

Fabian Society 1937, 'Selling Socialism?' A conference report from the New Fabian Research Bureau, Maidstone, 23–24 October.

Fletcher, W. 1988, Political Ads have Changed the Face of British Society. If That's Not Great Advertising, What Is?, *Marketing Week*, 11 March.

Forrester, A., Lansley, A. and Pauley, R. 1985, *Beyond Our Ken*, London: Fourth Estate.

Foster, S. 1985, Who Are they Now? How the Top 30 Agencies have Changed over the Past 50 Years, 1933–1983, *Campaign*, 29 March.

Hollins, T.J. 1981, The Presentation of Politics: The Place of Party Publicity, Broadcasting and Film in British Politics. Unpublished Ph.D. thesis, Leeds University.

Jones, G. 1967, Unpublished interview with Clem Leslie, 24 July, London School of Economics archive reference MORRISON 6/3.

Jones, G. 1973, Political Leadership in Local Government: How Herbert Morrison Governed London 1934–1940, *Local Government Studies*, June, pp. 1–11.

Keynes, J.M. 1936, *The General Theory of Employment, Interest and Money*, London: Macmillan.

L'Etang, J. 2004, *Public Relations in Britain: A History of Professional Practice in the Twentieth Century*, London: Lawrence Erlbaum.

London News 1937, Publicity in Politics, *London News*, May, p. 3.

Mandelson, P. 1988, Marketing Labour, *Contempoary Record*, Winter 1988, pp. 11–13.

McHenry, D. 1938, *The Labour Party in Transition, 1931–38*, London: George Routledge & Sons

Moore, M. 2006, *The Origins of Modern Spin: Democratic Givernment and the Media in Britain, 1945–51*, Basingstoke: Palgrave Macmillan.

Morrison, H. 1920, On the Fighting of a Municipal Election. In *The Labour Party Handbook of Local Government*, London: George Allen & Unwin.

Morrison, H. 1921, *The Citizen's Charter*, London: Labour Party.

Morrison, H. 1923, Can Labour Win London without the Middle-Classes?, *Labour Organiser*, no. 34.

Morrison, H. 1927, Back to Socialism: A Plea for 'Moral Uplift' in Labour Party Propaganda, *Labour Magazine*, August.

Morrison, H. 1937, Broadcast by the Rt. Hon. Herbert Morrison MP, Leader of the London County Council, transcript of BBC Regional broadcast, 24 February.

Morrison, H. and Daines, D.H. 1935, *London under Socialist Rule*, London: Labour Party.

Myers, K. 1986, *Understains: The Sense and Seduction of Advertising*, London: Comedia.

News Chronicle 1937, What Londoners Pay For, *News Chronicle*, 18 February, p. 10.

Powell, C. 2000, *How the Left Learned to Love Advertising: Social and Political Advertising by BMP 1970–2000*, London: BMP DDB.

Robson, W. 1937, London and the LCC Election, *Political Quarterly*, 8, pp. 194–195.

Scammell, M. 1995, *Designer Politics: How Elections Are Won*, Basingstoke: Macmillan.

Waller, R. 1988, *Moulding Public Opinion*, London: Croom Helm.

Weightman, G. and Humphries, S. 2007, *The Making of Modern London*, London: Ebury Press.

Wring, D. 2005, *The Politics of Marketing the Labour Party*, Basingstoke: Palgrave Macmillan.

10

ANTICIPATING THE AGE OF 'POLITICAL SPIN'?

An historical analysis of 1980s government communications

Ruth Garland

Introduction

The ideal of the well-informed citizen served by a watchdog media that holds governments to account, and a government that places accurate information in the public domain, is seen as a pre-requisite for representative democracy. In recent decades, however, this has been considered to be in trouble. Many accounts of central governing bureaucracies in Western liberal democracies claim that the balance of power has tilted in favour of politicians and away from the administrative arm of government (Eichbaum and Shaw 2010; Hustedt and Salomonsen 2014). This process is referred to as a form of 'top-down politicization' in which political parties become the 'principal agents' (Peters and Pierre 2004a:287). Within Westminster systems such as the UK's, which are characterised by an extreme form of executive dominance, the risk of 'party capture' of publicly sensitive functions such as government communication has traditionally been mitigated by a strict, albeit self-regulated, culture of impartiality (Lijphart 1999; Aucoin 2012). In the UK government press officers are bound by their propriety codes to provide information that is 'objective and explanatory' rather than 'party political' (GCS 2015:10). Yet from the late 1990s, a series of major controversies, such as the discredited dossier leading up to the 2003 Iraq War, and, more recently, the 2016 EU referendum campaign (Chilcot 2016; Halligan 2016; Herring and Robinson 2014) raised concerns that government communication activities were becoming increasingly partisan and untrustworthy, leaving the public under-served and disillusioned (Blumler and Coleman 2015; Foster 2005; Yeung 2006). As the Trump experiment indicates, public distrust in media and governing elites is widespread, and one response has been the rise of populism and more personalised forms of direct political communication through social media.

This chapter considers the generative role of changes in government communication practices in response to the rise of the new multi-channel environment during the 1980s. An historical case study approach is used to examine how the Conservative Thatcher administrations of the UK (1979–1990) exploited the opportunities of this challenging media landscape, in order to 'sell' an initially deeply unpopular neoliberal policy of economic and social transformation. The Conservative Party had successfully applied political marketing techniques during the 1979 election, and once in power sought to implement a more persuasive style of communication that later came to be known as 'political spin.'[1] They met resistance from a civil service culture determined to uphold values of impartiality that had been enshrined in the postwar information model of communication (Grant 1999; Moore 2006).

Many accounts relating to the UK case consider ministers and their politically appointed aides largely responsible for the decline in public trust in governments, blaming the practice of selectively trading privileged government information to serve party or personal interests. Critics claim this began in earnest with the 1997 New Labour government and is now so widespread as to become institutionalised (Jones 2006; Wring 2005). A series of critical government and parliamentary reviews into government communications also blamed political actors, and called for a return to a less partisan style of public communication in order to rebuild trust (House of Lords 2008; Phillis 2004; Public Administration Select Committee 1998, 2013). A consistent concern of these reviews was the informal media relations role of the rising numbers of temporary civil servants known as special advisers (or SpAds), the partisan officials appointed by and accountable to ministers and exempt from impartiality (Public Administration Select Committee 2000, 2012, 2013; Wicks 2003). This small but networked group of political operators whose media relations activities are largely unofficial, and hence deniable, has been demonised as people who practice the 'dark arts' of political spin (Blick 2004).

Despite these critiques, the ethical and strategic role of government press officers in briefing the news media has been consistently weakened since 1997, while SpAds remain key to government news management (Garland 2017). Meanwhile, direct communication such as marketing and advertising has all but ceased since the post-2010 budget cuts (Garland et al. 2018; Tee 2011). According to the *narrative of political spin*, public officials are victims of a political takeover of government communications. Yet this narrative may be too simplistic in at least two ways: first, ostensibly impartial public officials may allow loyalty to the government of the day to override their public interest obligations; second, politicians may behave in impartial ways that uphold the public interest. Rather than being mere victims, should public officials as well as political actors bear responsibility for the consistent decline in public trust in recent decades in what governments say (IpsosMORI 2016; Whiteley et al. 2016)?

This chapter draws on a systematic analysis of UK government documentary and archival evidence dating from the 1980s to argue that, during the Thatcher era, there were signs that politically driven media strategists were already coming into conflict with a civil service communications culture that resisted overt advocacy or persuasion – a tension that surfaced publicly after 1997. In the struggle to determine government narratives, the balance of power shifted towards ministers and away from civil servants, accepted routines were challenged and media considerations were prioritised. Archives show how the prime minister and her closest advisers, including her chief press secretary Bernard Ingham, challenged what they saw as civil service resistance, to develop a more persuasive and centralised approach to government media management of controversial issues, especially on the economy. At the same time, an analysis of one high-profile government campaign shows that a ministerial commitment to impartiality can disregard or override party interest. Indeed, as we shall see, the historical record challenges the long-accepted dichotomy between impartial civil servants (good), and partisan politicians (bad).

In the next section, I begin by outlining the methodological approach and reflecting on the generative role of history in influencing the actions of political and media elites, both in the UK and elsewhere. I then examine documentary evidence in relation to two critical moments in UK government communications during the Thatcher years that illustrate points of conflict and contestation behind the scenes: first, the role of the prime minister's press secretary Bernard Ingham, in the lead-up to the 1983 election; second, the struggle on the part of the minister for health to implement the world's first national AIDS awareness campaign in 1986–1987 against a prime minister, Cabinet and public opinion that held intolerant views about homosexuality. These findings will then be considered as possible antecedents to government communications during the post-1997 New Labour era and beyond. The chapter will conclude with some predictions about the direction of travel, and some thoughts on possible solutions to the problem of public distrust in government communication.

An historical case study approach to government communications

The 'qualitative, longitudinal deep case study method' used here is characteristic of the historical institutionalist approach common in political studies, which examines the interaction of institutions, ideas and agents over time (Bannerman and Haggart 2015:10). This involves selecting the case study and time period, identifying the institution and agents/actors to be studied, the mechanisms that strengthen or weaken the institutions, and the agents and ideas in play, and establishing who gains and who loses during a period of change. Certain groups may be favoured or excluded, options may be constrained or extended, and new debates and agendas may emerge as others recede or drift into irrelevance. Institutions are defined as the 'formal and informal procedures, routines, norms and conventions embedded in the organizational structure of the polity' (Hall and Taylor 1996:6). This approach seeks to overcome what has been referred to as a lack of transparency and rigour, where too little attention is paid to the clear application of historical concepts such as temporal comparison, turning points, the 'centrality of sequence,' and too little focus on specific actors' situational constraints and enabling factors in particular places and times (Stanyer and Mihelj 2016).

In his groundbreaking study of US public relations during the twentieth century, Cutlip demonstrated the value of detailed and contexualised case studies of what is usually a hidden and unaccountable activity. He concluded that to build public trust, PR practitioners must 'have the guts to say no to their bosses' (Cutlip 1994:774). L'Etang's study of British public relations through a combination of oral history interviews and archival analysis introduced the method of 'historical sociology' to the study of PR. She considered the symbiotic relationship between PR and the media to be 'crucial and of great sociological significance,' and argued that PR was not a neutral process (L'Etang 2009:3). She identified 1980s Britain as a moment when a 'massive communication effort' was required both to publicise the new privatisation process and to establish corporate identities for the new private utility companies. Rather than sidelining the history of government PR as mere propaganda, scholars should engage deeply with the customs and practices of PR in the light of the 'larger processes of transformation' taking place at the time (L'Etang 2008:321). A symbiosis, or mutual adaptation, between PR officials, governing politicians and media actors has been observed in recent Scandinavian research. An ethnographic study of a Norwegian executive agency found that civil servants who were closest to ministers were more 'media savvy' than other officials (Thorbjornsrud et al. 2014). Similarly, a documentary study of Swedish executive agencies found that officials sought to increase the media profile of their organisation as a way of pleasing politicians, hoping thereby to resist political interference (Fredriksson et al. 2015). Thus, although today's *narrative of political spin* upholds a dichotomy between civil servants and impartiality on the one hand, and politicians and partisanship on the other, in reality, the picture is more complex and fraught with power struggles that largely exclude both publics and parliaments.

Historical sources

Evidence derived from sources such as memoirs, biographies, government and parliamentary enquiry evidence sessions and interviews is all potentially subject to respondents claiming their particular 'place in history.' To establish chronology and provide a check on established narratives, three tranches of archived documentary evidence were systematically examined.

1. Archival records concerned with the presentation of government policy from 1981–1983 (PREM 19/720/721) and 1983–1986 (PREM 19/1775).
2. Documents from the Ingham archive held by the Margaret Thatcher Foundation dated May 1979 to April 1985.[2]
3. Recently released archived correspondence relating to the launch of the government's 1986–1987 AIDS/HIV awareness campaign (PREM-19-1863).

These data sets were analysed to test the main claims that underlie the *narrative of political spin* and to ask whether actions from the 1980s are linked through a chain of causality to more recent publicity failures such as the discredited Iraq WMD dossier of 2002, and the failed government campaign of 2016 to remain in the EU. The narrative claims that party news management was progressively brought into government while new partisan PR operators managed government information 'under the radar,' bypassing and disrupting the civil service communications hierarchy. Government communication increasingly operated in the party rather than the public interest, leading ultimately to a failure to serve the information needs of citizens and a consequent decline in public trust in government communications.

Strategic government communication: the Thatcher years

From the arrival of the first Thatcher government in May 1979, the prime minister's new chief press secretary, Bernard Ingham, an impartial civil servant rather than a political appointment by the PM,[3] and the Government Information Service (GIS), staffed by civil servants, faced pressure from incoming ministers for a more co-ordinated and promotional approach to government communication. In this section, I examine documents relating to the little-known (outside Whitehall) *Liaison Committee on the Presentation of Government Policy* that provide insights into the internal struggles between the prime minister, ministers and civil servants for control over government narratives at a time when the government's survival was threatened. I then examine correspondence relating to the 1986–1987 AIDS/HIV awareness campaign jointly championed by the secretary of state for health and the chief medical officer in the teeth of opposition from the media, the party and public opinion. Finally, I consider why we should rethink notions of impartiality and partisanship in government communication, and how these ideas link to the narrative of political spin.

The Liaison Committee: 1981–1983

The *Liaison Committee* was a longstanding but intermittent secret postwar body that was revived briefly in 1981, meeting monthly from the beginning of 1982 amid concerns that the government was not getting its message across. A Number 10 political adviser recalls how 'Mrs Thatcher was presented by much of the press as a hate figure and many in the party thought she was leading the country to destruction' (Hoskyns 2000:357). Voting intention ratings at the end of the year put the Conservatives in third place at less than 30 per cent (YouGov 2018).

Archived government documents show how the PM, her close advisers and a handful of senior ministers tried to develop a more compelling approach to economic presentation that included regular briefings from Conservative Party HQ, and a drive to turn around media and eventually public opinion. This meeting was so secret that it was not even known to most Cabinet members until March 1982. Civil servants in ministerial private offices referred to it as 'highly sensitive' and even not quite 'sanitary' (PREM 19/720/721). Key actors on the Committee were the minister responsible for coordinating government publicity Francis Pym; the PM's press secretary Bernard Ingham; the Conservative Party Research Department, which produced many of the briefing papers; and Mrs Thatcher, in her role as joint-chair (with Pym). The Committee initially focused on economic policy but then expanded its remit to tackle a range of priority issues such as industry, pay policy/employment, housing, nuclear defence and education.

The Committee's remit is explained in a briefing document produced by Pym's private office and circulated the day before the Committee's first meeting on 10 February 1982. This stressed the 'sensitivity of its proceedings,' explaining that 'no agenda has been issued for this meeting.' The Committee's terms of reference were 'to give guidance to MPs and others on the interpretation of government policy and to take such action as in their opinion is necessary to sustain public confidence in the Government.' Its priority was 'to identify those policy areas *likely to be of key political importance in the period approaching an election*' (my emphasis) by focusing on issues identified by Conservative Party HQ as being '*of primary importance in electoral terms.*' This would require 'a significant contribution from the Whitehall machine,' effectively enlisting supposedly impartial civil servants to an electioneering role.

A short note confirmed that the Committee had agreed to 'commission work on specific policy areas likely to be of special political importance' and '*most relevant in the run up to an election*' (my emphasis). These included the economy, industrial and employment strategy, and how the 1982 Budget was to be presented, all of which were then highly controversial. Despite the proceedings' sensitivity, the 'major work now in hand' meant that it would, after all, be necessary to prepare papers in advance and produce an agenda, but 'great care must be taken to preserve their confidentiality and the Party Chairman would distribute them personally.' Two days before the second meeting on 10 March, Ingham briefed the PM that 'it will be important to sell – and to sell hard – the Budget's promises especially as they affect industry.' Taking a distinctly partisan tone, he wrote that the government would be 'talking up political and economic confidence' at a time when 'the Labour Party is racked by a new Trot-induced row.' The next day he told the PM that she must 'sustain the momentum' and produce a comprehensive presentation plan 'before the election' (PREM 19/720–1). The election took place on 9 June 1983, almost a year after victory in the Falklands War, and, in the most decisive postwar election result since 1945, resulted in an increased majority for the Conservatives of 144.

Here we can see why this meeting, taking place on Whitehall turf and serviced by supposedly impartial officials, was so sensitive. Against convention, the Liaison Committee implicated civil servants such as Bernard Ingham in improper partisan practices. Civil service rules explicitly stated that civil servants could not participate in electoral campaigning, a rule that still applies today (GCS 2015). Although, strictly speaking, such preparatory activity taking place before the official election campaigning period (known as 'purdah' and lasting six weeks) did not overtly break the rules, it challenged them covertly and in spirit.

Accusations that Ingham stepped over the line separating government information from party publicity were made at the time. One of the few to even register the existence of the Liaison Committee, Young argued that Ingham's presence was 'a testimony to the intimate linkage even beyond the bounds of Whitehall propriety, between party and government machines,' a charge that anticipates later criticism of Alastair Campbell (Young 1989:299). Ingham was overwhelmingly committed to Margaret Thatcher, later stating in an interview with this author that 'I served the prime minister' and that his first responsibility was 'not to get her into trouble, to keep her out of trouble' (interview: 14/11/2014). This meant protecting her not only from the media but from political enemies within her own party. The fact that he managed this task for 11 years to her satisfaction, while leaving on good terms with the political correspondents (known as 'the lobby') in 1990, is a remarkable achievement after an estimated 5,000 press lobby briefings, but there were clearly times when he crossed the line into personal advocacy, paving the way for an overtly partisan director of government communications in the shape of Alastair Campbell (Seymour-Ure 2003; Watts 1997). Ingham's success with the lobby may also indicate ideological convergence as the media swung round in support of the Thatcher experiment after the 1983 election. His success as the PM's representative led to accusations that he failed as a medium for properly informing the public because he had become 'too partisan' (Cockerell et al. 1984:72), an accusation later levelled at Campbell (Moran 2005; Tumber 2000).

Yet such charges are not straightforward given the messy reality of government communications, and by Ingham's own ambivalence. His first loyalty may have been to the Prime Minister but from taking up his post on 1 November 1979, he fought to promote and defend the work of the GIS[4] under his leadership from what he saw as the scapegoating tendencies of ministers, although, when interviewed, he described the quality of the service that he inherited as 'very mixed.' Before taking up the post, in a detailed paper to the minister then in charge of presentation, he warned that the performance and morale of the service needed to be improved, stating that, although he was 'anxious to raise the reputation and status of the Government Information Service (…) it can only be done by a collective demonstration of effort and competence' (Memo 15/10, 1979). The archival record repeatedly shows him anticipating, pre-empting and resisting ministerial activism and then going on the offensive by driving through a more co-ordinated and disciplined approach on the part of the service. We see him roused to anger on several occasions by what he saw as interference in publicity matters by ill-informed ministers. A robust response was provoked in December 1981, for example, when the Chancellor, Geoffrey Howe, complained that press releases produced by civil servants were not persuasive enough and that press officers were not 'ideally deployed for the proper presentation of the overall economic message.' Ingham dismissed the complaint as 'gratuitous, so long as Ministers of the Government cut the Government to pieces.' He insisted on being included in meetings about the matter and offered to prepare a paper (PREM 19/720).

He also acted swiftly to pre-empt potential charges of party political bias. On 19 July 1982, the Treasury minister, Leon Brittan, proposed to members of the Liaison Committee that they change the rules about party political ministerial speeches. The Questions of Procedures for Ministers (QPM), the forerunner to today's Ministerial Code, permitted these to be circulated only through the party. Brittan proposed instead that they be circulated through the official government machine, in order to secure 'far more coverage' (PREM 19/720). Ingham wrote to the PM that day insisting that she should 'resolutely refuse' to change the rules since these were 'well-founded' and had served successive governments well by 'protecting Ministers from charges of misusing Government resources for Party ends and the GIS from the charge of party political bias.' Two days later, the Liaison Committee agreed that 'it would be presentationally unwise for this Government to be seen to be tinkering with the rules' and the idea was dropped. This incident provides one possible explanation as to why Ingham participated in the Liaison Committee: it put him in a position to detect and pre-empt ministerial activism that might undermine the government's propriety framework, and, perhaps more importantly, challenge his (and the PM's) dominance over government narratives. In her 1991 analysis of government news management during the Thatcher years, Scammell concludes that, given the complexities of the role, Ingham maintained his impartiality almost until the end. However, under the 30-year rule, she did not have access to the material presented here, which is far more incriminating (Scammell 1991).

The 1986–1987 AIDS/HIV awareness campaign

> It was a life and death situation. I'd been to San Francisco, where the wards were full of young men dying. Same in Germany, same in the United Kingdom. There was no time to think about whether it might offend one or two people. And history shows we were right – people took care and HIV cases went down.
>
> *(Norman Fowler, Health Secretary, 1981–1987,*
> *interview in the Guardian, 4/9/2017)*

The world's first national government-sponsored AIDS/HIV awareness campaign, *AIDS: Don't Die of Ignorance,* was launched in November 1986 with leaflets sent to every home in Britain followed in early 1987 by a hard-hitting film and television campaign produced by the ad agency TBWA (Duncton 2016). The campaign cost £5m (equivalent to £13m today), the most expensive government health campaign of its time, and was co-ordinated by a Cabinet committee chaired by the deputy prime minister, Willie Whitelaw. The ad was intended to shock – featuring apocalytpic imagery such as an iceberg, a volcanic exposion and a tombstone, and a portentious voiceover by the actor John Hurt stating that 'anyone can get it.' The government was accused of panic-mongering but the campaign was later hailed as one of the most successful health campaigns ever, both in raising awareness and changing behaviour, and its tactics were imitated all over the world (Kelly 2011). How did a government accused of promoting anti-gay sentiment with its restrictive legislation on sex education in schools ('Section 28' of the 1988 Local Government Act) manage to produce, in five months, a powerful campaign that explicitly referred to 'anal sex' and 'rectal intercourse' at a time when homophobia was widespread among the public, in government, the police and the popular press? Government documents covering the period from 28 August 1985 to 31 December 1986, released in 2016 by the National Archives (PREM 19/1863), provide an insight into how a politician, Norman Fowler, working with the chief medical officer, Sir Donald Acheson, won the argument against a reluctant prime minister.

One of the UK's first known AIDS sufferers, Terrence Higgins, died in July 1982 aged 37, but until the first needle exchanges opened in 1985, little was done about what then seemed a terrifying and inexplicable disease that mainly affected gay men and drug addicts. The disease was often depicted as a 'gay plague' and represented by traditionalists as punishment for drug addicts and gay men, rather than a general public health emergency. The chief constable of Greater Manchester Police, James Anderton, said at a police training event in 1987 that victims were 'swirling about in a human cesspool of their own making,' repeating it weeks later in a BBC interview (*The Daily Telegraph* 2012). By the summer of 1985, scientists were predicting that the total number of UK HIV cases could reach 300,000 if nothing was done, but it was clear that the issue of AIDS/HIV was heavily politicised, with the prime minister likely to line up on the side of the traditionalists.

The archived folder begins with a dossier sent to the prime minister's office on 19 September 1985, including a submission to ministers from Donald Acheson summarising the medical and public health issues relating to AIDS, and a reference to TBWA having 'been commissioned and briefed' to produce a public health campaign aimed at high-risk groups. Also in the dossier are copies of leaflets produced by the Health Education Council and Blood Transfusion Service aimed solely at high-risk groups. Norman Fowler raised the priority of the issue when he wrote to the PM on 25 September, copying in senior ministers, describing AIDS as 'one of the most serious public health hazards faced by this country for many decades.' He constituted a ministerial steering group, including senior civil servants and the chief medical officer, to coordinate government action. The following day, Margaret Thatcher was advised by her private secretary to 'stay clear of Aids!' and leave it to Norman Fowler. She decided not to attend the opening of a new blood products testing laboratory or to agree to the setting up of an official Cabinet committee to tackle AIDS.

By February 1986, the Committee had agreed on a hard-hitting text for a newspaper advertisement to launch in March. The tone of the debate shifted dramatically when, on 24 February, David Willetts from the PM's Policy Unit reported that 'Norman Fowler is proposing to place explicit and distasteful advertisements about AIDS in all the Sunday papers.' Responding to the draft text, Margaret Thatcher added a note stating 'do we have to do the section on risky sex? I should have thought it could do immense harm if young teenagers were to read it.' Correspondence between the Committee and Margaret Thatcher's office continued as she repeatedly objected to the explicit content of the ad and the tactic of placing it in mainstream media. The debate culminated in a letter from Norman Fowler on 10 March stating that the Committee was unanimous that 'the use of explicit references to sexual practices (…) are a regrettable necessity' and that not to include this information 'would be to jeopardise the public health unnecessarily.' Finally, Margaret Thatcher conceded with a resigned 'yes' and the campaign launched on 16 March. Having established a political powerbase independent of the prime minister in the shape of the steering Committee, and in alliance with the chief medical officer, Fowler used scientific argument and a public interest defence to launch a far more high-profile and explicit film and television campaign, but the debate wasn't over.

By the summer, Fowler reported on the success of the campaign and urged the PM 'not to lose momentum.' The Committee was proposing a further round of national advertising that would include the phrase, 'Anal sex (rectal intercourse) carries the highest risk and should be avoided.' Again, the PM's 'yes' appeared on the document. Two months later, Fowler proposed that in order to bring about the necessary 'breakthrough in public recognition' an AIDS leaflet should be delivered to every household in the country. The Cabinet secretary Robert Armstrong wrote to the PM on 21 October warning strongly that there could be 'half a million affected carriers' as the disease spread to the general population, including new-born babies, and that 'most of those who die will be young people.' He repeated the proposal made (and dismissed by the PM) a year before, that the authority of the steering committee be escalated by constituting it as a Cabinet sub-committee chaired by the deputy PM. This time, she agreed.

By the autumn, AIDS had become a hot topic in the media and pressure was building on the PM to agree to a major campaign. Bernard Ingham makes his first significant appearance in the archive on 29 October, telling Willie Whitelaw that he wanted the PM to be seen taking a 'close personal interest in the issue.' He reported his concerns that, at a dinner for 24 regional newspaper editors the previous week, Mrs Thatcher had seemed 'cautious on the idea of a house-to-house leaflet drop,' although the editors expressed strong support for a hard-hitting government campaign. By 7 November, she had said 'yes' to the leaflets, and her policy adviser David Willetts was now declaring that AIDS is 'the most important health issue this century,' noting that 'there was not a single complaint about obscenity in the newspaper advertisements.' Three days later, the Cabinet sub-committee met for the first time and agreed new newspaper advertising and poster campaigns, including one aimed specifically at young people, the house-to-house leaflet drop and a proposed TV campaign. The TV ad *AIDS: Don't Die of Ignorance* aired early in 1987. On 18 April 1987, Princess Diana was photographed shaking hands with an AIDS patient.

To put this campaign in today's context, despite repeated calls for more direct public communication (Phillis 2004; House of Lords 2008), there have been large cuts in government campaign expenditure: in 2013–2014, external communication by the government cost £237m, compared to £532m in 2009–2010 (GCS 2013). The body responsible for health promotion, the Health Education Council, was closed in 1987 and its successor, the Health Education Agency, was closed in 2000. Before it was shut down in 2012, the Central Office of Information (COI), the government agency that commissioned public campaigns, had been reduced to 500 staff, compared with 1,500 in 1970 (Hood and Dixon 2015). The 1986–1987 AIDS campaign was the outcome of a well-resourced system of direct communication that had been developed over decades. Given the cuts in such activity since 2010, which have led to a greater dependence on the much cheaper media news management over direct communication, it is doubtful that a campaign on this scale and speed could be run today.

Conclusion and recommendations

The historical case study approach complicates the narrative of political spin, challenging the long-accepted dichotomy between impartial civil servants (good) and partisan politicians (bad). This dichotomy remains an article of faith in Westminster systems such as the UK, although in practice it continually grapples with political imperatives and the messiness of everyday life. In the AIDS case study, we saw a government minister behaving impartially – that is, in consideration of the public good as opposed to personal, ideological or party interest. In the workings of the Liaison Committee, we saw a civil servant pushed over the edge in defence of what he saw as the prime minister's, and hence the government's, interest. There are some continuities with today. Many of the changes associated with claims of political spin after 1997, such as the central co-ordination of government presentation, the strategic drive for a coherent party/government narrative and the demand for a more persuasive style of communication, were already being introduced during the 1980s as the new Thatcher government sought public consent to implement its radical and initially hugely unpopular programme of privatisation and economic liberalism.

Ingham's 1982 appeal to the prime minister that an open breach of the code would be seen as 'protecting Ministers from charges of misusing Government resources for Party ends and the GIS from the charge of party political bias' reveals the importance of the *appearance* of impartiality. This continues today. Government press officers can claim to provide 'objective and explanatory' information to the public while, behind the scenes, special advisers covertly set the government news agenda and brief journalists, disguising a significant internal shift in what is deemed appropriate and acceptable. This is a major discontinuity with the 1980s. Instead of a dichotomous information regime within government in which officials and political actors act as a check on each other to reach a consensus on what should be placed in the public domain and how, we see a tripartite system where political actors and government press officers collude with journalists in providing political entertainment. Direct forms of communication, such as that exemplified by the 1986–1987 AIDS campaign, have given way to the participation by governments in an ever-expanding and speeded-up political news cycle. In this sense, the answer to the question – should public officials as well as political actors bear responsibility for the consistent decline in public trust in recent decades in what governments say? – should be 'yes.'

If political strategy is increasingly and covertly being allowed to determine what is placed in the public domain and what is withheld, public trust can only fall further. If a solution is to be found, it must open up to public scrutiny what has been a closed, self-regulatory system that lacks transparency. In doing so it must adopt mechanisms of accountability that uphold the doctrine of speaking truth to power, whether by civil servants, special advisers, ministers, parliaments or publics.

Notes

1 The first use of the term 'political spin' can be traced to *The New York Times* in 1984, in an article about the televised debate between the US presidential candidates Ronald Reagan and Walter Mondale. See www.theguardian.com/notesandqueries'query/0.5753.-1124.00.htm.
2 Archived with the Margaret Thatcher Papers at www.chu.cam.ac.uk/archives/collections/thatcher-papers/.
3 Not knowing who to appoint, the PM asked her private secretary Clive Whitmore to choose three candidates for the post of Number 10 press secretary. She and Clive only saw Whitmore's first choice, Bernard Ingham, for 20 minutes (Hoskyns 2000).
4 Later known as the GICS (1997), then the GCN (2005) and finally GCS (2013).

References

Aucoin, P. 2012, New Political Governance in Westminster Systems: Impartial Public Administration and Management Performance at Risk, *Governance*, 25(2), pp. 177–199.

Bannerman, S. and Haggart, B. 2015, Historical Institutionalism in Communication Studies, *Communication Theory*, 25(1), pp. 1–22.

Blick, A. 2004, *People Who Live in the Dark*, London: Politico's.

Blumler, J.G. and Coleman, S. 2015, Democracy and the Media – Revisited, *Javnost – The Public*, 22(2), pp. 111–128.

Chilcot, S.J. 2016, *The Report of the Iraq Inquiry*, London: House of Commons.

Cockerell, M., Hennessy, P. and Walker, D. 1984, *Sources Close to the Prime Minister: Inside the Hidden World of the News Manipulators*, Basingstoke: Macmillan.

Cutlip, S.M. 1994, *The Unseen Power: Public Relations – A History*, London; New York: Routledge.

The Daily Telegraph 2012, Margaret Thatcher Saved Career of Police Chief Who Made AIDS Remarks, 4 January. Available online www.telegraph.co.uk/news/uknews/law-and-order/8991935/Margaret-Thatcher-saved-career-of-police-chief-who-made-Aids-remarks.html.

Duncton, M. 2016, The AIDS Health Campaign. Available online http://blog.nationalarchives.gov.uk/blog/.

Eichbaum, C. and Shaw, R. 2010, *Partisan Appointees and Public Servants: An International Analysis of the Role of the Political Adviser*, Cheltenham; Northampton, MA: Edward Elgar.

Foster, C.D. 2005, *British Government in Crisis, or, The Third English Revolution*, Oxford: Hart.

Fredriksson, M., Schillemans, T. and Pallas, J. 2015, Determinants of Organizational Mediatisation: An Analysis of the Adaptation of Swedish Government Agencies to News Media, *Public Administration*, 93(4), pp. 1049–1068.

Garland, R. 2017, Between Mediatisation and Politicisation: The Changing Role and Position of Whitehall Press Officers in the Age of Political Spin. *Public Relations Inquiry*, 6(2), pp. 171–189.

Garland, R., Tambini, D. and Couldry, N. 2018, Has Government been Mediatized? A UK Perspective, *Media, Culture & Society*, 40(4), pp. 493–513.

GCS 2013, Government Communications Plan 2013/14, London: HM Government.

GCS 2015, Government Communications (*GCS) Handbook*, London: Cabinet Office.

Grant, M. 1999, Towards a Central Office of Information: Continuity and Change in British Government Information Policy, 1939–51, *Journal of Contemporary History*, 34(1), pp. 49–67.

Hall, P.A. and Taylor, R.C.R. 1996, Political Science and the Three New Institutionalisms, *Political Studies*, 44(5), pp. 936–957.

Halligan, L. 2016, A Pro-EU 'Study' Straight from the Ministry of Truth, *Daily Telegraph*, 23 April. Available online www.telegraph.co.uk/business/2016/04/23/a-pro-eu-study-straight-from-the-ministry-of-truth/.

Herring, E. and Robinson, N. 2014, Report X Marks the Spot: The British Government's Deceptive Dossier on Iraq and WMD, *Political Science Quarterly*, 129(4), pp. 551–584.

Hood, C. and Dixon, R. 2015, *A Government that Worked Better and Cost Less?* Oxford: Oxford University Press.

Hoskyns, J. 2000, *Just in Time: Inside the Thatcher Revolution*, London: Aurum Press.

House of Lords Communication Select Committee 2008, *First Report: Session 2008–9*, London: House of Lords.

Hustedt, T. and Salomonsen, H.H. 2014, Ensuring Political Responsiveness: Politicization Mechanisms in Ministerial Bureaucracies, *International Review of Administrative Sciences*, 80(4), pp. 746–765.

IpsosMORI 2016, *Veracity Index 2015: Trust in Professions*, London: IpsosMORI.

Jones, N. 2006, *Trading Information*, London: Politico's.

Kelly, J. 2011, HIV/Aids: Why were the Campaigns Successful in the West? *BBC News*. Available online www.bbc.co.uk/news/magazine-15886670.

L'Etang, J. 2008, Writing PR History: Issues, Methods and Politics, *Journal of Communication Management*, 12(4), pp. 319–335.

L'Etang, J. 2009, *Public Relations in Britain: A History of Professional Practice in the 20th Century*, London: Routledge.

Lijphart, A. 1999, *Patterns of Democracy: Government Forms and Performance in Thirty-Six Countries*, New Haven, CT: Yale University Press.

Moore, M. 2006, *The Origins of Modern Spin: Democratic Government and the Media in Britain, 1945–51*, Basingstoke: Palgrave Macmillan.

Moran, M. 2005, *Politics and Governance in the UK*, Basingstoke: Palgrave Macmillan.

Peters, P. and Pierre, J. 2004, *Politicization of the Civil Service in Comparative Perspective: The Quest for Control*, London: Routledge.

Phillis, R. 2004, *An Independent Review of Government Communications*, London: Cabinet Office.

Public Administration Select Committee 1998, *Sixth Report, Session 1997–98*, London: House of Commons.

Public Administration Select Committee 2000, *Fourth Report: Special Advisers – Boon or Bane?* London: House of Commons.

Public Administration Select Committee 2012, *Special Advisers in the Thick of It*, London: House of Commons.

Public Administration Select Committee 2013, *Future of the Civil Service: Gus O'Donnell Evidence Session*, London: House of Commons.

Scammell, M. 1991, *The Impact of Marketing and Public Relations on Modern British Politics: The Conservative Party and Government under Mrs. Thatcher*. PhD thesis, London School of Economics.

Seymour-Ure, C. 2003, *Prime Ministers and the Media: Issues of Power and Control*, Malden, MA: Blackwell.

Stanyer, J. and Mihelj, S. 2016, Taking Time Seriously? Theorizing and Researching Change in Communication and Media Studies, *Journal of Communication*, 66(2), pp. 266–279.

Tee, M. 2011, *Review of Government Direct Communications and the Role of the COI*, London: Cabinet Office.

Thorbjornsrud, K., Figenschou, T.U. and Ihlen, O. 2014, Mediatization in Public Bureaucracies: A Typology, *Communications – The European Journal of Communication Research*, 39(1), pp. 3–22.

Tumber, H. 2000, *Media Power, Professionals, and Policies*, London; New York: Routledge.

Watts, D. 1997, *Political Communication Today*, Manchester: Manchester University Press.

Whiteley, P., Clarke, H.D., Sanders, D. and Stewart, M. 2016, Why Do Voters Lose Trust in Governments? Public Perceptions of Government Honesty and Trustworthiness in Britain 2000–2013. *British Journal of Politics and International Relations*, 18(1), pp. 234–254.

Wicks, N. 2003, *Ninth Report of the Committee: Defining the Boundaries within the Executive: Ministers, Special Advisers and the Permanent Civil Service*, London: Committee on Standards in Public Life.

Wring, D. 2005, Politics and the Media: The Hutton Inquiry, the Public Relations State, and Crisis at the BBC, *Parliamentary Affairs*, 58(2), pp. 380–393.

Yeung, K. 2006, Regulating Government Communications, *The Cambridge Law Journal*, 65(01), pp. 53–91.

YouGov 2018, *UK Polling Report*. Available online http://ukpollingreport.co.uk/voting-intention-1979–1983 [accessed 9 November 2018].

Young, H. 1989, *One of Us: A Biography of Margaret Thatcher*, London: Pan Macmillan.

11

SPORTS PROMOTION AND THE CONSTRUCTION OF 'IRISH' IDENTITY

Nationalism, social exclusion and the Gaelic Athletic Association

Ian Somerville, David Mitchell and Owen Hargie

Introduction

L'Etang (2008) notes that public relations histories have tended to focus on institutional, organisational, professional and biographical spheres or have engaged with histories of ideas that have shaped concepts, theories and thinking about public relations. She suggests that other, perhaps less inward-looking, areas are ripe for exploration and that 'there are other approaches to PR history, for example its role in broader historical contexts (linked to causes and impacts) in political, economic, social, diplomatic and international histories' (2008:319). Elsewhere she also argues that '[A]lthough sport is used as a communications vehicle it has not been given adequate treatment within public relations literature (…) leaving considerable gaps in our understanding of PR's role in cultural relationships and processes in the sporting context' (L'Etang 2006:393). This chapter brings these threads together and explores the promotional history of sport in two senses. First, it examines the promotional activities of a major sporting and politicocultural organisation in Ireland, the Gaelic Athletic Association (GAA), by tracing some of its key communication strategies since its foundation almost 140 years ago. Second, it analyses how 'history' itself was deployed by the GAA as a promotional tool in the construction of an ethno-nationalist mythology that sought to secure and maintain the organisation's position as the pre-eminent sporting organisation in Ireland and at the same time promote a particular definition of 'Irishness.' Using empirical data from the 'Social Exclusion and Sport in Northern Ireland' (SESNI) research study, the chapter then explores some of the lasting impacts of these promotional strategies for today's deeply divided Northern Irish society. This is a story of how sports promotion was used in nationalist resistance against 'colonialism,' to construct a political and cultural identity, and to play a significant role in the exclusion of 'the other' in a deeply divided society.

Sport, promotional culture and 'social capital'

Across a wide range of actors (nation-states, NGOs, intergovernmental organisations, international sports federations, transnational corporations etc.) an international orthodoxy seems to have been established that sport promotes peace and prosperity (Giulianotti 2011; Darnell 2012). For example, the United Nations has highlighted sport as 'a powerful tool to support conflict prevention and peacebuilding efforts' (United Nations Inter-Agency Task Force on Sport for Development and Peace 2003:i). More recently the European Union has declared that 'Sport can also be a vehicle to promote social inclusion of minorities and other vulnerable or disadvantaged groups and contribute towards better understanding among communities, including in post-conflict regions' (European Commission 2011:4). This positive power of sport has been highlighted in PR scholarship too; Curtin and Gaither (2005:92) note that it is often 'overlooked in international public relations texts, yet sports can unify nations, promote social change and affect the national psyche, making it a powerful cultural agent.'

However, while sporting competition is often portrayed as a generator of goodwill, where different peoples and nations can come together under common values of respect and fair play, examination of its actual societal impact paints a much more ambiguous picture. George Orwell famously suggested that

> Serious sport (...) is war minus the shooting (...) There cannot be much doubt that the whole thing is bound up with the rise of nationalism – that is, with the lunatic modern habit of identifying oneself with large power units and seeing everything in terms of competitive prestige.
>
> *(Orwell 1968:42)*

While one doesn't have to entirely agree with Orwell's disparaging judgment on the nature of sport in modern times, it is clear that it is frequently deployed in questionable promotional activities. Sport has been utilised as an instrument of soft power (Grix and Lee 2013) by all kinds of (frequently unpleasant) regimes to boost national prestige and to promote the profile of populist politicians and state leaders. Organised, competitive sport can also serve as an opportunity for the expression of hostility, inter-group difference and often violence. The malign potential of sport is perhaps especially acute within deeply divided societies. Where people live close together, internal sporting contests are more regular than international competition, and inter-group enmity is often especially bitter and volatile (Sugden and Bairner 2000; Reiche 2011; Bell 2017).

So, how do we make sense of these opposing tendencies, or, as Donnelly (2011a) calls it, 'the Janus-face of sport'? A key concept that has been deployed to understand and explain the role of sport in people's lives is the notion of 'social capital' (Putnam 2000). Bailey notes: 'Since sports participation provides a focus for social activity, an opportunity to make friends, develop networks and reduce social isolation, it seems well placed to support the development of social capital' (Bailey

2005:76). However, it's important to remember that 'the relationship between sport and social capital has an equal chance of being either positive or negative' (Nicholson and Hoye 2008:12). Putnam (2000) argued that social capital has a 'dark side' in that the bonds of organisations and networks can also exclude outsiders from the privileges enjoyed by insiders. Indeed this 'bonding capital' can trump the 'bridging capital' potential of sport, which can frequently lead to segregation and exclusionary behaviour (Coalter 2007).

Thus, sport is easily co-opted into social identity or ideological struggles between 'us' and 'them,' and this is particularly the case in divided societies such as Northern Ireland. L'Etang notes that: 'Sport is as an arena for debate and discourses about elites, resource allocation, privilege, deprivation, exploitation, justice, nationalism, racism, gender, age, the body, ideologies, religion (…) Sports PR goes way beyond sport and is intrinsically political' (2006:390). Using the case of the GAA in Ireland, we explore the issue of promotional culture and sport, and more particularly the use of 'sports PR' to promote specific sociocultural or political ends.

Ireland, nationalism and the GAA

Some political histories argue the roots of the Irish conflict lie in attempts to integrate Ireland into the British state during the sixteenth and seventeenth centuries (Ruane and Todd 1996). In this narrative the movement of Protestants from Britain, mainly to the north of the island, created two distinct identity groups on the island: British/Protestants/'settlers,' most of whom valued the political link with Britain, and Catholics/Nationalists/'natives,' most of whom wished to sever that link. The conflict in Northern Ireland is thus framed by some academics (and journalists and politicians) in ethno-nationalist terms – in other words, the presence of two rival ethnic groups resulted in conflict (e.g., Hughes 1994; Whyte 1991).

This perspective has been challenged by revisionist political historians in recent times; for example, McGrattan (2010) notes that adopting ethnic antagonism as *the* explanation arguably tends to obliterate the salience of other questions surrounding gender, class, location and political choices at key historical moments. McGrattan suggests that:

> The ethno-national narrative is a superficially persuasive and easily comprehensible rendering of the 'Irish question'. (…) Previous conflicts are held up as examples of the return of ancient antagonisms, regardless of the fact that in those cases also the decisions of political elites were crucial in shaping the course of events.
>
> *(2010:10)*

Revisionist historians argue that we must ask how 'identities' are created and maintained. If we take them at face value there is the risk that political realities will be obscured and scholars may simply reproduce the stories that elites use/ have used to maintain their hegemony within their communities. White (2004) also points out that many contemporary political historians are extremely critical of ethnic nationalisms that are inventions of the recent past. Instead, the history of all European peoples is one based on waves of migration and 'the idea of fixed, separated peoples who lived in isolation of each other forming distinct national identities is a myth itself' (White 2004:332). He also observes: 'In the Irish context, even though the Celts began migrating to Ireland in the sixth century BC, no one identified themselves as Celtic until the late 18th or early 19th century' (White 2004:332). Modern genetics also seems to debunk notions of a distinct 'Celtic race' in Ireland or anywhere else, but, as Sykes (2006) notes, the myth 'is very entrenched and has a lot to do with the Scottish, Welsh and Irish identity; their main identifying feature is that they are not English.' The veracity of claims about the origins and distinctiveness of the 'Irish' or the 'Gaels' is not really the issue, of course; the genetic realities 'have no bearing on cultural history' (Oppenheimer 2006). It is the politico-promotional function of such narratives that matter, and it is here that sport came to play a central role in shaping a version of recent Irish history.

The 'Gaelic sports' are those that either have some claim to have originated in Ireland or were invented/developed in Ireland, and they consist of Gaelic football, hurling, camogie (women's hurling) and handball. Founded in 1884, the GAA formed part of the Gaelic revival, a cultural movement intended to redress the decline in indigenous Irish culture and an important component in the development of modern Irish nationalism. Within Northern Ireland, Gaelic games are played almost exclusively by the Catholic community, and the GAA, along with the Roman Catholic Church, has been one of the pillars of nationalist community life. A founding patron of the GAA was Archbishop Croke of Cashel, who 'linked the GAA with Catholicism from the outset, and it is a relationship that has not waned with the passing years.' (Cronin 2002:26). GAA clubs were formed in line with Catholic parishes, Catholic clergy usually played a central role in the local club and hurling and Gaelic football became the games of local Catholic schools (Butler and Ruane 2009). Devine and Devine (2004), in highlighting the strong link between the Catholic Church and Gaelic games, argue that this 'ensures there is a family atmosphere at matches and crowd control and hooliganism have never been an issue' (177). This may be largely true, but this very relationship could hardly be viewed as conducive to members of the Protestant community who may give some thought to attending or participating in these sports. Indeed, Ewart et al.'s (2004) research finds that for young Protestants, 'Gaelic sports were either seen as an integral part of the Nationalist-Irish culture or as a sectarian activity that largely excluded Protestants' (2004:42). This idea of the GAA being a 'cold house' for the Protestant Unionist community is compounded by the opening pages of the GAA Official Guide – Part One (Gaelic Athletic Association 2016), which states:

> Those who play its games, those who organise its activities and those who control its destinies see in the G.A.A. a means of consolidating our Irish identity. The games to them are more than games – they have a national

> significance (…) The Association is a National Organisation which has as its
> basic aim the strengthening of the National Identity in a 32 County Ireland.
>
> *(4–5)*

Thus, because of its Catholic, nationalist ethos, the GAA has historically been held
in low esteem by Protestants, being perceived as, at best, unwelcoming to non-
nationalists, and at worst, during the Northern Irish conflict, as a sectarian front for
the IRA (Cronin 2000).

To compound this alienation, the GAA Constitution historically included a
number of rules that in effect actively excluded the Protestant population. Until it
was dropped in 1971, the GAA under 'Rule 27' enforced a ban on members from
playing or attending 'foreign' games (such as rugby, hockey and soccer), or participating in social functions organised by clubs from non-Gaelic sports. Additionally,
'Rule 21' prevented members of the British security forces (in effect the Northern
Irish police) from joining the GAA, a ban that was removed in November 2001,
and 'Rule 42' banned 'foreign' sports from GAA grounds. This rule too was eventually amended in 2005 and Fulton and Bairner (2007) note that for many

> the issue of Rule 42 was not merely a defining moment in the history of
> the association or of Irish sport in general. It was seen, more fundamentally,
> as a defining moment in the recent history of Ireland, a measure (…) of the
> extent to which (if at all) Ireland had modernised.
>
> *(57)*

Nevertheless it is in Northern Ireland that these exclusionary rules have their most
enduring legacy; as Cronin (2000) points out, in Northern Ireland 'Gaelic games
can be seen as sports that support the Catholic population through its exclusiveness, stresses political aspirations that champion the cause of an Irish Republic and
that exclude the broad Protestant/Unionist population' (26). The central importance of sport to identity in Northern Ireland and the long history of refusal by the
GAA to permit their members to have any association with other sports had an
enormous impact on both the simultaneous bonding and exclusionary effects of
sporting cultures in Northern Ireland.

Promoting an 'Irish' identity: sport and the GAA

It is clear that from its foundation the GAA saw itself from within the prism of cultural struggle with 'foreign' games but also came to see itself as the key defender and
preserver of a particular kind of Irish identity, an identity that had little space for
diversity in regard to political viewpoint. Before examining the legacy of these policies for contemporary Northern Ireland, this section briefly explores some of the
main promotional and PR strategies deployed by the GAA to assert and strengthen
what it believed to be its rightful position as the pre-eminent sporting organisation
on the island of Ireland.

'History' as promotional strategy: the GAA and the 'Irish nation' myth

White (2004) suggests that in situations where nationalism challenges imperial power, sociocultural institutions are required and indeed can play a pivotal role in linking the masses with elite constructed national myths. He argues that in Ireland the GAA was particularly important in this regard in helping to promote and consolidate the Gaelic revival at the end of the nineteenth, century and indeed played a vital role in developing a unique sense of national identity in the twentieth century, one in sharp contrast to that of British identity:

> Nationalist ideals cannot be propagated without an institutional framework to disseminate the particular myth of the nation advanced by nationalist elites. One organization that was critical in the cultural realm that organized and symbolized the effort to 'invent' the modern sense of Celtic or Gaelic Irish nationalism in the late 19th century was the Gaelic Athletic Association (GAA).
>
> *(White 2004:335)*

The GAA, despite being founded in 1884, has always attempted to promote its sports as ancient activities, handed down from a Celtic race, which have existed for thousands of years. It has always been keen, in other words, to recruit 'history' as a key element in its promotional strategy. A typical GAA advert reads:

> WE'RE PLAYING HURLING
> It's an Irish Sport.
> It's 3000 years old.
> Yes, it's as fun as it looks.
> Find out more: Playhurling.com

Hurling is undoubtedly based upon an ancient game played with curved sticks and a ball-type object, as is hockey and the closely related Scottish sport of shinty, which seems to have been the version of 'hurling' played in the northern part of Ireland before the codification by the GAA in 1884. The fact that 4,000-year-old carvings in Egypt appear to show people playing something akin to hockey/hurling/shinty (Craig 2002:23) would suggest that the claims in the advert are rather dubious, except perhaps the final one. Actual historical facts would not have deterred Michael Cusack and his fellow GAA founders from their determination to identify uniquely 'Irish' games, despite plenty of evidence to the contrary Cusack was convinced that chess was also one of the Gaelic games (Rouse 2015). Debunking this mythologising about sporting origins is not really the key issue here, but it is important to recognise that this myth of an Irish 'nation' playing Gaelic games for thousands of years played a key role in the creation and subsequent maintenance of an Irish identity, particularly after independence from the UK in 1921.

Ideologies always tend to be conveyed through myths (Cronin 1999), although a peculiar feature of the GAA myth is that is tends to be uncritically adopted even by some scholarship in the area. For example, Devine and Devine (2004:180) claim that 'For centuries Gaelic games have been at the heart of the Nationalist community in Northern Ireland.' Underpinning their assertion appears to be the notion that 'Irishness' equals Irish nationalism and that Gaelic games belong to Irish nationalists. The actual historical record paints a different picture – Gaelic 'football' didn't exist at all in any distinctive sense before it's invention by GAA President Maurice Davin in 1885 (Rouse 2015). The case of hurling is more interesting, but here too the historical record contradicts Devine and Devine's (2004) equation of nationalism and Gaelic games. Hutchinson's (2004) historical study discusses at length the playing of the northern version of hurling across both communities in Ulster in the eighteenth and nineteenth centuries, where it had become by the mid-nineteenth century the most popular sport in strongly Protestant County Down. Hutchinson examines the numerous attempts to form a Scottish Irish Gaelic sports association in the nineteenth century and concluded that these discussions always fell apart for the same reason: the Scots wished to limit the focus to sport and culture, whereas many, but not all, on the Irish side viewed Gaelic games as a key element in promoting Irish nationalism. White (2004:335) notes that the 'GAA provided an important organisational mechanism for (…) creating and defining Irish popular culture in Gaelic terms.' Central to this was constructing a narrative that emphasised the separateness of the idea of Irishness and protected it from contamination by the 'British' populations of the islands they shared.

Spectacle, mega-events and sports PR

The GAA's central promotional strategy of constructing a nation-building myth demonstrates L'Etang's (2006) point that that sports PR frequently goes way beyond sport and is intrinsically political. However the organisation also engaged in activities with a more traditional PR function. After the partition of Ireland in 1921 one of the first major public events planned was the Tailteann Games, advertised through a wide range of promotional materials as the 'Irish Race Olympics,' to be held at the refurbished headquarters of the GAA, Croke Park, Dublin. It was originally due to be held on 6–13 August 1922, but the Irish Civil War delayed the actual event until August 1924. However, this delay was serendipitous because it meant that many of the competitors returning from the Olympic Games in Paris, which had ended the previous week (including 'stars' such as the swimmer Johnny Weissmuller), accepted invitations to come to Dublin to take part.

The Dublin sports spectacular turned out to be a PR masterstroke, a powerful promotional event to announce the new nation on the world's stage. Perhaps some of the glamour of the Paris Olympics transferred to the 1924 Irish games, but in truth it became a hugely successful event in its own right and proved as popular with the world's media as the Paris Games had been (Rouse 2015). As L'Etang notes the Olympics are 'the ultimate "mega-event", (…) due to their wider cultural significance shaped by a range of PR and media sources that set agendas, create or promote ideologies, shape myths and icons, promote goods and thus create international reference points and touchstones' (2006:390). The soft power benefits of the Tailteann Games to the newly independent nation were evident, with huge media coverage throughout the event via Pathé newsreels shown in cinemas globally and daily reports in *The Times of London* and *The New York Times*. The organising committee decided to repeat the event to coincide with the Amsterdam Olympics in 1928, which also guaranteed attendance by Olympic athletes and again, although not reaching the heights of 1924, the event was successful. The fact that the 1932 Olympiad was given to Los Angeles meant that there would be no geographical proximity and thus no Olympic stars travelling to the Tailteann Games. This, combined with a lack of funding support from the new elected Fianna Fáil government led by Éamon de Valera, ensured that this was the last time this kind of mega-event was held.

De Valera-led governments held power in Ireland for most of the next three decades, and the GAA was required to navigate through the political environment carefully during this period because De Valera, while not overtly hostile to the GAA, was never particularly supportive either. He was opposed to the GAA ban on participation in 'foreign' sports and his preference for rugby was well known (Fanning 2015). De Valera effectively killed the Tailteann Games by appointing an inter-departmental committee to look into the possibility of holding them again in the future, which resulted in the decision being perpetually deferred (Rouse 2015). Elected governments in post-independence Ireland generally seemed reluctant to offer the preferential treatment that many in the GAA regarded as their right, leading to frequent periods of heighted tensions and even outright hostility (Connolly and Dolan 2012). For similar reasons these tensions also manifested themselves in the organisation's relations with the Irish state broadcasters and indeed at times with the press, leading to an 'unconventional' approach to media relations for much of the post-independence period.

The GAA's media relations

Connolly and Dolan (2012:414) note that the conflation of Gaelic games and the GAA with the nationalist movement prior to, and during, the War of Independence 'fostered a sense of entitlement, often articulated and cultivated by GAA activists and administrators, for a primary position as the national sporting and cultural body in the new Irish Free State.' In 1936, the new national radio station, 2RN (Radio Éireann), began the policy of broadcasting results from different sporting events held around Ireland, which led the GAA general secretary to attack:

> The linking up of Gaelic results with the reports of foreign games. The Council considered this an insidious method of introducing non-Gaelic pastimes to the attention of the Irish public at large. It is a debatable question

> whether the advantages of Wireless publicity are not entirely neutralised by
> the manner in which it is provided at present.
>
> *(GAA/AC 1936)*

This obsession with the media coverage given to other sports in the broadcast
media, but also in the print media, became a recurring theme in the GAA's media
relations approach (see Cronin, Duncan and Rouse 2009:192). The GAA knew of
course that it relied on the media to cover and publicise its games, but as Connolly
and Dolan (2012:418) note, 'differences over the meaning of nationhood and
Irishness' caused frequent breakdowns in its relationship with the media. In 1954,
for example, the GAA banned the broadcasting of a national final due to the fact
that Radio Éireann planned to cover an international soccer match between the
Republic of Ireland and Scotland during half-time (Boyle 1992).

However, while 'nationalist rhetoric' remained a significant element in the
GAA's media relations well into the 1960s, by the end of this decade the expansion of television as a mass medium posed dilemmas for the GAA. For those who
held the position that it was not enough just to play Gaelic games, to be truly Irish
was to shun all other games as well; the decision by the national broadcaster, now
RTÉ (Raidió Teilifís Éireann), to begin to show rugby and soccer matches in the
1960s was hugely significant. The ban on attending 'foreign games' now seemed
particularly absurd and it was no surprise to see it dropped in 1971. A situation
where GAA membership was revoked for going along to watch Ireland play rugby
or soccer at a stadium, but not revoked for sitting at home and watching it on TV,
was patently ridiculous.

Connolly and Dolan (2012:420) argue that the fear that the medium of television could convert Irish people to other sports meant that there was a clear shift
in the approach to media relations by the end of the 1960s. Attempts to pressurise the media via ideological appeals to patriotic nationalism were replaced by
a different message over the next decade. In 1969 the GAA's official magazine
was arguing: '(...) soccer, rugby, golf or boxing. All of them deserve their share of
publicity. But they get it, and Gaelic games do not' (*Gaelic Sport* 1969:29, cited in
Connolly and Dolan 2012:420). Similar complaints were expressed at meetings of
the GAA's central council:

> RTE are carrying out a deliberate policy of downgrading Gaelic games due
> to the inadequate coverage and unfair treatment meted out in the past few
> years, so blatant it is beyond belief, and yet soccer, rugby, racing, snooker and
> other sports command extensive coverage to the detriment of the national
> games of Ireland.
>
> *(GAA 1974:24)*

The criticism now is not that RTÉ is covering other sports, but that there is a
perceived lack of comparative coverage or poorer quality of presentation for Gaelic
games by the national broadcaster. This marks a significant change, the era of media

relations by attempting to pressurise the media through discourses of 'nationhood' was coming to a close and now the message became one of cooperation: 'The Association and the Media need one another and we must endeavour to use the media to the Association's best advantage. We must treat their representatives with respect' (GAA/AC 1977).

By the end of the 1970s, the GAA was beginning to see itself as one of a number of competitor sports, which must use the amplifying role of the media in promoting itself in the marketplace, and this led to attempts to professionalise its communications/PR approach.

> The competition for space in the media is now intense. Daily decisions are made in newspapers about the news value of different items. All sports are in competition here (...) To provide a proper system of information each county should have its own active PRO [public relations officer] (...) and the main task is to provide information re county activities to national and provincial papers and to train clubs in the value and use of publicity re club activities.
>
> *(GAA 1979)*

Connolly and Dolan (2012:423–424) note that by the end of the twentieth century and moving into the twenty-first, specialist public relations functions such as 'director of communications,' 'communications manager,' 'brand manager,' 'sponsorship manager' etc., and the knowledge and techniques they bring, are now perceived to be an indispensable requirement if the GAA is to be successful in its competition 'with other sports for a share of an expanding and more differentiated sports media space.' This change in approach is indicative of the GAA's sense of entitlement becoming less pronounced and it has been accompanied by a movement away from an era where 'nationalist rhetoric' was the dominant discourse in GAA public statements and media relations to an era of 'selling the games' (Connolly and Dolan 2012) in a competitive sporting market.

However, the pace and extent of this transition was not universal across the GAA. In deeply divided Northern Ireland the GAA remained 'strongly embedded within a cultural narrative which fused Irish nationalist politics, Gaelic games and Irish music and language with Irish identity' (Connolly and Dolan 2012:424). While no one can directly blame the GAA for the violent conflicts in Ireland it is clear that its successful promotion of Gaelic games as an integral element of Irish nationalism and its draconian exclusionary rules did help produce a society in Northern Ireland in which sport is one of the significant markers of communal identity. Just as the GAA constructed an historical narrative to promote a specific kind of Irish identity, so this narrative helps shapes the present perceptions of identity. The GAA case also points to a wider lesson, when sports promotion becomes entangled with the promotion of a political ideology this will have political consequences. Using data from our recent research project we briefly explore in the next section some of these consequences for Northern Irish society today.

Exploring the legacy of ethno-nationalist sports promotion in Northern Ireland

Drawing on data from our project[1] on social exclusion and sport in Northern Ireland, we analyse two key findings below: the first focuses on current interest in the GAA sports across Northern Ireland's communities; the second explores whether or not participants feel that the GAA today is taking active steps to become more inclusive.

Interest in GAA sports

If we examine the figures for interest in GAA sports as indicated by TV viewing, it is clear that the committed TV audience for Gaelic games is almost exclusively made up of those from the Catholic/Nationalist community background (see Figure 11.1). While some Protestant/Unionists state they watch GAA a little on TV, the vast majority of this community express no interest.

It was also clear from the interviews that even those Protestants who occasionally watch on TV feel uncomfortable about actually attending a GAA event. Indeed, while Protestants participants frequently expressed admiration for Gaelic sports, talking about their speed, athleticism and excitement, they were conscious of being outsiders. A 72-year-old Protestant man who said he enjoyed watching Gaelic sports on TV would, however, never contemplate actually going to a game: 'But that's their game. (…) It's their national sport and you have to respect that.' Protestant attitudes to the GAA in Northern Ireland are frequently complex; for example, a 38-year-old Protestant man admitted to having mixed feelings about the GAA; he was open to the sports, but more sceptical about the organisation:

> If I was in a work environment or something and five guys said look do you want to come and play Gaelic for us, we're short tonight, I'd have no problem going along, or if they said, do you want to come and watch? I'll go for the

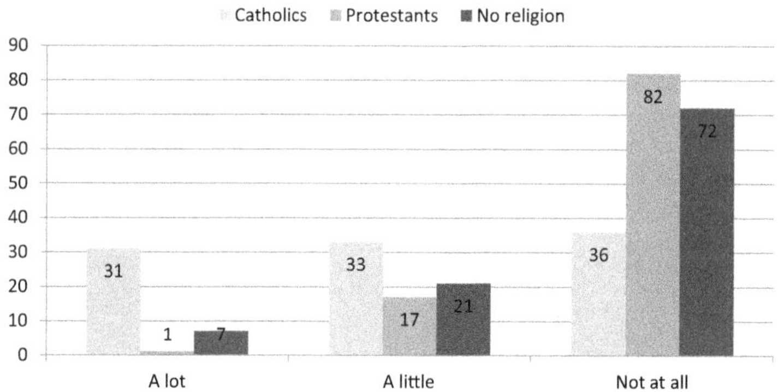

FIGURE 11.1 TV viewing of Gaelic games in Northern Ireland – results by religion

craic of a big game. The GAA and the actual organisation itself… I would still struggle with its kind of ethos, that it's still kind of quite nationalist and not totally tolerant, you know.

The interviews with participants from a Catholic community background revealed a mixture of both a high level of interest and some criticism of the GAA. The passionate commitment to the GAA of some Catholic interviewees was clear, as was its importance to their sporting and social lives. Nevertheless, there was broad understanding of why Protestants may not find the GAA appealing. A 42-year-old man who had played Gaelic all his life was conscious that certain aspects of the GAA – such as the playing of the Irish national anthem – discouraged Protestant interest: 'Obviously Gaelic is still a predominantly nationalist sport, (…) but it could be made more open. Like the idea of playing the anthem before matches, I still don't get. I don't understand why you need a stamp, a political song or a national anthem on top of a sport.' Other Catholic participants attributed not just its Irish nationalism but its 'Catholic identity' as off-putting for Protestants; one noted: 'I think that [GAA] sport has got its own problem, inherent problem, because it's a Catholic-dominated sport'; another said:

> I think the GAA should be for both sides of the community. (…) There's people that see the GAA as a Catholic organisation, but I see it more of a sport, so there is definitely improvements that could be made.

Is the GAA becoming more inclusive?

Although almost 40 per cent of Protestants in our survey held the view that the GAA was or was probably taking active steps today to welcome them (see Figure 11.2), in the interviews it was noticeable that they not could name any actual

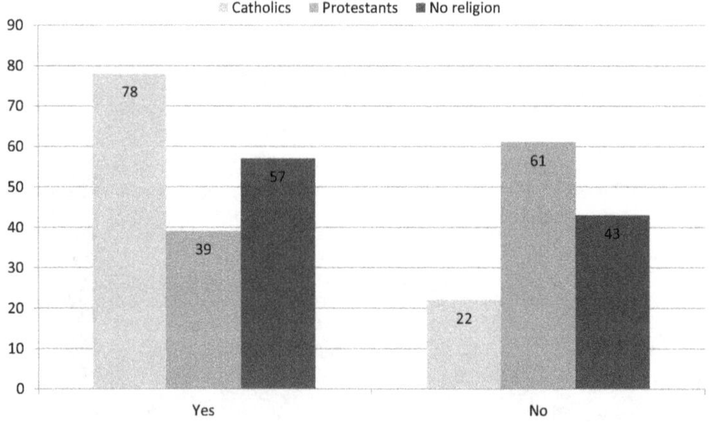

FIGURE 11.2 The GAA is taking active steps to welcome all traditions in Northern Ireland – results by religion

initiatives or promotional activities that targeted their community. The majority expressed the view that as far as they could tell the GAA had little interest in encouraging them to get involved.

Protestant interviewees tended to focus on feelings of exclusion. One 58-year-old Protestant man stated:

> I personally would find the GAA would not be accommodating to my community. For me to go along and be a supporter or a spectator, or for my children to participate, no. Let's be honest, I'm not welcome (…) they're not coming out to my community.

Another participant, a 65-year-old Protestant man, similarly couldn't recall any attempts by the GAA to reach out to Protestants: 'I think that there's no [GAA] publicity that would suggest to Protestants that they would be welcome.'

Although frequently Catholic interviewees expressed a wish to see the 'de-politicisation' of the GAA in order to make it more attractive to the Protestant community, some were concerned about rapid cultural change in the organisation. They recognised there were members of the organisation – an older generation with strong memories of the 'Troubles' – for whom the traditional symbols of nationalism were meaningful. One Catholic participant noted a danger of dividing the Catholic community itself over the issue: 'if you're talking about cultural change within the sporting dimension, if you make big leaps, you will exclude people who have a strong identity.' Others, however, disagreed with the cautious approach; a 52-year-old Catholic man argued that it was time for the GAA to be more direct. He said 'They [the GAA] could go out and actually say that people are welcome, no matter what religion they are.'

Discussion and conclusions

In the context of sport and identity politics, the GAA is of significant interest because its history provides a particularly vivid case study of how sporting promotional culture is not merely limited to the outputs of the promotional professions but is intertwined with 'active practices' (Davis 2013), across diverse sociopolitical spheres, which have impacted on the everyday experiences of people in Ireland for over a century. The GAA's promotional activity – the deployment of a mythical sporting history, the early use of mega-events, its eventual development of professional media relations – on one level can be viewed as a highly successful example of sports promotional activity. This is because these activities not only ensured the rapid growth of newly invented/codified sports in Ireland but also were a key element in constructing an Irish national identity in the newly independent Irish state. However, the data from our research project on social exclusion and sport indicate some of the less-positive consequences that this campaign has bequeathed to today's post-conflict generation in Northern Ireland.

Sean McCarthy, the president of the GAA in 1933, publically stated that if you were not a 'Catholic and a member of the GAA you could not be a good Irishman' (Keating 2017). While we can't ignore the political context of the time, it is significant that the head of a sporting organisation felt entitled to both articulate a perspective that denied the idea of an 'Irish' identity to the Unionist/Protestant population, and to exclude the possibility of any engagement between the GAA and that population that shared the island of Ireland with his community. Edward Said (1993) made the point that just as every empire is characterised by hybridity, so it is inevitable that every postcolonial society is left deeply marked by hybridity too. As White (2008:90) notes, 'Perhaps all that was achievable by Irish nationalists was to create an identity and realise that the impact of colonisation was far too great to leave anything other than a hybrid culture.' For much of its history, the GAA's public discourse and its promotional activities opposed any notion of hybridity. For example, the idea that you could be Irish and British was rejected in favour of a nation-building project based on a mythic 'pure' Celtic identity. Yet identities, of course, can be multiple; many people consider themselves to be both Scottish and British, or English and British. Indeed, in Northern Ireland many people consider themselves to be Irish and British.

It is probably fair to say that it is only more recently that the GAA has come to recognise this and there is no doubt the organisation has taken steps in recent years to reconcile its past role as a key instrument of a monocultural manifestation of Irish nationalism with a new modern multicultural and inclusive Ireland. Partly this has been forced upon it; as Connolly and Dolan (2012) highlight, the movement towards PR professionalisation, while indicative of a general PR-isation of culture, also illustrates something more significant about a changing Irish society. The movement away from GAA idealogues and their 'nationalist rhetoric' towards a focus on 'selling the games' is also a movement away from a sense of entitlement to a special status.

In relation to Northern Ireland it is also clear that the GAA is today genuinely attempting to engage with the Unionist/Protestant community. Danny Murphy, Director of the Ulster GAA, stated that the GAA was committed to 'building a shared future and a better future for everyone on this island' (Murphy 2012) and the past few years have seen the development of some cross-community initiatives. However, the findings of our SESNI study indicate that there remain perceptions, from both Protestants and Catholics, that the GAA is an organisation exclusively for Catholics and Nationalists and in order to follow through on its stated aims around a shared future it is time for the GAA to invest in proactively developing public communication strategies to rectify these perceptions.

Above, we discussed how the building of social capital is dependent upon 'bonding' and 'bridging' rhetoric (Dryzek 2010). More specifically, Dryzek (2010) explains that the impact of bonding *political rhetoric*, in societies where deep divisions exist, serves 'to deepen divisions with outgroups [and] (…) to move groups to extremes' (Dryzek 2010:238). Adapting slightly Dryzek's concept from its political science context into the realm of the promotional, we could argue that the

GAA proved particularly adept at bonding *promotional rhetoric*. However, this success produced a context where the bonding social capital, which helped in building and maintaining a Nationalist/Catholic community identity, had the effect of excluding the possibility of bridging across to those with a Unionist/Protestant community identity. The GAA's promotional history demonstrated that it was for a long time very successful in developing *bonding* promotional rhetoric to build social capital for one section of the population on the island of Ireland. The organisation now needs to show it is just as adept at producing *bridging* promotional rhetoric, to more effectively communicate and demonstrate its inclusivity, and thereby encourage people from all traditions and backgrounds to play and watch Gaelic games.

Note

1 Our project employed a questionnaire survey (n. 1210) and semi-structured interviews (n. 104). For details of sampling and data analysis see Hargie et al. (2015).

References

Bailey, R. 2005, Evaluating the Relationship between Physical Education, Sport and Social Inclusion, *Educational Review*, 57, pp. 71–90.

Bell, J. 2017, Green and White Army: The Structuration of a Social System? Unpublished PhD thesis. Jordanstown, Northern Ireland: Ulster University.

Boyle, R. 1992, From our Gaelic Fields: Radio, Sport and Nation in Post-Partition Ireland, *Media, Culture & Society*, 14(4), pp. 623–636.

Butler, D. and Ruane, J. 2009, Identity, Difference and Community in Southern Irish Protestantism: The Protestants of West Cork, *National Identities*, 11(1), pp. 73–86.

Coalter, F. 2007, *A Wider Social Role for Sport: Who's Keeping the Score?*, Abingdon: Routledge.

Coalter, F. 2010, The politics of Sport-for-Development: Limited Focus Programmes and Broad Gauge Problems? *International Review for the Sociology of Sport*, 45, pp. 295–314.

Connolly, J. and Dolan, P. 2012, Sport, Media and the Gaelic Athletic Association: The Quest for the 'Youth' of Ireland, Media, *Culture & Society*, 34(4), pp. 407–423.

Craig, S. 2002, *Sports and Games of the Ancients*, London: Greenwood Press.

Cronin, M. 1999, *Sport and Nationalism in Ireland: Gaelic Games, Soccer and Irish Identity Since 1884*, Dublin: Four Courts Press.

Cronin, M. 2000, Catholics and Sport in Northern Ireland: Exclusiveness or Inclusiveness?, *International Sports Studies*, 22, pp. 25–41.

Cronin, M. 2002, Catholics and Sport in Northern Ireland: Inclusiveness or Exclusiveness? In Magdalinski, T. and Chandler, T. (eds), *With God on their Side: Sport in the Service of Religion*, London: Routledge.

Cronin, M., Duncan, M. and Rouse, P. 2009, *The GAA: A People's History*, Cork: Irish Academic Press.

Curtin, P.A. and Gaither, T.K. 2005, Privileging Identity, Difference and Power: The Circuit of Culture as a Basis for Public Relations Theory, *Public Relations Review*, 17(2), pp. 91–115.

Darnell, S. 2012, *Sport for Development and Peace: A Critical Sociology*, London: Bloomsbury Academic.

Davis, A. 2013, *Promotional Cultures: The Rise and Spread of Advertising, Public Relations, Marketing and Branding*, Cambridge: Polity Press.

Devine, A. and Devine, F. 2004, The Politics of Sports Tourism in Northern Ireland, *Journal of Sport and Tourism*, 9, pp. 171–182.

Donnelly, P. 2011, From War without Weapons to Sport for Development and Peace: The Janus-Face of Sport, *SAIS Review*, 31, pp. 65–76.

Dryzek, J.S. 2010, Rhetoric in Democracy: A Systemic Appreciation, *Political Theory*, 38(3), pp. 319–339.

European Commission 2011, *Developing the European Dimension in Sport*. Available online http://eur-lex.europa.eu/LexUriServ/LexUriServ.do?uri=COM:2011:0012:FIN:EN :PDF [accessed 28 September 2018].

Ewart, S., Schubotz, D., Abbs, F., Harris, D., Montgomery, L., Moynagh, C., Maguire, G. and Livingstone, S. 2004, *Voices behind the statistics: young people's views of sectarianism in Northern Ireland*, National Children's Bureau. Available online www.ncb.org.uk [accessed 28 December 2018].

Fanning, R. 2015, *Eamon de Valera, A Will to Power*, London: Faber & Faber.

Fulton, G. and Bairner, A. 2007, Sport, Space and National Identity in Ireland: The GAA, Croke Park and Rule 42, *Space and Polity*, 11, pp. 55–74.

Gaelic Athletic Association (GAA) 2016, *The Official Guide: Part One*. Available online https://learning.gaa.ie/sites/default/files/2016%20Official%20Guide%20-%20Part%201%20%281%29.pdf [accessed 23 January 2019].

GAA 1936, An Chomhdháil Bhliantúil (Annual Report/Convention), Dublin: GAA.

GAA/AC 1974, Minutes of Annual Congress, Dublin: GAA.

GAA/AC 1977, Minutes of Annual Congress, Dublin: GAA.

GAA 1979, An Chomhdháil Bhliantúil, Dublin: GAA.

Giulianotti, R. 2011, Sport, Peacemaking and Conflict Resolution: A Contextual Analysis and Modelling of the Sport, Development and Peace Sector, *Ethnic and Racial Studies*, 34, pp. 207–228.

Grix, J. and Lee, D. 2013, Soft Power, Sports Mega-Events and Emerging States: The Lure of the Politics of Attraction, *Global Society*, 27(4), pp. 521–536.

Hargie, O., Somerville, I. and Mitchell, D. 2015, Social Exclusion and Sport in Northern Ireland, Office of First Minister and Deputy First Minister, University of Ulster, pp. 386. Available online www.executiveoffice-ni.gov.uk/publications/social-exclusion-and-sport-northern-ireland [accessed 29 September 2018].

Hughes, M. 1994, *Ireland Divided: The Roots of the Modern Irish Problem*, Cardiff: University of Wales Press.

Hutchinson, R. 2004, *Camanachd!: The Story of Shinty*, Edinburgh: Birlinn Press.

Keating, A. 2017, A Politically Inconvenient Aspect of History: The Unpublished Official History of the Gaelic Athletic Association of 1934, *Sport in History*, 37(4), pp. 448–468.

L'Etang, J. 2006, Public Relations and Sport in Promotional Culture, *Public Relations Review*, 32(4), pp. 386–394.

L'Etang, J. 2008, Writing PR History: Issues, Methods and Politics, *Journal of Communication Management*, 12(4), pp. 319–335.

McGrattan, C. 2010, *Northern Ireland, 1968–2008: The Politics of Entrenchment*, Basingstoke: Palgrave Macmillan.

Murphy, D. 2012, Building a Constructive Friendship? Available online www.community-relations.org.uk/about-us/news/item/956/ulster-gaa-leader-in-respect-pledge/ [accessed 3 January 2019].

Nicholson, M. and Hoye, R. (eds) 2008b, Sport and Social Capital: An Introduction. In *Sport and Social Capital*, Oxford: Butterworth-Heinemann, pp. 1–20.

Oppenheimer, S. 2006, *The Origins of the British: A Genetic Detective Story of the English, Irish, Scottish, and Welsh*, New York: Carroll & Graf Publishers.

Orwell, G. 1968, In Front of Your Nose. In Orwell, S. and Angus, I. (eds), *The Collected Essays, Journalism and Letters of George Orwell, Volume 4: In Front of Your Nose, 1945–1950*, London: Secker and Warburg.

Putnam, R. 2000, *Bowling Alone: The Collapse and Revival of American Community*, New York: Simon and Schuster.

Reiche, D. 2011, War Minus the Shooting? The Politics of Sport in Lebanon as a Unique Case in Comparative Politics, *Third World Quarterly*, 32, pp. 261–277.

Rouse, P. 2015, *Sport and Ireland: A History*, Oxford: Oxford University Press.

Ruane, J. and Todd, J. 1996, *The Dynamics of Conflict in Northern Ireland: Power, Conflict and Emancipation*, Cambridge: Cambridge University Press.

Said, E. 1993, *Culture and Imperialism*, New York: Vintage Books.

Sugden, J. and Bairner, A. (eds) 2000, *Sport in Divided Societies*, Aachen: Meyer and Meyer.

Sykes, B. 2006, *Saxons, Vikings, and Celts: The Genetic Roots of Britain and Ireland*, New York: W.W. Norton.

United Nations Inter-Agency Task Force on Sport for Development and Peace 2003, Sport as a Tool for Development and Peace: Towards Achieving the United Nations Millennium Development Goals. Available online www.un.org/sport2005/resources/task_force.pdf [accessed 29 September 2019].

White, T. 2004, Mythmaking and the Creation of Irish Nationalism in the 19th Century, *Studi Celtici*, 3, pp. 325–339.

White, T. 2008, Redefining Ethnically Defined Conceptions of Nationalism: Ireland's Celtic Identity and the Future, *Studia Celtica Fennica*, 5, pp. 83–96.

Whyte, J. 1991, Interpreting Northern Ireland, Oxford: Clarendon Press.

12

A CRITICAL DISCOURSE ANALYSIS OF JONATHAN SWIFT'S *DRAPIER'S LETTERS*

Public advocacy and nationalism in Ireland, 1724–1725

Kevin Hora

Introduction

When the seven political pamphlets that formed the *Drapier's Letters* first appeared as a collection in 1735, its author, Jonathan Dean Swift (1667–1745), enjoyed a gleeful Latinism on the frontispiece. A decade earlier, as the pseudonymous Drapier, he had waged a propaganda campaign against a royal patent to increase Ireland's copper coinage, giving voice to a nascent Anglo-Irish national identity. In the collected edition, a quote from Horace accompanied an engraving of Swift on his dean's throne: *Exegi Monumentum Aere perennius* (I have made a monument more lasting than bronze). *Aere*, bronze, phonologically echoes *Éire*, and Horace was recast in praise of Swift, who accepted the plaudits for defending Irish national identity against English encroachments; I have, Swift punned, forever made a monument to Ireland. Swift's immodesty was well-founded – he was at the height of his influence, esteemed in the Anglo-Irish nation, and had thwarted the English political system where he had learned to practice propaganda. This chapter charts Swift's origins and journey to political activism through pamphleteering, and suggests that he is a key figure in the proto-history of Irish and British public relations. It examines the *Drapier's Letters* as a nation building text in Irish public relations history, beginning by outlining the background to Swift's activism and critiquing his understanding and use of the words kingdom, nation, Ireland and country through a critical discourse analysis following Fairclough's three-dimensional framework of textual exploration. It avoids the tempocentrism that suggests the history of public relations must inform the present, preferring instead to highlight the campaign as an important antecedent from which aspects of public relations theory and practice are visible, namely nation building and rhetoric. Inasmuch as it presents a biography of Swift as a public relations forebear, it eschews a great-man perspective in favour of a 'description, explanation and analysis of one character in public relations' past' (Opdycke Lamme 2015:51–53).

Locating Swift

Swift's reputation rests largely on *Gulliver's Travels*, but the basis for its adoration is, like Swift himself, elusive and contradictory. It is both children's classic and public affairs primer; former Labour leader and Swift biographer Michael Foot deemed it essential reading for political careers. In it, Swift created childish neologisms, revelling in scatological and sexual crudity (Glendinning 1998:179–181; Nokes 1987:317–318). Though his best-known work, alongside his legacy as cleric, progenitor of the Anglo-Irish literary tradition, essayist, poet, satirist and humanist, it obscures his public relations credentials. Swift, a product of the English Glorious Revolution and the European Enlightenment, was also a pamphleteer and propagandist, uniquely contributing to the emergence of proto-public relations in two countries.

Born to an English family in Ireland, Swift's formative years were spent between both countries, perhaps contributing to a sense of dualism in defining his identity. He was, self-avowedly, an Englishman born in Ireland, and a member of the Ascendancy class – a Protestant, Anglican hegemony that 'monopolized law, politics and "society"' (Foster 1988:170) in order to subjugate Catholicism and Presbyterianism. He read for a doctorate in divinity in Trinity College, Dublin and, taking holy orders, received the living of Kilroot, a poor parish near Belfast with limited potential for advancement (Tucker 1983:10–11). He quit for England within two years, and applied himself to pamphleteering, gaining a degree of notoriety for *The Battle of the Books* (a treatise defending the philosophy and wisdom of the Ancients against modernity) and *A Tale of a Tub* (a satirical allegory of Christianity). In London, perfecting skills in satire and spin, he became a propagandist for Queen Anne's Tories, the Anglican, royalist party that evolved into the Conservative Party. Glendinning defends Swift compromising his talent as a wordsmith for hire, observing that it was his formidable intelligence arguing any cause that necessitated his political activism. Fauske (2002:4–5) similarly asserts that Swift's public affairs activities were indicative of a political tactician with deeper interests than partisan principle.

Swift the propagandist emerges from this period. Hailed as the pre-eminent satirist in the English language, like many public relations pioneers, journalism was Swift's vocation. Foot, a Fleet Street veteran, dubbed Swift 'the prince of journalists' for his 1710–1711 editorship of the Tory weekly, single-article broadsheet *The Examiner* (Foot 1966:9). Appointed by Queen Anne's Lord High Treasurer, Robert Harley, Swift fused propaganda and journalism, excoriating Whigs (the Tories' constitutional monarchist rivals) while praising the government in 'a dazzling display of political journalism hardly ever equalled since' (Tucker 1983:44–45). Harley chose well: Swift was among the Tories' most influential propagandists (Glendinning 1998:101–102). However, by 1713, with London advancement unattainable, Swift was appointed Dean of St Patrick's Cathedral, the cynosure of Irish Protestantism; he considered it a financially ruinous snub (Nokes 1987:181). For much of the next decade Swift played the churchman to impoverished Dubliners of all faiths, avoiding overt intervention in public affairs. However, Swift's apparent lost decade was more contemplative and politically engaged than previously supposed (Fauske 2002:4–5). Once feelings of separation from London dissipated, Swift began to advocate for Irish interests (Nokes 1987:266). His first public affairs polemic since leaving London, *A Proposal for the Universal Use of Irish Manufacture* (1720), was an anti-colonial pamphlet berating English textile producers whose imported products harmed the Irish economy and national sovereignty (Moore 2010:26). Textiles were a pretext for a deeper polemic; the pamphlet asserted the Irish parliament's right to administer its own financial affairs free from English interference, and its publication 'was a "media event" that shaped public opinion and historical action' (*ibid.*:29).

Wood's Halfpence and the *Drapier's Letters*

Encouraged by the response to this polemic, Swift's next public venture also framed an economic principle to assert national identity. Using the *nom de guerre* M.B., a drapier of Francis Street, proximate to his cathedral, the *Letters* were Swift's contribution to a public affairs campaign against a coinage patent awarded by George I to William Wood in 1722. Ireland had no mint but needed more small-denomination coin – the most common coin, a Portuguese *moidore*, was worth 30 shillings (Fauske 2002:126). Wood, an English iron merchant, obtained the patent by bribing the king's mistress for the right to mint copper coin at a rate equivalent to one-quarter of Ireland's total coinage over 14 years (Tucker 1983:76). Swift exaggerated gossip that Wood could only profit by adulterating his metal (Ward 2004:75). The patent was awarded without consulting Irish interests, and fears grew of inflation and a flight of precious-metal coins from Ireland (Nokes 1987:280). It was symptomatic of the way English interests prevailed over Irish. Though both kingdoms were nominally equal, Ireland was treated as a colony whose land, capital and human resources were exploited by the British fiscal-military state evident by the early 1700s (Moore 2010:1–2).

Swift's Drapier was a loyal Everyman and the *Letters* are public affairs polemics with multiple standpoints and arguments targeting distinct publics. Swift's public affairs strategy balanced fact and linguistic dexterity, a blend that may not be quite acceptable in a modern, ethically codified profession yet was, for the time, audacious in translating the pamphlet from printed word to social discourse. He educated and informed the populace on the metallic composition of the coins, the Westminster parliament's unconstitutional treatment of Irish affairs, and cautiously alluded to the bribe Wood had paid. But he also denigrated Wood as a profiteering adventurer, and exhorted readers to shun Wood's coin. Officials in Ireland and Britain were made to understand the dangers in forcing the coins on the populace, yet the Drapier could not appear treasonous (Ewald, Jr. 1968:170–171). Exposing corruption and advocating political action contrary to government wishes was hazardous – a £300 reward failed to unmask the Drapier, widely known to be Swift, and the publisher, John Harding, was charged, by order of Swift's old friend the Lord Lieutenant, Lord Carteret, with printing treasonous documents (Nokes 1987:288–289). Harding died of ill health soon after, and it was his widow, Sarah, to whom Swift entrusted publication of the Drapier's sixth letter, and from whom he recalled the manuscript when Carteret announced Wood's patent had been withdrawn (Nokes 1987:293–294).

The *Drapier's Letters*: a critical discourse analysis

Originating in critical linguistics, exploring structural linkages between language and society (Tyrwhitt-Drake 2005:11), critical discourse analysis (CDA) examines language in its social practice context, establishing a relationship between discourse and power, its nature, beneficiaries and consequences. It has evolved from studying linguistic units to multi-disciplinary inquiries of complex social phenomena (Wodak and Meyer 2009:2) and lends itself to multi-disciplined approaches, here history, public relations and linguistics, exploring the historical propagation of national identity through primary texts. Fairclough's model, which shares similarities with gobbet writing and other historiographical approaches, incorporates micro-, meso- and macro-layers (Shahbazi and Rezaee 2017:99–100). The micro-layer is the text: the author's explicit and implicit meaning, and rhetorical flourishes. The meso-layer is the discourse practice, which explores the text's physical production and consumption. The macro-layer, the sociocultural milieu where the text is situated, deals with hegemony and hidden power (Titscher et al. 2000:151; Shahbazi and Rezaee 2017:100). Historians of public relations have identified progressive ways of exploring the past while remaining cognisant of the distortions caused by modern lenses such as CDA, and L'Etang (2016:29) observes public relations history's rhetorical origins and broadening scope from 'language within the context of written records and the dissemination of written ideas' to performative, visual and monumental communicative forms that bring public relations' primary-source material into CDA's ambit.

Micro-level

The *Drapier's Letters* were a series of five pamphlets published during the coinage controversy in 1724. Swift wrote two further pamphlets but, with the controversy resolved, did not publish them until the first collected edition. This chapter uses Davis' 1966 edition of the *Letters*, which retains much of the textual formatting of the original pamphlets with only slight editorial intrusion. The first five letters, contributing to the discourse, form the basis of this analysis. They appeared at infrequent intervals addressed to: the Shop-keepers, Tradesmen, Farmers, and Common-People of Ireland (March); Mr. Harding the Printer (August); the Nobility and Gentry of the Kingdom of Ireland (August); the Whole People of Ireland (October); and the Honourable the Lord Viscount Molesworth (December). The clarity in identifying and addressing distinct publics in each letter, and the letters' escalating urgency, suggests something of Swift's ability to strategise his contribution. Swift wrote pseudonymously to foment public opinion against Britain's treatment of Ireland as a vassal kingdom, and gave much thought to his publics. Rather than attempting

TABLE 12.1 Frequency of nouns identifying Ireland, Letters I–V

Noun	Frequency	Total
Kingdom	107	111
Kingdoms	4	
Ireland	102	112
Irish	10	
Country	20	33
Countrymen	13	
Nation	18	24
Nations	6	

to influence politicians directly, his strategy unfolded on a middle-class bourgeoisie whose livelihoods were at risk from adulterated coinage, and with whom he held common affinity, and then to influential members of society, the citizenry at large and, finally, Molesworth, who, despite having been a Whig member of parliament in Dublin and London, shared intellectual ground with Swift regarding Ireland's constitutional position. The pamphlets, a mixture of political fact, advocacy and propaganda, roused public ire against Wood and were instrumental in the patent being withdrawn.

In this epistolary quintet, Swift uses one proper noun and three nouns, with a derivative of each, either a plural or adjectival form, to identify the realm – these are the basis of a nation building analysis. Swift commonly allows these ostensibly similar words to stand on their own as markers. However, when he creates noun phrases, distinctions emerge.

Swift's 'Kingdom,' abridged from Kingdom of Ireland, is an administrative entity co-equal to England comprising the machinery of government, an economy, and populace loyal to the King. He refers to '*all the* Officers *in the Kingdom* (Civil and Military)' on whom daily administration depends, and to the Privy Council and House of Commons of the Irish Kingdom, stating that the latter 'represents the whole People of the Kingdom.' 'Whole' is an adjective appearing 16 times in conjunction with the Kingdom or its people. But Swift observes a hierarchy: 'our Ancestors reduced this Kingdom to the Obedience of England.' These ancestors were Protestant settlers from Elizabethan to Williamite times who established English rule of law in Ireland. All people in Swift's kingdom are subjects, but the Ascendancy is pre-eminent. It is this, partly, that makes Ireland 'a Kingdom distinguished for its Loyalty.' The four references to 'Kingdom' are Swift's attempt to ensure that Ireland remains equal to England: the two kingdoms '*shall be for ever knit together under one.*' Swift also highlights his singularity as an English-trained propagandist, and membership of the Ascendancy. In his habit of writing and engaging in discourse, 'wherein I differ from almost the whole Kingdom,' native Catholics and Presbyterians, the King's subjects, are excluded for lack of Englishness.

'Ireland,' the second half of the abridged title, has similar meaning to 'Kingdom.' References to the machinery of the state – parliament, Privy Council and crown offices like the Lord Lieutenancy – account for 19 of 102 uses. There is a stronger sense of an economic identity as Ireland than as a kingdom, mainly in commercially minded Letter I. More significant are nine noun phrases linking Ireland with 'depend,' 'depending,' 'dependent' and 'dependency,' with the referent being the Declaratory Act of 1719 (6. Geo. I, c. 5). This law reduced the Irish parliament's power so that Ireland became subservient to and dependent on English monarchs, while the English – not the Irish – House of Lords became the appellate court for Irish judicial decisions. Dependency is the crux of the Drapier's arguments – Swift asserts Irish economic independence from English interference. His appeal to the bourgeois merchant class, a mainly Protestant body, is that they reject the coin; they are the '*True English People of Ireland*, who refuse it; although we take it for granted that the *Irish* will do so too.'

'Country/countrymen' most often appears in a noun phrase with a possessive pronoun. This is reinforced with the inclusion of 'own' on three occasions in Letters Four and Five, perhaps in exasperated emphasis. Negation is evident with the phrase 'Betrayers of their Country' twice – Irishmen who support Wood can never be part of Swift's 'dear' or 'poor' country. The Drapier says he would quit his campaign for a sinecure on Molesworth's Yorkshire estates (Letter V) but with regret 'for leaving my Countrymen under the Dread of the brazen Talons of Mr *Wood*' (emphasis in the original), a denunciation rich in metaphor. 'Country' is a unifying noun, and perhaps the most emotive term Swift uses given its connotations of sharing possession of an identity without reference to class or religion.

'Nation/Nations' identifies the Ascendancy as a superior class in Ireland. It appears eight times as the noun phrase 'the whole Nation.' Swift refers to 'the whole Voice of the Nation' and 'Representatives of the Nation in Parliament' – this when the Irish parliament represented Protestant values only. His identification of an Anglo-Irish nation is more clearly established with the phrase: 'This Nation flourished extreamly [*sic*], till the Time of the Massacre, 1641,' the referent being the 1641 Rebellion, when Catholic insurgents committed atrocities against Protestants, including non-combatants. Swift's use of the plural is a form of comparative opposition to advocate Ascendancy Ireland's superior status to Britain's new-world colonies. It does not appear until the fourth letter, when Swift's discourse had expanded from its primary target of Wood's halfpence into a defence of the rights and privileges of the Ascendancy.

Meso-level

The physical appearance of the individual letters, especially their covers, matches Swift's rhetoric: concise, stylish, wry. A parenthetical reassurance on the first cover that it is 'Very proper to be kept in every family' hints at mischievousness, and a document of public importance. Burgeoning mercantilism and an Anglophone book publishing trade second only to London (Moore 2010:2) gave Swift his platform. He expressed delight that 2,000 copies of his first letter sold within months, including to Westminster MPs, and sold out, he chided Harding in the second letter, because the printer had not anticipated demand. By 1725, the first letter had been reprinted in one of the Irish newspapers that had emerged in the early 1700s, after the lapsing of the restrictive Licensing of the Press Act 1662 (14 Car. II. c. 33) in 1695 (Higgins 1989:195). *Pue's Impartial Occurrences* appeared in 1703, the *Dublin Gazette* and *Flying Post* in 1706, and the *Dublin Journal* at the tail end of Drapier's affair in 1725 (Foster 1988:183; Mac Con Iomaire 2012:3). The well-developed newspaper culture allowed Swift to stir public opinion, albeit that most newspapers 'were for, by, and about the ruling Anglo-Irish Protestant minority' (Moore 2010:47). Likewise, their readership was 'male, metropolitan and inclined to aggregate with like-minded peers' in the guilds, who were influential in the city's governance (Ward 2004:10). A typical guild member socialised in Dublin's newly popular coffeehouses, which fostered a lively journalism trade, and were concentrated near St Patrick's Cathedral and Dublin Castle, the centre of English power in Ireland (Mac Con Iomaire 2012:2–5).

Macro-level

Why was there so little focus on Catholics and Presbyterians in civic society? More numerous than the Ascendancy, the Catholic élite, diminished with James II's defeat by William of Orange, and Ulster-Scottish Presbyterianism, mistrustful of all but its own devices, had been supplanted by an Anglican minority 'isolated from the masses by the great gulf of its religion' (O'Mahony and Delanty 1998:37–38). Since Henrician times, Irish Protestants had defined their citizenship through loyalty to the monarch. Locke's *Second Treatise on Civil Government* (1690) introduced the liberal concept that rights and liberties sustained by constitutional limits on government trumped duty-bound citizenship (Lyons 2018:33–34). By Swift's era, Ascendancy Ireland had developed institutions and laws as protection against native Irish and English interference. Sectarian laws reduced Catholic land ownership to 14 per cent of the country by 1704, forbade them to carry arms, vote and be educated abroad, and required the registration of Catholic clergy. The Anglican Archbishop William King openly advocated for the permanent debarring of Catholics from all public office (Foster 1988:153–156). Presbyterians, likewise barred from public office, and suffering similar sectarianism, were, however, enfranchised. Clearly, neither Catholics nor Presbyterians had influence to exert, and, echoing the maxim that issues create publics, Swift's publics were defined by the economic and sovereign issue of Wood's halfpence – Irish-born bishops, resident landowners, lower clergy, the electorate and guilds (Fauske 2002:74).

Swift's was one voice in a larger discourse of journalists and propagandists, and he was not unique as a Protestant cleric pamphleteering on Irish socioeconomic affairs. By the 1740s Ascendancy clergy and gentry were dissecting public affairs with increasing frequency and reliability (Rees 2015:87–89). Bishop George Berkeley, arguably Swift's equal in intellectual and philosophical public affairs, published his influential economic treatise *The Querist* a decade after the coinage controversy. King and Bishop Francis Hutchinson contributed to political and economic discourse with largely benign views on non-Protestant natives. Hutchinson, an agricultural economist (Sneddon 2007:292–293), and Berkeley were to the fore in advocating economic nationalism where Protestant ethics were essential to developing a sound Irish economy (*ibid.*:296). Crucially, their involvement had the form of non-political patriotism (*ibid.*:290) though as members of the Irish House of Lords King, Berkeley and Hutchinson were steeped in political as well as episcopal practice. They were also less strident in their pamphleteering than Swift.

Public relations' antecedents

Swift and nation building

Extending the macro exploration, what proto-public relations insights appear? Public relations theories of nation building tend to start with the twentieth century, but societies were constructed through contemporary communications channels in the early modern period. Swift's Ireland was a deeply divided society, and recrudescent violence loomed ominously in the Ascendancy psyche, besieged domestically and disdained by Britain. This matches the definition of division offered by Somerville et al., though their inclusion of further, modern criteria are less useful to historians of public relations (2017:2). Much of the recent impetus in studying public relation's role in nation building comes from African and Asian states, where there have been sometimes harmful consequences on national cohesion (Taylor and Kent 2017:10). From an historical perspective Ireland also experienced comparable social schisms with the creation of an Ascendancy master narrative of national identity. In the *Letter to the Whole People of Ireland*, Swift writes: 'OUR *Neighbours* (…) have a strong contempt for most Nations, but especially for *Ireland:* They look upon us as a sort of *Savage Irish,* whom our Ancestors conquered.' Bloor and Bloor (2007:87) suggest the concept of nationality is complex for those with more than one nationality, or an affinity with a distant homeland. Such dislocations were manifested in Ascendancy Ireland; though domestically dominant, Swift's public was increasingly the poor cousin in the Anglo-Irish relationship. Moreover, Catholic Irish saw them as English, yet in their sister kingdom they were Irish.

Central to inventing and sustaining national identity, master narratives are propagated through educational and cultural means (van Alphen and Carretero 2015:514). Swift's pamphleteering is a perfect example of how the Ascendancy's inherently defensive master narrative, predicated on constant expectation of threat from Catholic insurrection and the downgrading of its co-equal status with England, was propagandised. While his antipathy towards Wood's halfpence was real, it was a cause Swift selected to further the master narrative of a Protestant kingdom governed by and on behalf of a Protestant people; in the *Letter to Molesworth* the Drapier expressed his 'Zeal for his present Majesty and His Protestant Line.' Opdycke Lamme and Miller Russell (2010:291) observe that public relations techniques can 'inspire devotees to fight for their faith, to enhance national identity through the association with faith' so that, ultimately, religiosity becomes part of the nation's sociocultural identity. From this, Swift's Ascendancy hegemony shows marked similarities to the primordialist approach to nation building, typified by 'competing loyalties between groups based on long-standing stereotypes, beliefs, and traditions' (Taylor 2000:185). Primordialism sustains 'the idea that national identities are eternal and everlasting' (Karaaslan Şanli 2018:437) and constant repetition of this narrative suited the besieged Ascendancy mindset.

Swift and the public sphere

Ascendancy Ireland's enthusiastic propagation of national identity illustrates Moore's theory that 'modern nations are first created in the press, suggesting that the identity and sovereignty of the polity are inextricably bound to the success of their mediation in print.' (2010:214). Swift inhabited the prototypical environment Habermas proposes as a voluntary civic association coalescing on a commonality of purpose with discursive reason among equals. This environment was possible because the pamphleteer and journalist emerged in print-based opposition to authority (Thorne 2001:532–533). Leeper (2005:712) makes claims for the public sphere as an inclusive space for rationality and opinion-forming that sustains democratic society and, hence, is important to public relations. In Swift's Dublin, a vibrant Ascendancy public sphere existed, with mercantilism having gravitated from taverns towards fashionable coffee shops and the newspapers they provided (Mac Con Iomaire 2012:3). Conditions for the public sphere were set: a monarchy with power circumscribed by parliament, a relatively free press and a bourgeoisie. These conditions permitted a public discourse that formed a bulwark against the tyranny of arbitrariness in political decision-making (McNair 2003:19). The *Drapier's Letters* could hardly have been written otherwise.

Bentele (2005:709) observes three functions of the public sphere, transparency, validation and orientation. Transparency allows for all points of view; validation matches two-way symmetrical communication in that actors are willing to moderate their standpoints; and orientation is persuasive. Habermas' expresses misgivings that public relations transformed the public sphere from a locus of opinion-forming to one where performance by actors creates opinion (Leeper 2005:711, col. 2). Moloney, likewise, suggests that the presence of a public sphere is no guarantor of good public relations, as persuasiveness is incompatible with the discursive public sphere (2000:152). A Foucaultian interpretation of history, where power relations shape every individual discourse, and discourse is inescapably connected to its context, may support his view. Moreover, 'each discourse is structured by powerful people who have an interest in embedding discursive mechanisms allowing to minimize [*sic*] the risk of a change in social power relations' (Wehmeier 2015:94). Swift's pamphleteering contributed to a nation building discourse, where social power relations were visible as social capital, 'a social phenomenon in that it exists only in relationships among actors' (Sommerfeldt 2013:284). At the risk of applying modern views to the past, if, as Bonanno suggests (2018:387) public relations and rhetoric create social capital, Swift's advocacy helped create a distinctive Anglo-Irish social capital based on economic concerns and hegemonic self-identifying membership.

With Swift and his Ascendancy public sharing commonalities such as language, religion and a bifurcated Anglo-Irish identity, an identifiable category of socially significant people emerged. Identities are constructed and construed by social groups, culture and religion – either the downtrodden and oppressed, or, as in Swiftian discourse, an hegemony that assumed not only leadership but domination across society's, political, cultural, economic and ideological interests (Fairclough 1995:76). Hegemony builds alliances (similar to public relations coalition-building) in order to integrate rather than dominate subordinate or less socially significant groups across a panoply of discourses (*ibid.*). From constant two-way communication the outcome of discourse is consensus, not victory (Fiske 1990:176). This parallels the Grunigian paradigm's fascination with symmetry. The dominant hegemony creates national identity, a construct inculcated in subordinates through nation building mythology.

There is, nonetheless, evidence that Swift does not quite conform to classic definitions of the public sphere, the German *Öffentlichkeit*, a public space that functions as an outcome, and therefore a quality of the public communication system in society (Ihlen and van Ruler 2007:245). Swift lived in a constitutional monarchy, not a democracy. He was not inclusive, writing with a Protestant pen, largely omitting Catholics and Presbyterians from his pamphleteering. His finest satirical pamphlet, *A Modest Proposal* (1729), suggested breeding the young of Catholics as a native food source: it was a methodically constructed *reductio ad absurdum* that defied rationality yet, badly digested by critics, earned opprobrium. Alongside contemporary Tory satirists, John Gay and Alexander Pope, Swift entered public affairs debates 'with more force than finesse' and near-hysterical disdain of the printing press' socially equalising effect in permitting widespread contradictory, corrosive pamphleteering at odds with their notions of classical discourse (Thorne 2001:533–534). Indeed, the modernity Swift had railed against in *The Battle of the Books* – and which, in the Ascendancy memory, had produced rebellion, a republic and regicide (*ibid.*:536) – was unconducive to building knowledge and understanding. It had instead created 'an insane proliferation of argumentative standpoints' (*ibid.*:534–535) – or, as modern public relations would understand it, a multiplicity of publics competing for attention.

Swift and rhetorical proto-public relations

Swift's prime legacy as communicator may be as a rhetorician. In contemporary public relations rhetoric has emerged as a contested though important field of inquiry. An early intervention by L'Etang laid clear rhetorical benefits to public relations 'not only in its communicative function but (...) in the claim to be contributing to a better society and by assisting the flow of information' (1996:117).

Mackey (2003:3), more sceptical of the evolution of rhetorical studies of public relations, nonetheless suggests that a central component of any civilisation is 'public relations properly revealed as a key expression of contemporary rhetoric.' For Porter, too, rhetoric is a valid public relations technique: the need to understand human character through research and dialogue leads to advocacy (2010:130). Heath accepts advocacy is needed to co-create meaning and give voice to self-interests (2001:32). Weigand considers rhetoric 'to be *rooted in human beings' interests and needs.* It is in the end the need to maintain one's position in the community which is part of human beings' nature' (2008:3. Emphasis in the original). This echoes Taylor and Kent's observations that shared norms and values produce deeper societal relationships (2017:11).

Whether this was a true reflection of Swift's Ireland is moot, but rhetorical public relations can palliate 'naive realism and platonic notions of absolute truth' (Ihlen 2010:59). Marsh, acknowledging the platonic nature of absolute truth, cedes that it 'allows Plato's ideal rhetorician to lie to persuade the unenlightened' (Marsh 2013:240). Swift's strategy was persuasive, using devices contemporary practice would deem suspect, notably expressing one group's social superiority. Swift wrote when the effect of language on a Ciceronian-style *res publica* was more important than philology (Bishop 1998:11). While his era valued literary linguistic precision and communicators who exercised 'control over language, to effect efficient and harmonious communication with others' (*ibid.*:8), Swift's Drapier inclined to censoriousness and bombast – an efficient rhetorician, but not a harmonising figure. In this, Swift's rhetoric was 'instrumental, intentional, unidirectional, formulaic, and agonistic' (Cissna and Anderson 2008:39). This demonstrates the cleavage between rhetoric and the Grunigian paradigm, which, with inherent nervousness of persuasion, overlooks the rationality and agency of receiving publics (Porter 2010:130) and meaning-making through dialogue and discourse (Miller Russell and Opdycke Lamme 2016:746).

Aristotle's three types of rhetoric, deliberative, forensic and epideitic, provide clarity for public relations practice (Kent 2011:553). The *Letters* show shades of forensic rhetoric, a judicial, legalistic construct, in Swift's propagation of Ascendancy Ireland's right to constitutionalism: by 'The Laws of GOD, of NATURE, of NATIONS, and of your own country,' the Drapier's countrymen enjoyed the same freedom as their English counterparts. Irish Protestants had erected an edifice of state institutions and laws to safeguard against internal and external adversaries, and saw themselves as 'beneficiaries of an independent Irish constitution' in a dual monarchy with England (Kelly 1989:86); it is this element of nationhood that Swift particularly defends. Epideixis is also apparent in Swift's linguistic flourishes and convincing creation of a character, the Drapier, competent to speak for the mass of his peers. In his *Letter to Harding*, the Drapier avers that his pamphlet is intended 'for all my Countrymen. I have no Interest in this Affair but what is common to the Publick.' But Swift's strategy leans towards deliberative rhetoric that, being future-orientated, attempts to construct something better from the prevailing conditions and issues. That those he exhorted to act were an élite bent on self-preservation is unsurprising: 'not everyone acts in the best interest of society. Individuals are often guided by self-interest and held in check by social convention and the will of others' (Kent 2011:553) Swift's rhetoric succeeds, partly because of his forceful language, but mostly because he invests in understanding the interests and needs of his publics.

Conclusion

A 'great-man' analysis of Swift would offer up the Hibernian Patriot, a populist title bestowed on him for his advocacy and propagandising for an Irish nation. It is as simplistically seductive as it is reductive: Swift, his complexities and inconsistencies probed, emerging as the dominant figure in eighteenth-century Ireland, and as a lodestar for modern public relations. But public relations history is much more complex: 'Public relations historical work is the process of thinking and writing about the history of meaning generation and the circulation of discourses, ideas and networks linked to agency, structures, power, hegemony, ideology and communicative action' (L'Etang 2014:659). A critical examination suggests it is Swift's rhetoric and pamphleteering, not a psychohistorical analysis of personality, that shows his influence on public relations. While avoiding the tempocentrism that can wheedle undue regard, Swift's proto-historical public relations credentials stem from his ability to engage in discourse in the public sphere through persuasive pamphleteering; from his ability in framing issues for maximum propaganda value; and from his success in propagating national identity. The *Letters* use advocacy and propaganda practices of their time, largely unacceptable by modern mores, but rooted in techniques that remain unchanged today: rhetoric and persuasion, identifying issues and addressing their attendant publics with targeted messages. Swift signed off his fifth letter with a eulogy to 'my most loyal and innocent Country-men; to whom I owe so much for their good Opinion of me.' It may be judged a permissible flaw that Swift himself had created that opinion.

References

Bentele, G. 2005, Public Sphere (Öffentlichkeit). In Heath, R.L. (ed.), *Encyclopaedia of Public Relations Volume 1*, London: Sage, pp. 709–710.

Bishop, J. A. 1998, Language at Work in Jonathan Swift. Unpublished PhD thesis, University of Newcastle.

Bloor, M. and Bloor, T. 2007, *The Practice of Critical Discourse Analysis. An introduction*, London: Hodder Education.

Bonanno, J. N. 2018, Capital as the Lens that Bourdieu Pierres through: Public Relations, Social Theory, and Rhetoric, *Public Relations Review*, 44(3), p. 385–392.

Cissna, K. N. and Anderson, R. 2008, Dialogic Rhetoric, Coauthorship, and Moments of Meeting. In Weigand, E. (ed.), *Dialogue and Rhetoric*, Amsterdam: John Benjamins B.V, pp. 39–54.

Davis, H. (ed.) 1966, *The Drapier's Letters and Other Works 1724–1725*, Oxford: Basil Blackwell.

Ewald, Jr., W. 1968, M.B., Drapier. In: Jeffares, A.N. (ed.), *Swift*, London: MacMillan, pp. 170–191.

Fairclough, N. 1995, *Critical Discourse Analysis: The Critical Study of Language*, Essex: Longman/Pearson Education Limited.

Fauske, C. J. 2002, *Jonathan Swift and the Church of Ireland, 1710–1724*, Dublin: Irish Academic Press.

Fiske, J. 1990, *Introduction to Communication Studies*, 2nd edn. London: Routledge.

Foot, M. 1966, *The Pen and the Sword. A Year in the Life of Jonathan Swift*, London: MacGibbon and Kee.

Foster, R. 1988, *Modern Ireland 1600–1972*, London: Penguin.

Glendinning, V. 1998, *Jonathan Swift*, London: Hutchinson.

Heath, R.L. 2001, A Rhetorical Enactment Rationale for Public Relations: The Good Organization Communicating Well. In Heath, R.L. (ed.), *Handbook of Public Relations*, London: Sage.

Higgins, I.K. 1989, *The Sentiments of a Church-of-England Man: A Study of Swift's Politics*. Unpublished PhD thesis, University of Warwick.

Ihlen, Ø. 2010, The Cursed Sisters: Public Relations and Rhetoric. In Heath, R.L. (ed.), *The SAGE Handbook of Public Relations*, 2nd edn. Thousand Oaks, CA: Sage, pp. 59–70.

Ihlen, Ø. and van Ruler, B. 2007, How Public Relations Works: Theoretical Roots, *Public Relations Review*, 33(3), pp. 243–248.

Karaaslan Şanli, H. 2018, Public Relations Activities During the Nation-Building Process in Turkey, *MANAS Journal of Social Studies*, 7(4), pp. 435–447.

Kelly, P. 1989. Archbishop William King (1650–1729) and Colonialism Nationalism, In Brady, C. (ed.), *Worsted in the Game. Losers in Irish History*, Dublin: Lilliput Press, pp. 85–94.

Kelly, J. 1991, Jonathan Swift and the Irish Economy in the 1720s, *Eighteenth-Century Ireland / Iris an dá chultúr*, 6, pp. 7–36.

Kent, M.L. 2011, Public Relations Rhetoric: Criticism, Dialogue, and the Long Now, *Management Communication Quarterly*, 25(3), pp. 550–559.

Lamme, M. & Russell, K. 2010, Removing the Spin: Toward a New Theory of Public Relations History, *Journalism & Communication Monographs*, 11 (4), pp. 281–362.

Leeper, R.V. 2005, Public Sphere Discourse. In Heath, R.L. (ed.), *Encyclopaedia of Public Relations Volume 1*, London: Sage, pp. 710–712.

L'Etang, J. 1996, Public Relations and Rhetoric. In L'Etang, J. and Pieczka, M. (eds), *Critical Perspectives in Public Relations*, London: International Thompson Business Press, pp. 106–123.

L'Etang, J. 2014, Public Relations and Historical Sociology: Historiography as Reflexive Critique, *Public Relations Review*, 40, pp. 654–660.

L'Etang, J. 2016, History as a Source of Critique. History and Knowledge, Societal Change, Activism and Movements. In L'Etang, J., McKie, D., Snow, N. and Xifra, J. (eds), *The Routledge Handbook of Critical Public Relations*, Abingdon, Oxford: Routledge, pp. 28–40.

Lyons, M.A. 2018, Concepts of Citizenship in Ireland During an Era of Revolutions, 1688–1798. In Ellis, S.G. (ed.), *Enfranchising Ireland? Identity, Citizenship and State*, Dublin: Royal Irish Academy, pp. 33–51.

Mac Con Iomaire, M. 2012, Coffee Culture in Dublin: A Brief History, *M/C Journal – A Journal of Media and Culture*, 15(2), May. Available online http://journal.media-culture.org.au/index.php/mcjournal/article/view/456 [accessed 28 June 2019].

Mackey, S. (2003), Changing Vistas in Public Relations Theory, *PRism*, 1(1), pp. 1–9.

McMinn, J. 1987, A Weary Patriot: Swift and the Formation of an Anglo-Irish Identity, *Eighteenth-Century Ireland/Iris an dá chultúr*, 2, pp. 103–113.

McNair, B. 2003, *An Introduction to Political Communication*, 3rd edn. Abingdon, Oxon: Routledge.

Miller Russell, K. and Opdycke Lamme, M. 2016, Theorizing Public Relations History: The Roles of Strategic Intent and Human Agency. In *Public Relations Review*, 42(5), pp. 741–747.

Moloney, K. 2000, *Rethinking Public Relations. The Spin and the Substance*, 1st edn. London: Routledge.

Moore, S.D. 2010, *Swift, the Book, and the Irish Financial Revolution. Satire and Sovereignty in Colonial Ireland*, Baltimore, MD: The Johns Hopkins University Press.

Nokes, D. 1987, *Jonathan Swift. A Hypocrite Reversed*, Oxford: Oxford Univesity Press.

O'Mahony, P. and Delanty, G. 1998, *Rethinking Irish History. Nationalism, Identity and Ideology*, Basingstoke: Palgrave.

Opdycke Lamme, M. 2015, Where the Quiet Work is Done': Biography in Public Relations. In Watson, T. (ed.), *Perspectives on Public Relations Historiography and Historical Theorization: Other Voices*, Basingstoke: Palgrave Macmillan, pp. 48–68.

Porter, L. 2010, Communicating for the Good of the State: A Post-symmetrical Polemic on Persuasion in Ethical Public Relations, *Public Relations Review*, 36(2), pp. 127–133.

Rees, G. 2015, 'The Most Miserable Scene of Universal Distress': Irish Pamphleteers and the Subsistence Crisis of the Early 1740s, *Studia Hibernica*, 41 (January), pp. 87–108.

Shahbazi, M. and Rezaee, M. 2017, Reflection of Ideology on Translation: A Critical Discourse Analysis Perspective, *Journal of Applied Linguistics and Language Learning*, 3(4), pp. 97–101.

Sneddon, A. 2007, Bishop Frances Hutchinson (1660–1739): a Case Study in the Eighteenth-Century Culture of Improvement, *Irish Historical Studies*, XXXV(139), pp. 289–310.

Sommerfeldt, E.J. 2013, The Civility of Social Capital: Public Relations in the Public Sphere, Civil Society, and Democracy. *Public Relations Review*, 39(4), pp. 280–289.

Somerville, I., Hargie, O., Taylor, M. and Toledano, M. 2017, Introduction: Public Relations in Deeply Divided Societies. In Somerville, I., Hargie, O., Taylor, M. and Toledano, M. (eds), *International Public Relations: Perspectives from Deeply Divided Societies*, Abingdon, Oxon: Routledge, pp. 1–8.

Taylor, M. 2000, Toward a Public Relations Approach to Nation Building, *Journal of Public Relations Research*, 12(2), pp. 179–210.

Taylor, M. and Kent, M. 2017, Nation Building in the Former Yugoslavia: A 20-year Retrospective to Understand How Public Relations Build Relationships in Divided Societies, In Somerville, I., Hargie, O., Taylor, M. and Toledano, M. (eds), *International Public Relations: Perspectives from Deeply Divided Societies*, Abingdon, Oxon: Routledge, pp. 9–26.

Thorne, C. 2001, Thumbing our Nose at the Public Sphere: Satire, the Market, and the Invention of Literature, *PMLA*, 116(3), pp. 531–544.

Titscher, S., Meyer, M., Wodak, R. and Vetter, E. 2000, *Methods of Text and Discourse Analysis*, Sage: London.

Tucker, B. 1983, *Jonathan Swift*, Dublin: Gill and MacMillan.

Tyrwhitt-Drake, H. 2005, *A Critique of Critical Discourse Analysis*, s.l. Unpublished thesis, University of Reading.

van Alphen, F. and Carretero, M. 2015, The Construction of the Relation between National Past and Present in the Appropriation of Historical Master Narratives, *Integrative Psychological and Behavioral Science*, 49(3), pp. 512–530.

Ward, J.G. 2004, *Reading Swift and Ireland, 1720–1729. Constituencies, Contexts and Constructions of Identity in Jonathan Swift's Occasional Writings of the 1720s*, s.l. Unpublished thesis, University of Leeds.

Wehmeier, S. 2015, Historiography (and Theory) of Public Relations History. In Watson, T. (ed.), *Perspectives on Public Relations Historiography and Historical Theorization: Other Voices*, Basingstoke, Hampshire: Palgrave Macmillan, pp. 85–114.

Weigand, E. 2008, Rhetoric in the Mixed Game. In Weigand, E. (ed.), *Dialogue and Rhetoric*, Amsterdam: John Benjamins B.V, pp. 3–22.

Wodak, R. and Meyer, M. 2009, Critical Discourse Analysis: History, Agenda, Theory and Methodology. In: Wodak, R. and Meyer, M. (eds), *Methods of Critical Discourse Analysis*, 2nd edn. London: Sage, pp. 1–33.

INDEX